Appointment for Murder

Appointment for Murder

THE STORY OF
THE KILLING DENTIST

Susan Crain Bakos

G. P. PUTNAM'S SONS   NEW YORK

G. P. Putnam's Sons
Publishers Since 1838
200 Madison Avenue
New York, NY 10016

Library of Congress Cataloging-in-Publication Data

Bakos, Susan Crain.
    Appointment for murder : the story of the killing dentist / Susan
Crain Bakos.—1st American ed.
        p.   cm.
    ISBN 0-399-13341-0 : price
    1. Engleman, Glennon—Fiction.   I. Title.
PS3552.A439A87   1988   87-35914 CIP
813'.54—dc19

Typeset by Fisher Composition, Inc.

Printed in the United States of America
1   2   3   4   5   6   7   8   9   10

ACKNOWLEDGMENTS

Special thanks to:
  Jack Heidenry, who encourages and inspires me
      in every project I undertake;
  my agent, Nancy Love, and editor, Stacy Creamer,
      who helped shape the book;
  Mel Pine, who read and critiqued the initial proposal;
  Richard Alex Bakos, for hours spent in the microfilm
      room and on the phone tracking down leads;
  the Bureau of Alcohol, Tobacco, and Firearms, and
      particularly Bill McGarvey for invaluable assistance
      in getting the details right;
  Gordon Ankney and Robert E. Trone, who saved and
      shared everything, including their courtroom notes;
  Bea Miller, Judith Keltner, Cynthia Schipper,
      Michael Gothberg, and Dana McAuliffe, who
      contributed their journalistic insights, over several
      bottles of champagne in various St. Louis bars—
      and especially Judith, who also gave me the key to
      her Brentwood condo.
  And finally to Nick Miranda for his honesty, dignity,
      and courage in retelling the story.

                              —Susan Crain Bakos

FOR JACK KAPLAN

CONTENTS

PROLOGUE:

The Newlyweds

Noon, Sunday, September 5, 1976, Pacific, Missouri

A young couple in their mid-twenties, dressed in jeans and T-shirts, walked along a path in a wooded area adjacent to a small pond. Behind the path a wall of white rock was broken by caves—jagged openings emitting cool, faintly musty smells. The sun streamed through the leaves of the trees—leaves already turning to autumn shades. A stagnant scum clinging to the edges of the pond had dried in mossy clumps on the narrow, sandy shore, proof that the water level had receded during the hot, dry summer. On this day, however, the temperature hovered near eighty, not quite so hot, and the beads of perspiration on each of their foreheads didn't threaten to run.

The big amusement park, Six Flags Over Mid-America, was one exit back on Highway 44. He'd wanted to stop there to look at the new motorcyles at the auto show; she'd promised him they would later. As they walked toward their destination, they passed a family—mother, father, and two young children—who had apparently come to explore the narrow caves. The young woman smiled at the mother of two and said hello. The men exchanged nods.

"Cute couple," the wife said; and they heard her say it, but they did not look at each other surreptitiously and grin.

"Cute" was the right adjective for the two of them. He was

twenty-six, tall with dark blond hair and a darker mustache, reasonably attractive, a lineman for Southwestern Bell Telephone Company. The doctor, whom she trusted completely, had said he was a good choice for marriage. Certainly he was the sort of man a working-class mother would pick for her daughter: He had modest but solid financial prospects and lacked imagination, which the economic reality of the working class and the sexual routine of marriage require. Both attributes made it likely he would stay married.

She was a dental assistant, twenty-four, petite and shapely, her Mexican heritage evident in her olive coloring and deep dark eyes. Her sexuality stood away from her, touching uncomfortably on her body contours, the way a stiff new negligee made of the cheapest lace, worn to please a man, touches the body. The couple had dated in high school before she dropped out in the tenth grade. They'd met again later at a party when he'd accidentally sprayed her with beer while inserting the tap into a keg of Busch.

When she told her employer about her renewed acquaintance, the doctor had said that he was the right one and instructed her to call him every two or three days. She had done that and followed his instructions, which he'd repeated over and over—for the doctor never said anything important less than dozens of times. And each time he repeated his instructions in the gentle, reasonable voice he nearly always used with her. Among other things, he had taught her how to touch her young lover's genitals with her hands and her mouth until he began thrashing around in the manner the doctor described as wild. Before the doctor told her how to perform this complicated ritual, she'd thought it was enough to place a few shy kisses, when asked, on the man in his private place, like a little mother making the boo-boo go away.

She had become very good at pleasing the lineman, mainly because she was accustomed to doing what she was told, especially when someone as powerful as the doctor commanded; and so they had married in October of 1975. They were still newlyweds as they walked along that path toward a particular cave, less than a half hour's drive from their St. Louis home, yet she had already been pregnant with their child and aborted it with his consent.

She was a few steps ahead of him when they approached a cave in the white cliff wall. Having walked through this with the doctor the week before, she knew where they were going. She had even parked her orange '71 VW in the spot where the doctor had parked his dark blue car. Her husband trailing behind seemed irritable, as if he were following her reluctantly through K-Mart in search of something *she* felt they needed for their home, something she thought she couldn't buy without his approval. He asked her again what it was she wanted him to see and when would they get there in the same tone he would use to say, *Why don't you pick out any damn lamp you want?* This time she ignored the question. Perhaps he regretted not packing the picnic lunch she'd originally suggested.

She kept walking, her hands in the front pockets of her Levi's, her head bent forward so that the shiny chestnut hair grazed her cheeks. Her mind was on the other man, not her husband. She was listening for sound but she didn't know what sound he might make. A twig snapping perhaps. She heard only the chirping hum of birds and insects in motion and flies buzzing around the pond scum. A fat blowfly circled her face. Gingerly she swatted at it, she didn't want its stomach to explode fly eggs onto her hand, her face. She shivered at the idea, at the nasty harbinger of death. But this really won't happen, she thought; it will fail again as it had failed two other times, though there was no way she could dare to let it fail—not now. Yet even as she advanced to the mouth of the cave, she couldn't shake the feeling that it wouldn't work this third time. The sun would keep shining—it was such a pleasant day—and in a few minutes she and her husband would get back in their car and return to the home they shared.

She was very pretty, even if she looked a little sad as she walked ahead of her husband. Images of the doctor kept running through her mind. His leering face was in front of hers as she sat on the counter in his office, where he had touched her breasts, vulnerable through a soft gauze shirt, her crotch protected by the stiff cloth of blue jeans. She'd said no, praying he would believe she had the strength the word implied. His hands on her private places, revolting as a father's touch would be, disgusted her. She was there to talk about the plan, and he was whispering to her so a patient in the next room wouldn't hear. "When we have an intimate moment, we'll discuss the others," he told her, withdrawing his hand from her breast. "It will reassure you to hear about the others." That was the only time he had touched her breasts. He said it would make them closer to have this plan; and then he removed his hand in deference to her wishes. She was grateful that he had.

She knew who the others were, Eric Frey and someone named Bullock. The doctor seemed to think talking about them would excite her, make the space between her legs turn wet in anticipation of him, but it never had. The doctor's face changed when he talked about what he had done to the two men. His features turned proud, fearsome; his was the face of some vengeful, primitive god, part animal, part man. Though she tried, she couldn't remember Eric Frey's face—she had only been nine years old—but she remembered Sandy's. She remembered swimming in the pool with her sister Nedra at the apartment complex where Sandy Frey lived with her baby after Eric's death. The baby girl looked just like the doctor; her features were the doctor's softened by baby fat. She sometimes watched the baby when Sandy and the doctor went out, always with his hand on Sandy's back or lower, cupping her ass, as he guided her out the door. Yes, she had envied Sandy going out with the doctor though she didn't want his hands on her the way they were always on Sandy. What she wanted was his approval, his continued protection. He had told her she could live in an apartment complex with a pool too.

"How much further?" her husband called behind her. He didn't sound angry, only bored, resigned. They looked like so many handsome young couples who already know the marriage isn't working out: she grimly in the lead, he following with mounting irritation. "Are you sure you know where you're going?" he said.

She had tried to give him reason to divorce her, meeting other men at nightclubs, coming home to him, long after he'd turned out the lights and gone to bed, with the smell of liquor and those men on her breath, her body. She deliberately placed the smells on her body, rubbing her face against aftershave-scented cheeks, absorbing the scent like garlic to offend him. How many times had she slowly taken off her clothes where he could see from the bed so he would know from the disarray of her underthings that she had allowed another man to fondle her? Sometimes she had even created the disarray herself, hurriedly twisting a bra strap, hiking up her panties beneath her jeans furtively in the car before coming into the house; and she couldn't do any more than that.

"How much further," he said. It had stopped being a question. She felt he meant to follow her down the path until she got tired of leading. He would show her who had the greater endurance, wouldn't he?

Maybe he was afraid to divorce her because he thought she would want a share of the house he owned before marriage. He still ridiculed her for her mother's wedding gift: a bowl of home-made tamales. Her face never failed to burn when he did so. *My parents gave me the down payment for a home, and your mother gave us tamales.* Maybe he thought she would try to take what he had because she had nothing. He would wait her out; and the waiting made her crazy. Yet she was afraid to do any more than give him just cause.

The doctor could be so cruel and kind. When the doctor got mad, she wasn't afraid he would beat her, but she wasn't exactly sure what he would do. His anger was so secretive. She knew it was there, but she didn't know what he was going to do about it. What form would it take when it spewed out of him? Not knowing made her frightened and gave him even more power over her.

She stopped in front of a cave and turned toward her husband. A shot rang out. He slumped forward, falling at her feet, according to plan. She never really believed it would happen, that the plan would work—that her husband would be murdered—until he fell there at her feet. She wanted to take it back then, to turn the clock backward five minutes or less, time enough to grab his hand and run with him quickly the opposite way. His hands reached for her on the way down as they had sometimes reached to pull her into bed, not because he loved her so much—because she was his, branded by his ring, his name. She took a step backward.

"I've been shot. Get help," he whispered; and then her husband died, facedown in the sand, blood and then clear spinal fluid bubbling from the wound in his back, the acrid stench of rotting weeds blowing over him. Behind her a large target, an X shape made from duct tape, partially blocked the entrance to the cave. Budweiser beer cans hung from trees. She began to scream.

The doctor rushed from the bushes, the rifle in his hand. His eyes were wild, exuberant. He grabbed her arm, shook her roughly, and commanded, "Shut up! Stop screaming! Calm down!" She couldn't stop screaming. For a minute she thought he would shoot her too. He stood with his hand on her arm, his eyes glittering fiercely. She had told him if anything goes wrong, please shoot me too. *Please shoot me too*. His breath was coming hot and hard; he was panting obscenely. She thought he would shoot, but he threw the gun into a pile of leaves, not far from a half-empty bottle of Boone's Farm strawberry wine, and disappeared into the bushes again.

The little family they had passed on the path was suddenly running toward her. One of the children was dragging a blanket and a child's pillow stuffed into a Mickey Mouse pillowcase. Her hand pointed to her husband's face, smashed down in the sand, which filled his nose and mouth. She was screaming. In her head, she can still hear the scream.

PART ONE:

Murder Seven

"... St. Louis, ... a place where location of residence was of prime importance ..."—Tennessee Williams, who never forgave the city for its rigid neighborhood boundaries

Monday afternoon, January 14, 1980

Rosie Sutterfield was afraid of dentists. Yet, with relatively little trepidation, she yanked open the door at 4630 Gravois marked G. ENGLEMAN, D.D.S., 9:00 A.M. TO 5:00 P.M. EXCEPT THURS, SAT 9:00 A.M. TO 12 NOON, WALK IN—and walked in. Her new dentist had been recommended by her daughter as a "gentle, kind, and not expensive man," and the recommendation had been seconded by her neighbors. His office sat in the big revolving shadow of Bevo Mill, a restaurant built into an old rock mill that had taken on the dignity assumed by anything standing long enough to outlive its purpose. The Mill physically anchored the South Side as the Arch, another slightly foolish St. Louis monument, anchored the riverfront; and it was fitting, she thought, that Doc, who was held in such high regard by South Siders, should work near the base of the anchor. She found him to be all her daughter promised and more. In fact, she felt as if she'd known Glennon Engleman all her life. Unlike other dentists she'd encountered, he was "down to earth," the highest compliment Rosie could pay a professional man.

On the afternoon of the fourteenth, she didn't have an appointment. Like most of "the Doc's" patients in that neighborhood, where taxidermy shops and pawnbrokers still filled space and each block housed at least one person who read tarot cards or cast horoscopes, Rosie followed the invitation on the door and walked in whenever she had the time and the cash for dental work. The Doc disdained the paper niceties of middle-class dentistry: embossed appointment cards, personal checks, and bills sent in envelopes that could be turned inside out to become return envelopes. He preferred a cash-paying, walk-in trade. On occasion, he was known to lower the price, often considerably and sometimes to nothing, for hardworking people who couldn't scrape together enough money to have their festering teeth pulled, even on a pay-what-you-can, when-you-can basis. On the other hand, he had no use for those who carried green cards entitling them to government-paid medical care, especially blacks. Once he had been investigated by the Civil Rights Commission for refusing dental care to a black woman.

"Freeloaders!" he snorted, whenever the subject of welfare came up in the office or in one of the neighborhood bars. He patronized the most parochial of gathering places, where at least one burly truck driver per week would tell a harrowing story about driving in convoys through that dangerous city, New York. ("It's so dangerous up there, I'm afraid to drive into the city alone. They'll break into your truck while it's moving and throw your load onto the street. You could get killed up there for no reason.") If the "freeloaders" were white, Doc, picking up his dental drill or lifting the occasional beer, called them "hoosiers"; if black, they were "niggers." Whatever their color, he insisted, "The country would be better off without the lazy sons of bitches." To the truckers, he said, "If you get killed here, it's for a reason"; and they solemnly agreed this was how life should be.

His opinions were fiercely held, and he was as likely to share them with his patients as his poker buddies. The patients for the most part agreed with him, though few could match the extreme degree of his feelings. He had taken the credo of his peers and invested it with more passionate hatred than they could ever conceive. These peers, patients and buddies, came from white frame homes, which represented a step up the ladder from the projects where they grew up, with living rooms paneled in fake wood and dining tables decorated with plastic bouquets. Or they came from small, neat, red brick houses where the jockey boys in blackface, retired to basements in big northeastern cities, still tended the gates; and they felt no shame about those gleaming black statuary faces, a sign to all of their view of the proper role for blacks. Mainly they were the sons and daughters of Anheuser-Busch brewery workers. Many were brewery workers themselves; their drink of choice was Busch beer. Each spring fresh coats of pink paint were applied to their concrete lawn flamingos. Pickup trucks, predominantly red Fords, Jeeps, and Chevrolet Impalas with rusted spots on the fins and dented bumpers lined the streets in parking spaces their owners considered inviolate. Fistfights were not uncommon in winter when someone pulled his car into the regular spot, carefully shoveled clean, "belonging" to a neighbor. Inside the bars, fistfights were common in any season. The Doc, who didn't participate in public brawling, considered himself above such behavior and especially looked down on drunken women, packed tight into jeans and spilling out of halter tops, who slugged it out over some man, their mouths dripping obscenities. "Bitches from hell," he called them.

Hostility was never far from the surface on the South Side, even on the better streets where residents more often threatened to sue each other than resort to fisticuffs, and cutting the grass was a weekly duty, like religion used to be, from the first of April through the first of October. A good neighbor didn't run the mower before seven A.M., especially on weekends; and if he did, he might make someone mad enough to take a swing he wouldn't otherwise take. The social gradations of the South Side, which appeared to outsiders to run together like a melting, seven-layer Jell-O salad, a favorite potluck dish, were very distinct to the residents. To them it was simple: The layers above wherever one stood were people who believed "their shit don't stink"; and the layers below wherever one stood were all degrees of "hoosiers," which in St. Louis means white trash, not Indiana's refugees, the label many outsiders flung at South Siders in general. There was little tolerance for blacks—especially on those streets inhabited by whites who had fled the black invasion in north St. Louis—or for Jews, gays, or "uppity" women. Doc was a local hero on all levels. Many would recount his good deeds, their sentimentality as freely expressed as hatred, their eyes glistening unashamed as they spoke.

Three people were ahead of her when Rosie Sutterfield walked in Doc's office on January 14 and signed the book, open on the ledge of the tiny square window between the waiting room and the office. She sat down, picked up a *Newsweek* magazine, and read about the disco craze of '76. She wondered if she and her friend Bernie should go to a disco or if it was too late because they were too old or the time had passed. The magazine *was* four years old. Ethel Merman had even made a disco record, she'd heard. Did the Doc disco? Her thoughts always came back to Doc, the strong magnetic center of this little part of the world. Bernie'd had a brief flirtation with a dentist. Rather, the flirtation was all on the dentist's side. Bernie, a devout and divorced Catholic, could only continue to receive communion as long as she didn't date. Rosie now wondered if the Doc was Catholic. She knew the nuns from a nearby convent were patients of his. She'd seen him fussing over one of them in the waiting room, calling her "Sister."

Rosie considered pulling out her compact to powder her nose, then didn't. Her skin really didn't get that shiny anymore; and without her glasses she might not see where she was applying the fresh makeup and accidentally leave traces of pressed powder caked around her nostrils. She wouldn't want the Doc to notice her makeup was sloppily applied while examining her mouth. He had told her she looked like a younger Lucille Ball, which she took as a compliment and kept in mind whenever she painted the exaggerated bow shape over her natural lip line. She liked a man who noticed things. After ten minutes the woman sitting next to her commented on the soothing aqua shade of the office walls.

"Ain't it restful?" she asked Rosie, who replied it was.

"I especially like the framed Monet prints," Rosie said in a husky voice that hinted she smoked too many cigarettes. She picked up the "ain't" and noted with a little pleasure that the other woman clearly didn't know who Monet was. Naturally she expounded. "He told me his ex-wife did the framing," she finished. "I thought that was nice. He seems like the sort of man who would stay friends with his ex-wife, doesn't he?" And she couldn't resist adding, "Not like that ex-husband of mine."

Dr. Engleman opened the door and asked, "Who's next?"

He was the most prosaic of men: balding, of average height and build, round in the gut, yet giving off the air of grandiosity with the requisite faint scent of the dentist, a blend of disinfectant, mouthwash, and medicine. Rosie, like so many middle-aged divorcées and widows of the South Side, wanted to think he was more than he was because of his professional status and mirrored this image of him in the smile she gave him.

He was wearing the same white coat, black pants, shoes, and socks that he always wore, and she thought his meager wardrobe indicated he had no woman to take care of him. The woman who didn't know Monet went inside. Rosie looked at the framed prints again and wondered if the attractive blowsy blonde she'd seen in the office was his ex-wife or not. She was trying to decide if the two matched as a couple. The dentist wasn't exactly a handsome man, even if head on you didn't notice his tummy so much. The blonde, who wore scarves covering her hair, was a little on the heavy side, especially in the hips, but she was still very pretty. She looked better, but he had charisma; and he talked about restaurants a lot. Rosie was proud of her own trim body, but she didn't eat as many restaurant meals as she would have liked, unless you included the Famous-Barr employee cafeteria, which she didn't. She sneaked a look in her compact. Satisfied, she finished reading about the disco craze.

She was restlessly flipping through her third magazine, wondering what was taking so long when the Doc opened the door and said, "Be with you in a moment. It won't be much longer now." He had such a gentle, almost effeminate voice. The first time she'd heard it, she'd thought, briefly, he was one of those funny guys. Rosie and the woman waiting with a teenage girl smiled back at him. The girl, overweight and greasy from her hair to her sneakers, didn't look up from her own magazine.

"She needs a tooth pulled," the woman confided after he had shut the door again. Most of Doc's patients, in fact, needed teeth pulled. "We never had to wait this long, even when it's crowded.

It's nerve-racking to wait so long when you know you have to have a tooth pulled." Rosie nodded sympathetically and wondered if her makeup would hold out. "This is real unusual. He ain't that crowded either. She's lucky the tooth's in back where it don't show."

"Sorry to keep you waiting so long," he told Rosie as he was finally leading her back to an examining room. She breathed the familiar medicinal smell recalling discomfort and pain, but she sniffed another note in that bouquet too, something beneath the disinfectant, something almost smoky, an odor she couldn't place; and she was good with smells in spite of her smoking. In the corridor, they passed a young man, blond and clean-cut, wearing a red plaid shirt and jeans. The Doc had been hiring kids for odd jobs around the office since he began practicing dentistry. In the early days he had been a Scout Master and had taken the entire Miranda family, eight fatherless Mexican children and their beleaguered, widowed mother under his wing. When neighborhood people talked about his good deeds, they usually listed his kindness to kids, and especially the Mirandas, in that column. Rosie hadn't heard anything bad about him since she'd begun asking around about him—and how often could you say that about a dentist? Dentists specialized in gouging people, in the wallet and in the mouth. The Doc was such good husband material, she didn't know why he was divorced. Probably his wife, if she was that blonde, had run around. That blonde didn't look like she'd be any better than she had to be.

Inside the room, the Doc said, "Hop on up in the chair."

"Well, I don't know if I can hop, but I'll get up there." She said her line in what was now their standard exchange as he prepared the needle full of painkiller. He liked patter, the greetings and punch lines often repeated. *Hot enough for you?* he would say in August; *Think it will snow?* in January. Or to his ex-wife Ruth, *Why don't you quit while you're still only a short distance behind?*

"That needle gets bigger every time," Rosie said.

"Again I apologize for the delay," the dentist said, smiling at her, holding the needle poised in his right hand while he positioned her jaw with his left. "Hold still now. Just a quick prick." He jabbed, and she flinched. "I'm still having work done on the building. Nobody you hire can ever do anything without supervision, you know. Let me know when it's numb, will you? I always end up doing a lot of the work myself, had to let my practice go for a while when I first got this place a few years ago so I could do the remodeling. If you want something done right, you have to do it yourself."

"Isn't that the truth," she tried to mumble. His fingers, clean and white and small, inserted the packing in her mouth. Her own fingers reflexively gripped the edges of the chair as he began to poke and prod for the cavity she knew was there. He hadn't taken X rays because he didn't much believe in them. He said he used them only sparingly. They were "overused" by other dentists, who only relied upon them to "line their pockets," not help their patients. He kept talking while he worked on her mouth. That was one thing she really liked about him—he talked the whole time she sat in his chair, so she didn't feel nervous. And he knew so much about so many things. He could talk everything from politics to art. She was behind him a hundred percent when he railed against the I.R.S., the big utilities, banks, and insurance companies that ripped them all off, and the niggers who had taken over downtown and ruined it. They both remembered when downtown was a good place to be. She thought he was the best dentist she'd ever had. When he was satisfied that she could feel nothing in the area surrounding her bad tooth, he picked up the drill and flicked the switch. She closed her eyes and took a deep breath as he brought the whirring instrument into her mouth.

He worked quickly, talking all the while. He was really wound up today, she thought, going on and on for some reason about "Jews, money grubbers, and lawyers." Rosie knew a few Jews at work, but she hadn't formed much opinion about them as a group. She regretted not being able to speak so she could adroitly change the subject. When the work was finished, she handed him fifteen dollars in cash. He noted in a ledger book her name, no address, and how much she had paid. She marveled once again at how little he charged. As he told her to come back in a week or ten days, she fancied his eyes held hers for longer than was absolutely necessary. She left his office with a smile on her face.

Rosie had to take two buses from Engleman's office on Gravois to her home on Cherokee Street. While she waited for the first bus, she checked her watch, which said 4:40 P.M., and lamented the fact that Doc's tardiness had made it likely most of the junk shops on Cherokee Street would be closed by the time she walked past them toward her home. She forgot about the missed possibility of finding an addition to her collection of flow-blue pottery, however, when she got off the bus at Grand and Gravois.

While Rosie was boarding her first bus, Sophie Marie Berrera, another middle-aged south St. Louis divorcée, was walking slowly toward her car, a 1975 red Ford Pinto parked behind the dental lab she owned and operated in rented space on the second floor of the Grand View Arcade Building on South Grand, not more than ten minutes from Engleman's office. The car had been sitting in that parking lot since Vincent Day, her deliveryman and ex-brother-in-law, returned from making his deliveries in it at 10:18 A.M. If she had looked under the left front tire, she would have seen the pressure device, two pieces of balsa wood and an electrical connector, which would explode the dynamite placed under the driver's seat as soon as she put the car in reverse and drove over the pressure switch. But she didn't look. Sophie was a homely woman who had long ago adopted the attitude and expression associated with such looks: Her body held in bitter control, she usually looked down when she walked and avoided the faces of others.

On March 20, 1979, someone had tried to kill Berrera with a bomb planted outside her garage. That bomb, eight sticks of dynamite and an electronic detonator in a green plastic garbage bag, got soaked by rain and failed to explode. Since then she'd been telling people she knew she would "get it" someday. She kept the police emergency number on a pad by her phones at work and home. For a while she lived her life more carefully, dropping a planned suit against Dr. Glennon Engleman, who owed her nearly $15,000 in back lab bills, and immersing herself in her interests, her four grandchildren and her activities in national, state, and local dental associations—which filled the hours she might have spent with a man if she'd had one. Then she inexplicably changed course again and told her lawyer, William Gartenberg, to file the suit, saying, "If someone's going to get me, there's nothing I can do about it. If it be, it be." Six days before her death, while Engleman was at a Scout meeting with his ten-year-old son, she paid a neighbor for an Avon order, proudly displayed pictures of her new granddaughter, and laughed off the questions, "Do you have any idea yet who planted that bomb last year?" and "Are you still scared?"

She was a believer in astrology and read her daily horoscope. Apparently from a cursory reading of the stars she didn't get any sense that "it" would be on January 14, 1980, or she might have checked the underside of her car before turning the key. Thirty pounds overweight and wearing a dark red shade of lipstick similar to the one favored by Rosie Sutterfield, she walked slowly toward the Pinto. At fifty-nine, she had apparently reached a place which is home ground to middle-aged women not wanted by men, the point where she wouldn't be pushed by anyone anymore.

According to Vincent Day, she'd been working at the lab already when he arrived at nine A.M. Perhaps she was too tired at the end of the day to be cautious. She was also wearing open-toed shoes. Earlier the temperature had climbed near fifty, but now it was back down to forty, and perhaps her feet were cold. In any case cars were parked on either side of her own, obstructing her view, and Sophie wasn't one to bend at the waist without considerable provocation.

A neighborhood resident noticed her walking toward the car, shoulders slumped, her eyes downcast—and wondered if something was troubling Sophie. She opened the trunk and placed an attaché case inside. Then she walked to the driver's side, unlocked the door, and got in.

At 4:45 she put the car in reverse. The blast shattered windows in adjacent buildings, scattered glass and pieces of Sophie over the street. It sent the steering wheel of the Pinto onto the sixth-floor roof of a nearby apartment building. Flying debris shot holes in the windshields of cars. Bits of flesh and blood were pasted on the Diplomat apartments like bugs plastered to the windshield of a car on the open road. Sophie's feet were severed from her body and landed separately, with stockings in place from the arch down and toenail polish unchipped. A piece of an ear with the earring still attached would be found one hundred feet away from the car the next day.

The largest remaining part of Sophie, her head and torso, arms and right hand, hung outside the car. Her face was singed, and at the moment the blood had abruptly drained out of her body, its expression was one of anger and surprise. The first officer on the scene reported "the lower portion of her anatomy destroyed" when he radioed for backup. Later, the coroner's report would describe her death as "caused by massive explosion injury of abdomen and lower extremities." Anyone near enough to see her mutilated corpse knew the technical description was inadequate.

When Rosie Sutterfield got off the bus at Grand and Gravois, a block from Grand and Miami where the explosion had just occurred, she saw the crowds and the fleet of emergency vehicles, police, fire, and ambulance. She smelled death, the peculiar blend of gasoline, burnt body parts, and dynamite vapors, that accompanies car bombings. A boy yelled, "They're finding fingers over there! Fingers with the stuff hanging out the open ends!" She hurried to make the connection to her next bus. It was, she thought, another gang bombing; she would learn enough about it on the six-o'clock news. There had been a number of organized-crime bombings on the South Side—rival gangs fighting over control of labor unions. She didn't need to see some man's fingers with the stuffing hanging out. If they were going to do that to each other, she didn't have to look.

"What makes a person want to see a thing like that up close?" she asked another woman boarding the bus. They sat down together. To keep their minds off the tragedy of a stranger's scattered fingers, Rosie began to talk about her visit to the dentist. He was, she told her companion, such a good and gentle man. The companion said, Why, yes, she'd heard of him, she'd heard that too.

At the same time, roughly five minutes after his mother had been torn apart by the bomb, Frederick D. Berrera, Jr., entered a meeting at the same downtown Famous-Barr department store where Rosie Sutterfield worked in the photo studio. A former employee of the dental lab, the younger Berrera owned his own business, Aries Audio Enterprises. The sales call at Famous was the last he had scheduled for the day. It was moving to a satisfactory conclusion, and he was mildly irritated when the meeting was interrupted at 5:20 P.M. by a phone call from one of his employees.

"What do you want?" he snapped. When he was told his mother had been the victim of a car bombing in the vicinity of the lab, he calmly put down the phone, excused himself, and drove to the bomb scene. He pushed through a mass of people, including a man operating a small home movie camera, to reach the tape that read, POLICE LINE. DO NOT CROSS. He identified himself to investigating officers who represented the St. Louis Police Department and the U.S. Bureau of Alcohol, Tobacco, and Firearms; then he identified his mother's body. The police would consider him a potential suspect because he appeared to have no reaction at all to his mother's death as he stood alongside her remains.

Within ten minutes he was telling the press, "She baby-sat for my children on Sunday. I feel like I'm sleeping. I know I'm going to wake up tomorrow and suddenly this will hit me."

Berrera and the authorities waited while the crowd continued to swell. Vincent Day, the deliveryman, arrived. Sophie's immediate neighbors, who had already heard she was the victim, hung at the edge of the mass, dabbing at their eyes. Several cops were already talking to people, asking the questions, "Did you see anything?" and to the neighbors who knew her, "Can you think of anyone who had a motive for killing her?" Others were combing the area for pieces of the car and pieces of Sophie, which were deposited in plastic bags and labeled by location.

"What are they waiting for?" strangers waiting for the ultimate finale, the removal of the corpse, asked each other. "When are they taking the body out?"

Several more police and fire vehicles parked along the 3500 block of Miami Street to obstruct the view of spectators as much as possible. The stretcher was brought to the side of the red Pinto, crumpled and twisted as if it had been squeezed in a huge vise until the middle snapped. People strained to see, standing on tiptoe, climbing on car hoods, trash cans, fireplugs. They hung outside windows. A father put his young son on his shoulders and asked, "Can you see? Can you see what they're doing now? What are they doing now?" Someone told him to hush. The body was being removed.

What was left of Sophie Marie Berrera, wrapped in sheets, covered half the stretcher.

That evening, while Rosie Sutterfield was watching the six-o'clock news, the first report in which the victim was identified, she would have been shocked to know her kindly neighborhood dentist was en route to a South Side police station for questioning about the murder. He was quickly identified as a potential suspect by Berrera's son, her ex-husband, her daughter Linda Marie Owens, and a friend and neighbor who had each separately recounted the story of the lawsuit that had been dropped after the first bomb failed, then picked up again.

Another South Side woman was watching the six-o'clock news that night too: Ruth Jolley Engleman, Glennon Engleman's third ex-wife. When she heard that Sophie Marie Berrera had been killed by a car bomb, she thought she knew immediately who had done it and why. Worse, she was sure she would be next. She would not have been surprised to learn her ex-husband was riding in a police car.

Ruth usually wasn't home in time to see the early news, but she had stayed home from work at Gateway Account Services because she and David, her son by Engleman, both had a cold that day. She listened to the brief initial report in horror. The announcer said, "St. Louis detectives were already trying to fit together the puzzle of why Sophie Marie Berrera, a quiet, middle-aged south St. Louis divorcée, was killed by a car bomb."

He did it, he really did it, she thought. The phone rang and she recoiled, sure it would be him, laughing, bragging, warning.

"Is Dr. Glennon Engleman there, please?" a man's voice said.

"Who's calling?" she asked. Since the divorce, a year and a half before, she hadn't told people who called that he no longer lived there. There was security in letting people think a man, a doctor, lived in your house. Usually the callers were patients, and she would tell them to try the office. Why discuss your personal life with strangers? She didn't tell KMOX-TV anything either. "What is this about? Are you really KMOX-TV and why would you want Glennon?"

"We want to talk to him about a bombing that occurred in south St. Louis," the man replied. "Will you take my telephone number and ask him to call?"

She didn't take down the number recited. When he said thank you and hung up, she was almost afraid to replace the receiver, afraid the phone would ring again with another TV station or a newspaper—or the police. Her strong square jaw trembled. Stockily built, she looked like she'd grown up poor and tough in the projects, as she had, where she'd learned to take punches as well as throw them. In one spectacular fight with Glen, while she was in the process of divorcing him, she'd grabbed his legs as he was walking away from her up the circular steps in her living room, pulled down his pants, and sunk her teeth into his thigh. She'd held on as well as any junkyard dog. The blond hair dye didn't hide her true roots. Not much scared her. Her ex-husband, however, scared her now.

When she'd met him, she was only twenty-one, badly in need of dental work; and he was married to someone else, a librarian named Edie, whom he called his "sweet and light-headed wife." He told Ruth the black panty hose she wore with her Bermuda shorts made him horny as hell. They'd had sex in the dental office on a cot he pulled down from the rafters during her second visit to have a cavity filled. He'd dazzled her with his oral virtuosity. That man did everything with his mouth, talked like nobody she'd ever heard talk, and made love as well with his mouth as he did with the body part most men thought was sufficient to do the job. The words and the saliva flowed. He cajoled and extorted, threatened, enlightened, entertained with his lips, his tongue. His vocabulary was matched by the variety of the secret strokes his tongue could perform on her body. Just seeing him moisten his lips could get her going. And he held out the promise of a better life. Sex and a better life. Ruth was determined to make a better life for herself than the one she'd had growing up. Glennon Engleman was the first man she'd met who had any idea what constituted a better life—and he was one of the few South Siders able to finance one.

When she finally came to understand all he was really capable of doing—to her as well as to others—she grew afraid. At first she thought she was crazy for believing his stories; then she thought he was the crazy one for telling them. She had tried to divorce him several times. When she finally managed to do it, in self-defense she'd kept his name and clung to the identity he'd wanted her to have. Though divorced, she felt like an occupied country; the enemy troops hadn't withdrawn. She wasn't free yet. Retaining the title of "Mrs. Engleman" and granting him occasional conjugal rights had made her safer, she thought. Until now.

Two hours later when the *Post-Dispatch* called, she said she was the ex–Mrs. Engleman; she didn't know where her ex-husband was. Her voice trembled as she said it. She sensed that she had made a decision, even then.

"We want to talk to him about the car bombing," the woman said. "We understand he's been taken into custody now. Who's his attorney? Can you tell us that?"

"Does he need an attorney?" Ruth asked.

"Well, if he's been taken into custody, he does."

"I'm the ex–Mrs. Engleman now," Ruth repeated; and again she didn't write down the number given. When she hung up the phone this time, she knew what she had to do: She had to call his sister, Melody, with whom he'd lived since their divorce, and his best friend, Bob Handy, to show her concern for Glen, to make sure the message got back to him that she wouldn't say anything to anyone. She was so afraid she would be next. He had to believe he could trust her while she bided her time, figured out what she could do.

"They just never give that poor guy a break, do they?" she said first to Melody; then to Bob, her voice reduced to a flat, placating whine, she repeated the spiel word for word, obsequiously, as though she were selling newspaper subscriptions or aluminum siding over the phone. She was begging these people to have mercy on her. "They are just always after him about something . . . Well, have him call me if you hear from him. Tell him I called." She knew she hadn't fooled them, especially Melody, who despised her. Melody would do anything for her brother; and the looks they exchanged spoke of a deeper bond than any she could understand between brother and sister. When she first met Glen, he'd talked casually about taking Melody to dances or the movies, as if they were dates. No, she couldn't put anything past his sister. She hoped she could still fool *him*. As long as he still wanted her in bed, she could surely still fool him. But how long would that last? He'd let her know little boys didn't need their mothers past a certain age; and David was nearing that age.

While Ruth was making her calls, Detective Ron Lingle of the St. Louis PD and Special Agent John Bobb of ATF were talking to the Doc. They couldn't get his consent for a polygraph or a test of his hands for explosive residue. He wasn't worried about Sophie's lawsuit, he insisted, because he would have won it. While he didn't exactly cooperate, he certainly didn't reserve the right to remain silent either. In fact, he seemed to enjoy flaunting his knowledge about both Sophie's work habits and the making of bombs. He let them know he was familiar with the delivery schedule followed by her driver—and that the Pinto was used for those deliveries. Largely, however, for three hours, he railed against Sophie Berrera.

"She was cheating me, charging me more than she did anyone else! And I had proof of that. I would have won a lawsuit against her, and I regret not having the chance to do so. She was a greedy, avaricious bitch! She and her Jew lawyer were trying to bleed me, and she's got what she deserved," he said. "That bitch worked her husband Fred until he had a heart attack, and then she took everything from him. She was cruel to Pop [Ed] Hoffman, her deliveryman before he died. I'm not sorry she's dead. She got what she deserved."

Finally, Lingle and Bobb drove him back to the office on Gravois where he voluntarily surrendered the January 14, 1980, page from his appointment book to verify his alibi. They thought he was considerably more rabid in his views than the typical South Sider, but on the other hand, he wasn't extreme to a degree unknown in that part of the city. Feelings ran high on the South Side, especially where money and racial or ethnic origins were concerned. More important, the victim's son, the man who had watched so impassively as her mutilated body was yanked free of the twisted metal, stood to gain more from her death than the dentist she was suing. They thought the dentist had a screw loose, but that didn't necessarily make him a killer.

"If I'd been responsible for the bombing," he told them in his parting shot as they left the office, "I would have hired someone else to do it."

The Doc made some phone calls before he went back to Melody's house, but none of those calls were to Ruth. He was careful of what he said to the people he called in case the line was tapped.

"It isn't the crime they'd think I'd commit," he did say. "It's inhumane. They would say, 'Oh, Doc could kill all right, but he wouldn't kill this way, endangering other lives, here in south St. Louis where he's lived all his life. Why that bomb could have killed one of his patients for all he would know . . . And Doc wouldn't do that . . .' That's what they'd say . . . I'm not worried, that's what they'd say."

Tuesday morning, January 15, 1980

"Jesus Christ, you think he used enough dynamite for the job?" McGarvey said to no one in particular. Smoking a cigarette, he was standing in front of an apartment building that had been sprayed with the blood of Sophie Berrera. Dried bits of her clung to the bricks. The odor of her death still hung in the air. The stench of a bomb death was similar to that of a bad accident, and he'd inhaled some of those in his years with the Illinois State Police. The smell never failed to depress him. Sometimes he carried it for days inside his nostrils. It weighed him down with each breath. He shook his head in disgust, exhaled smoke, and threw the half-finished cigarette down. He ground it into the pavement with the toe of his shoe. "Hell of a mess, isn't it?"

Because the use of a bomb makes murder a federal crime, William J. McGarvey, a special agent with ATF, was part of the team at the bomb site early on Tuesday morning, examining the evidence and knocking on doors. Tall, dark, and lean, he wore a drooping mustache and longish hair hung over from the '70s, a look compatible with the hangover he was suffering that morning. He had recently turned thirty-three, and he was a cop's cop, no glory hound. He hadn't seen much glory since he joined the Air Force to serve in Vietnam but spent it as an aircraft electrician stationed at Scott Air Force base in Belleville, Illinois. There was little reason to think he would find it in ATF, Alcohol, Tobacco, and Firearms, an agency still living down their original main function, chasing moonshiners in the South—and even less reason to think he'd find it sifting through the remains of Sophie Berrera and her red Ford Pinto.

Like the other experts, he had all but ruled out a mob link in the bombing. The mob doesn't kill old ladies and the mob doesn't use more dynamite than the job requires, as this maniac had done. Unnecessarily endangering anyone but the designated hit isn't professional. It was a miracle that no one else had been hurt by the bomb that killed Sophie. McGarvey was one of many thinking along the same lines and chasing down leads, over a hundred of them, including every known crazy in the nearby vicinity. Dr. Glennon Engleman looked more interesting than promising as a lead.

"What do you think about this dentist," he asked Steve Alsup, from the city's bomb and arson squad.

"Seems farfetched, doesn't it?" Alsup shrugged his shoulders, shook his head. "It isn't likely that a neighborhood dentist, no matter how hot-tempered, would be responsible for a car bombing."

"Right. More likely he'd shoot her in front of witnesses. Let's look at him anyway," McGarvey said, his voice deep, distinctive, the way a gravelly voice might sound if all the edges of the individual bits of gravel had been worn smooth. It gave away nothing. His questions weren't even questions. His voice didn't go up at the end of the sentence. Like his face, it kept his secrets. He was convinced an investigator could do a better job if he looked like he might be selling insurance or manufacturing microprocessors, so he tried to look like he might be selling insurance. He was holding a sheaf of papers in his hand, reports from the officers who had conducted interviews the night before and notes on the dentist's visit to the station house. Shaking the papers briskly, he said, "He's divorced. Why don't we talk to the ex-wife."

McGarvey then did what a good cop does with a male lead: He began looking for the ex-wife.

She was looking for her ex-husband.

Ruth had been awake at five A.M., waiting for the delivery of the paper. The coverage on that morning of the fifteenth centered on the victim and the bomb scene. The dentist who had been questioned by police wasn't named and wouldn't be until the next day. Ruth read the articles twice and tried to tell herself it was nearly over, that because he wasn't identified as the murderer today, she was safe. She kept David home another day to be safe in case he wasn't well yet and to provide her with company. They baked cookies and watched television together. She nibbled and paced, dodging David's questions asked in his still babyish sing-song voice, and waited for the dentist who had been questioned by the police to call. When he didn't call by two P.M., she dialed the office, knowing he would answer the phone.

"I guess you heard Marie bought it last night," he told her, the satisfaction obvious in his voice. "She brought it on herself."

"Glen, David has been home from school sick. He had a fever of a hundred and one, so I kept him home from school. Why don't you stop by here after work and see him?"

He tried to talk about Sophie Marie Berrera again, but she wouldn't let him. After securing his promise to stop by, she hung up the phone. She wanted him to see her as the mother of his sick child, needed by the child. More important, she wanted him to think, *Ruth's not going to say anything to anybody. She wouldn't call me today if she was a threat to my security. I don't have to worry about Ruth. I can come to the house after doing something like this without worrying about her saying anything to anybody.*

You understand that, don't you, Glen? she said to herself. You don't have to worry about me.

She put on fresh makeup and the black panty hose he loved. The skirt she selected, a red-and-black-striped wool blend, ended above her knee, where all of her skirts had ended since the '60s. To match the skirt, she chose a bright red blouse, polyester blend, with a floppy bow tie. But she stopped herself from fluffing the pillows under the bedspread. She couldn't do that yet, not tonight.

He didn't get there until 9:15. She was helping David with his homework when she heard him come up the steps, whistling. *Whistling*, after he'd made her stew all day!

"Hey, babe!" he called. "Hey, bub!" He came right in the door as if it was still his house, as if he owned them. Well, didn't he?

"Dad!" David cried happily. He ran into his father's arms. Just like some TV sitcom family, she thought. After looking at David's throat, he told him to finish his homework so he could go back to school tomorrow. She sat next to him on the sofa.

"I was at the police station cooling my heels last night," he told her, his hand resting proprietarily on her knee. His fingers, she noted, were as white and clean as usual. She had often marveled that he managed to do so much manual work on his own buildings without ruining his hands.

"I don't want to hear about it," she said, inclining her head toward her son. "Sometimes I feel like this house is bugged. I don't want you to talk about it now."

David finished the work and went upstairs. Glen sat next to her, his hand on her knee, calling her "babe" and telling her over and over again that Sophie Berrera had gotten what she deserved. *She bought it. She brought it on herself.*

"You know she worked poor Fred, that poor bastard, to death," he said. "As soon as he got divorced from her, his health improved. You know she was never in the office before ten; and Fred was always there at seven A.M., opening up, doing a day's work before she ever got out of bed."

She was sure he had told her only days before that *Sophie* had been in the habit of arriving at work by seven A.M. Hadn't he said she was such a greedy woman she couldn't wait to get to work and start making money? Tonight she wouldn't call him on this. She was afraid to talk back to him, but she did it, gauging his mood, trying to estimate how far it was safe to go before she had really pushed him too far and he blew. When she did call him on something, she pushed the words out the way a downed boxer pushes himself up from the floor, afraid he will get hit again before he can finish standing up. Tonight she would keep her mouth shut because she knew what he was doing: justifying Sophie's murder.

At ten o'clock Glennon Engleman eagerly turned on the news, flipping from channel to channel to see if someone would mention his name. He said he hated the attention of the cops and the news media, but she thought he thrived on it. He delighted in being a suspect, then slipping out of the authorities' grasp. One reporter said an anonymous caller had reported seeing three young men, one black, in coveralls, around the car. Ruth asked him if three young men had been involved, and he shook his head no.

"They make everything up as they go along," he said derisively. She wondered if he'd had someone phone in the tip to confuse the cops. That would be like him, one of the games he would play with them. Hadn't he bragged before about pulling off his crimes under the noses of the stupid cops? She thought he was disappointed when the news commentators didn't mention his name—though he would have yelled if they had. That was Glen—a contradiction.

She turned her head away from him and called David downstairs. Her sudden decision to do that surprised her as much as it did Engleman.

"Glen, David has some questions about this story, about what's going on," she said to him while David stood unsure on the staircase. "Will you tell him the police talked to you because you knew her, because it happened in your neighborhood?"

"Yes, I knew her," he said. "I knew her well. They asked me questions because I knew her very well."

David nodded, his eyes clear and untroubled, as shiny as the blond hair on his head she'd just shampooed with Johnson's baby shampoo. He still hated to get soap in his eyes. The child believed what his father said. He would accept any story his father gave him unless she countered it with the truth—but she didn't dare do that as long as Glen was around. Ruth shivered. Satisfied, Engleman sent his son back upstairs and turned toward her.

"What was the point in that?" he asked, his hand clamping around her wrist, shaking it slightly.

She shrugged. "He has questions." He let the matter drop because, she thought, he wanted to spend the night. She didn't ask, and he was disappointed when she didn't. In fact, he left mad. She knew she could have him there any night she wanted him; and after he was gone, she berated herself for not being smart enough to want him tonight.

While the dentist was driving back to Melody's brick mansion in the central west end, McGarvey was sitting at a desk in far less elegant surroundings, his dingy office in the Federal Courts Building on Market Street. His long legs were stretched out, his feet crossed at the ankles on his desk. He was smoking another cigarette and reading a police report that detailed Engleman's interview of the previous evening. The guy sounded like a jerk— a pseudo Nazi from the South Side. He would have to show this stuff to Terry Adelman, one of the U.S. attorneys who worked in the building, a little Jewish guy. They'd laugh about it together. As far as McGarvey was concerned, the interview only proved the dentist was extremely prejudiced and outspoken. If he'd killed Berrera, would he talk so openly about his feelings?

Ruth Engleman's address, scribbled on a piece of yellow paper, was on top of a stack of papers.

Wednesday, January 16, 1980

On Wednesday morning the papers said a south St. Louis dentist had been questioned, and the *Globe-Democrat*, in the continuation of the story, named him: *Dr. Glennon Engleman*. The name stood out from the page. Ruth had planned to go back to work that day, but while reading the story she lost her nerve. She called the office to say she wouldn't be in. A coworker, Virginia Rutledge, took the call.

"I'm not coming back to work today," she said, "because of the newspaper coverage and so on. I think I need another day for everything to cool off."

"Oh, what are you talking about?"

"Well, if you haven't seen it, Virginia, just forget the whole thing. I don't feel like going into it with you," Ruth said, her anger building. The woman *had* seen. She read the papers, and she wouldn't have missed an item like that. Did she look down on Ruth for having been married to a man like Glen? Well, of course she did. "I just won't be in today."

That forced Virginia to admit she had read the papers. "Look, Ruth," she said sympathetically, "I think you should talk to someone about this if you're afraid. And I know you're afraid. You should contact the FBI."

"If you know someone that you could get me in touch with, then I'll do it. But I've tried to talk to the St. Louis Police Department about him before, another time when he was threatening to do something—and they wouldn't listen. They acted like they thought I was crazy, just another ex-wife out to get her husband. Another psycho broad." Her voice cracked. She was angry at herself for the cracking voice, the display of weakness. "Virginia, I'm so afraid."

"Listen, you have to do something about this. You can't let this continue. I know someone. I'll call him for you, Ruth."

She hung up the phone, expecting nothing from Virginia, angry at herself for letting her fear show—and hoping her ex-husband would call and say, "Babe, hey, babe." How she hated the kind of pity women like Virginia gave to women like her! What good was that pity against him? She wanted him to call. *Hey, babe, I'll let you live another day.* He had threatened to kill her when David reached fourteen. He was only ten. She had four years, didn't she? He wouldn't do anything to her yet, would he? And maybe he wouldn't really do anything at all, as long as she kept pleasing him, as long as her mouth and her "pussy," as he preferred to call that part of her anatomy, remained open to him. Perhaps she was wrong after all to think Sophie's death foreshadowed her own. It was even more possible that Sophie's death would force him to be careful, at least for a while. Well, wasn't it?

"We want to ask you a few questions," Steve Alsup began, launching his spiel like every TV cop she'd ever seen, introducing himself and McGarvey. As a result of Virginia Rutledge's call—or so she thought—she'd already been interviewed by the FBI, who had politely said they weren't the right agency for the job. She might have been trying to arrange a trash pickup for an outsize item. At times like that she thought Glen was right in all he said about the authorities. They could be fooled so easily. He'd done it often enough, hadn't he? And he'd certainly got a kick out of doing it. On Wednesday evening her hands trembled briefly as she let two more cops in the house and closed the door behind them.

McGarvey was already sizing up the two-level townhouse, the condominium of Tavistock Circle. It was, he thought, decorated the way he'd expect a doctor's wife to decorate a home: tasteful, quiet. The dining-room set appeared to be solid oak. The surfaces were immaculate, and no objects of south St. Louis kitsch art sat on the tabletops or bookshelves.

"Most of the books are his, Glennon's," she said as he quickly perused the titles, largely nonfiction, an eclectic collection with heavy concentration in the occult and history, particularly German history during the period of the Third Reich. Jesus, McGarvey thought. Of course, he would be a Hitler enthusiast. There was also a shelf of volumes on police investigative techniques. He turned his attention back to the dentist's third ex-wife. It was a little difficult to reconcile Ruth Engleman, short and stubby and garbed in a bright, short dress, with her house; she didn't appear to be put together by the same hand. But one thing was clear: The woman was extremely nervous.

"You don't have to answer any questions, of course," Alsup continued. She nodded and looked past him straight into McGarvey's deep brown eyes. He was kidded about his effect on women. Certainly his large, sad eyes were part of it. He had the kind of eyes that inspired trust—exactly the kind Ruth was looking for. "We can't make you answer any questions you don't want to answer," Alsup continued, but she and McGarvey already knew she had no other choice.

"I don't really know anything," she said, pulling a tissue from the box on the coffee table, twisting it in her hands. She crossed her legs and made an attempt to smooth her skirt down over hefty thighs. The hem wouldn't cover her knees. "I have suspicions, a lot of suspicions. But if I say anything, what happens to me?"

Again she looked into McGarvey's eyes. He wondered if she was smart enough to know that he, and not Alsup, could offer the immunity that would protect her for life. In his initial estimation, she possessed modest intelligence, an intelligence possibly clouded by her feelings, whatever they were, for her ex-husband.

She might or she might not have the story on the dentist—who might or might not have even the most peripheral involvement in this murder. She might or might not be crazy, but she was definitely scared. More important, she was looking for something, *someone*, to trust. If he could make her believe he was the one, then he could get everything she had, whatever it was worth. At that point he didn't think it was much, but he'd been surprised before.

"You can trust us," he said decisively. One foot was restlessly tapping the floor; his hands were clammy. Without looking at Alsup, he knew the other cop had also sensed he was the one Ruth would trust. Alsup would let him lead. The key was in deciding immediately who would be more effective in dealing with an informant and going with the gut reaction. There was no room for ego in this. It didn't matter why an informant leaned toward one and not another. "If you help us, we'll protect you."

"He's threatened to kill me," she said. "He's let me know my life isn't valuable to him after David gets a little older. And he'll do it—kill me; he's done it before. Killed. He's killed people before. More than Sophie. You just don't know."

"Tell us," he said, leaning toward her, resting his elbows on his knees. For all her strength, she was a woman who put her ultimate trust in powerful men. He figured that much out in the first sixty seconds. "We can't help you if you don't talk to us."

Ruth didn't tell them everything the first night. She told in outline form a long and incredible story, beginning with Bullock and ending with Berrera, tossing odd bits of factual information they seized upon to check later as the story rushed out, the way one might grab keepsakes rushing past in a flood. She put each alleged murder on the table as if it were a grisly carcass she'd disinterred from a shallow grave. When they didn't flinch at one, she piled on another. She was exhausted when they left, promising they would return. It was impossible to tell from their faces if they had believed her or not. Surely they would check on the things she had told them and see she was telling the truth. How long would it take them to put him away? And what if they didn't? She bolted the door when they left.

Saturday, January 19, 1980

On Thursday night, the Doc had come back, whistling up the steps, calling out, "Hey, babe, hey, bub." Already she felt like a ball in a Ping-Pong game between Glen and McGarvey. Already she'd known that's how it would be. If McGarvey won, she would be free; and if Glen won, she would be dead. He said he was taking David to Clarksville on Sunday to watch the eagles fly south. "Babe," he'd said, his hand on the back of her neck, his fingers kneading the muscles. "Babe, you're tense." She was.

Friday, McGarvey and Alsup had returned.

"They're going to watch the eagles fly south," she told McGarvey, "a real nice family thing to do, isn't it? I don't go with him when he takes David to places like that, because he might shoot me in some isolated spot while David was a few feet away, hidden by a clump of trees. Who would believe he had done it, killed me with my own child so close, his own child? And David would be hysterical of course. He would be soothing this hysterical child. He said he was taking David to Clarksville on Sunday, and he wanted him Saturday too. I said he couldn't have him both days, not both days."

On Saturday morning, she went to ATF headquarters and made her first detailed statement. She had chosen to trust McGarvey, partly because he seemed strong, compelling, in control, but also because he held out the promise of federal immunity and relocation, a better life. Or possibly she trusted him because he seemed exactly like the opposite of the man her ex-husband had become: He was the good to Glen's evil. When she was very young, she'd believed in Glen's version of the better life. She didn't anymore.

Less than a week after Sophie Berrera's death, Ruth Engleman had turned against her ex-husband.

PART TWO:

The Incredible Story

McGarvey: Ruth, are you aware that you are being recorded here? Ruth: Yes, I am.

Monday, January 21, 1980

McGarvey was reading the transcripts of the tapes from the interviews he, Alsup, Ron Lingle, and John Bobb had conducted with Ruth Engleman on Saturday and today. The early questions had been innocuous, benign. He had promised her they would be. Still she flinched at the first one. *State your name and address.* He'd looked at her and thought of someone in the dentist's chair, flinching from the needle prick, the shot of painkiller that always hurt worse than the drill, because it was the only thing you actually felt. *How long have you lived there and who lives with you? My son, David. Can you tell us when you married him, Ruth? Yes, it was April 15, 1967.*

He was alone in the office. The story she had told in the accumulated fifty-six pages of manuscript he held was the most bizarre tale he'd ever heard. They'd gone looking for the person who had committed a single murder, Sophie Berrera's; and if they were to believe Ruth, they'd found a man who had killed more, possibly several more, people. Even more unbelievably, that person was a professional man, a dentist who treated the poor without charge and took his son to Scout meetings. Yet a few of the details she'd given them had already checked out. How would she know about the physical evidence found at a murder site— evidence not disclosed to the press—if someone close to the murder hadn't told her? McGarvey lit another cigarette, recrossed his legs, began reading again from the beginning. What bothered him most was that Sophie's murder didn't fit the pattern Ruth described for the others.

Furthermore, most of what she claimed the Doc had told her had been said while they were married, which would make it evidence inadmissible in court. They had told her they needed to have her testimony corroborated by what she could get the Doc to tell her while she was wired. She had reluctantly agreed. She was disappointed at first. Had she really expected her word to be enough to nail him? Did she think she could get rid of a troublesome ex-husband that easily? He had promised her safe passage, a new name in a new city for her and David in exchange for her testimony. He was taking a chance by promising so much so soon, but he felt he'd had no choice. If everything she had said about the Doc was true, would they really be able to keep her safe? More important, could everything she said possibly be true? Clearly she wanted to get her son away from his father. Probably she had good reason for wanting to do that. The man had a violent temper, strong prejudices, and a sex drive that wouldn't quit. Was all that reason enough for what she was trying to do to him?

> RUTH: *I know of incidents that he said he was going to do, as far as murdering people . . . and incidents that he has done.*
> MCGARVEY: *Can you be specific here, Ruth?*
> RUTH: *Before we were married, just before we were married, his sister Melody and I were talking about something. I don't remember what. And suddenly she told me that it wasn't true, what some people had said, that Glen hadn't murdered the Bullock man. Glen came into the room then, and he was very angry. He was angry at Melody, ranting and raving and throwing things around. "Yes, I killed him!" he shouted. "Yes, I did!" He wanted me to know that he had.*

Murder One: James Bullock, December 17, 1958

On December 17, eight days before Christmas, glamorous Italian-born actress Pier Angeli divorced young singer Vic Damone, tearfully claiming he was "insanely jealous." Women in Doc's neighborhood would relish that story a few months down the road when the fan magazines rehashed it, turning it into beauty-shop reading material, since few of them read the papers except for the ads. The St. Louis department stores were running modest ads for Christmas goodies from ladies shoes with stiletto heels and dangerously pointed toes for $5.00 to baby dolls, complete with their own diapers and little buggies, for $2.50. The pretty Mexican girl who would become a widow on Labor Day, 1976, was only six years old, too young to read about movie stars or peruse the ads. She came from a very poor family, and much of what she and her seven siblings would receive that Christmas would come through the Doc's largesse, cash slipped into her mother's pocket when no one was looking.

Her big brother Nick, seventeen, had been following the Doc around, doing his odd jobs, absorbing his wisdom since before she was born. On the evening of the Bullock murder, he was doing something special for the Doc: Nick was timing buses, the ones that ran during the weekday evening hours from south St. Louis to downtown. He didn't know why he was timing buses, but he figured it fit somehow into one of his mentor's schemes. Helping Doc made him feel more important than anything else in the world. Doc had taught him how to steal while presenting his round cherubic face to the world. "Crime is the only way to get ahead," Doc often told him. "You won't ever have anything if you live your life within the law."

Doc didn't describe his crimes in detail yet. Rather he let Nick find out about them, a little at a time, so he absorbed only the information he was ready to accept. He'd discovered Doc's first insurance scam, for example, because he spent so much time reading to make his vocabulary as good someday as the Doc's. His favorite place to read was in the corner of Doc's basement in the house he'd recently bought on Compton. One day he'd gone down there to read and found the motor to a boat Doc and his brother Gene had built and reported stolen. The boat, sans motor, was found at the bottom of a lake. The insurance was collected. Then Nick found the motor and put two and two together. He didn't tell the Doc he had.

Nick would do anything the Doc required of him. And why not? Doc would do anything for Nick. He'd called him one cold morning a few years back, the first bitter day of the season, when he had no coat to wear to school. He was crying to Doc that he didn't want to go to school in the cold without a coat. The sting of the weather would be equaled by the sting of the kids laughing at him because he was poor. "Stay there," Doc said. "I'm coming over." He had knocked on their door with his own new coat in hand. The coat fit Nick, who was bigger than most boys his age. "Keep it," Doc said. "It's yours." Sure, he would do anything for Doc. Who else would give him a coat? Would treat his mother with respect, as though she were a rich white woman, not a poor Mexican?

While Nick was timing buses, James Stanley Bullock, twenty-seven, was stringing Christmas lights around his modest little bungalow in the Richmond Heights section of the city. With his slicked-back hair and serious countenance, he was the epitome of an upwardly striving middle-class husband, 1958. At seven P.M., as *The Price Is Right* was just coming on the screen of their black-and-white console television, he kissed his bride of six months, Ruth, a kindergarten teacher, and left his two-tone 1957 Plymouth sedan for his night classes at St. Louis University. An employee of Union Electric Company, he was studying finance. His route, normally over the expressway or down Lindell Boulevard, should not have taken him past the Art Museum, and he should have arrived at class around 7:20 or 7:25, depending on traffic. At 7:30 his class began without him.

At 7:37 P.M. a motorist traveling on Fine Arts Drive saw in the glare of his headlights a most unusual sight: A stockily built man wearing a brown hat and a dark, possibly blue, topcoat stood with a gun over another man lying in the road. When the gunman had apparently made sure his victim was dead, he ran away into the night. The motorist got out of the car at the same time another motorist behind him got out of his car. The two men ran around the Art Museum in search of the guard, who called the police. The three stood in front of the building beneath the inscription ART STILL HAS TRUTH. TAKE REFUGE THERE and waited while the blood poured out of James Stanley Bullock.

It was a slow night, so on-duty St. Louis detectives John Vining and Phil Dwyer were grabbing their dinner at a Christmas party at The Pink Elephant bar in midtown when the call came into the station. The dispatcher found them at the bar and sent them to the crime scene, where a patrolman reported the dead man had been seen moments before he died, his face pouring blood, running from behind the museum toward the statue of Louis IX on his horse, a man brandishing a gun behind him. They stood by as James Stanley Bullock was lifted from the dark red pool in which he had been lying and placed on a stretcher. His blood-caked face made it hard to tell where he'd been hit—or what he'd looked like only an hour before when his young wife had put her hand to his cheek while he kissed her good-bye. He had been shot twice in the head and once in the left shoulder by .22-caliber bullets. His chest contained the lead from half a dozen shotgun pellets, the type known as "birdshot," which constituted a fourth shot. He died shortly after he was placed in the ambulance.

Vining and Dwyer followed the patrolman to the victim's car, a two-tone 1957 Plymouth sedan parked at the dead-end of the L-shaped service drive that leads behind the museum. Its engine was still running, the driver's door wide open. The two young detectives exchanged glances. The area behind the Art Museum was a known meeting ground for homosexual men.

"That engine's been going quite a while," Vining said. "Look at the patch it's melted around the car. He was waiting for someone when he got killed." They walked around the car, Dwyer making notes on a report sheet. "Look at this," Vining said, pointing to the inside of the car where blood flecked the windshield and dashboard, the seat coverings and steering wheel. "He was shot in the car."

"Better call in the license plates for an ID," said Dwyer, picking up a hat from the rear floor. The initials on the sweatband read J.S.B. Bullock was already being tagged dead on arrival at City Hospital while the cops were reading those initials in his hat. The media circus known as the Bullock case officially began. It would have all the elements common to unsolved murders: opportunists, those people anxious to get something out of the ultimate life tragedy, from the grieving widow to promotion-minded cops to convicts in prisons eager to take another rap in exchange for small favors; rumors of sexual misconduct on the part of the participants, persistent rumors that swirled like the muddy whirlpools of the Mississippi; and genuine pathos in the story of an unsuspecting victim, pathetically ordinary and naive, and his equally ordinary survivors.

The detectives assigned to pick up the victim's next of kin for the grisly task of identifying the body had no idea this victim had been murdered. They thought he'd been run over by a car when they knocked on the door of the modest duplex in Richmond Heights, doffed their hats as the petite brunette answered, and told her that her husband had been killed in an "accident" in Forest Park. Her perky demeanor wilted faster than the cheap home permanent used by the twin in the TV commercials—the one who *didn't* have the Toni, the very commercial which was playing on the television set in the room behind her. She nearly swooned. Did she have any idea what her husband was doing in Forest Park that night? She didn't, she said; and another set of young cops exchanged glances. Her husband, they feared, had been getting some queer action on the side. Maybe, it occurred to them, he'd been deliberately run down by someone who hated queers, a fag baiter gone a little crazy. Or killed by his creep boyfriend.

The lady closely resembled the actress who played Beaver Cleaver's teacher in the comedy series *Leave It to Beaver.* Her eyes held that same wide, innocent, easily startled gaze. She leaned against the sturdy cops. They asked if Bullock had any close relatives in the area because they were afraid the sweet little thing wouldn't stand up to the task of identifying her husband's body alone. She told them Bullock had been raised by his aunt, Mrs. Walter Duerbeck, after the death of his parents when he was a young child. The pathos quotient increased.

They drove a few blocks to the aunt's house, where they learned she was at choir practice. Then they followed directions to the church, picked up the aunt, and headed downtown to the city morgue. When they arrived, the grieving widow refused to leave the police car. Geraldine Duerbeck, who had identified the bodies of his parents before him and raised this nephew with her own family, ignored the arm offered by an Irish cop and walked alone toward the sheet-covered body on the slab. James Bullock's face had been washed, but the bullet holes, one between the eyes, one near the top of the head, and one in the place where the neck and left shoulder join, gaped open at her.

"This is my nephew, James Stanley Bullock," she said in the steady voice of an American Gothic survivor claiming another of her dead. "Could you give me just a moment alone with him?"

In the police car the pretty widow dabbed at her eyes. She thought she was pregnant, she said, and the shock of seeing Jimmy could make her miscarry. She and Jimmy had been married in June; of course they wanted a baby, and if this baby was going to be all she had of him . . . she sobbed. He was going to graduate from St. Louis University next June, around the time of their first anniversary, so that he could get a better job than the clerk's position he held at Union Electric. They had no marital problems; they were *absolutely* happy!

"He strung the Christmas lights on our house before he left for school tonight!" she sobbed.

Nervously, the young cop, James Hackett, tried to remember the things he should ask a woman whose husband had died in an area where he had no logical reason for being—and finally he said, "Have you been married before, Mrs. Bullock?"

The question startled her. "Yes," she said. She had been married before, briefly, to Dr. Glennon Engleman, a dentist. She seemed to grow nervous and stared past the cop out the window.

Ruth and the young dental student she wed in 1953 and divorced in 1956 never lived together as man and wife, but she didn't volunteer that information in the police car. For the whole of their marriage, he lived at home with his mother, Annora, a reclusive woman he also called Madre with self-proclaimed psychic powers, while the bride shared an apartment, sanctioned for student housing, with some girls who were also students. Frequently, the young couple had sex in the backseats of cars, fierce couplings made possible by garter belt and stockings and the audacity of a woman who shunned panties. He usually came within seconds of entering her, but he was able to get hard again if she talked dirty to him. He loved to hear her talk dirty about sex, but would admonish her if she said "damn" any other time.

Perhaps they didn't set up housekeeping because the Doc believed he wasn't enough for her sexually. Her desires, he told friends, were "voracious." Or maybe she didn't want to live with his mother. He had made it clear to Ruth that he would never leave his mother. Or perhaps it was because he couldn't stop comparing his marriage to his sister Melody's. She had married well above her station; he had not. He'd complained to his mother that he felt deserted by Melody, "Miss Pretty Two Shoes," after her marriage. While he had sex in cars, his sister, who'd married Bill Gonterman, son of wealthy business owners, got her name in society pages for sponsoring charities, attending private parties. *Miss Pretty Two Shoes, dressed in peach silk moire offsetting her golden curls . . .*

"The older she gets, the more she'll be like me," his mother consoled him, her favorite child. "Wait and see. All of this will fall away."

Whatever the reason they never lived together, the young couple had parted on good terms. She went to him for money, and sex, from time to time; and he had convinced her he had the power to do more for her now than any man ever would. They had sex in his office on a sleeping bag he kept hidden in the rafters. He still preferred her dressed, except for panties, which she seldom wore anyway. "Get down on all fours," he had growled in her ear just the day before; and he had taken her hard from behind, the metal teeth of his zipper slapping her thigh. He liked her best this way, possibly it was because the position gave him the illusion of control over a woman who could not be controlled.

"In fact," she said out loud in the police car to the nervous and diffident cop, "he still fixes my teeth."

That caused the man to start. It was twenty years before the children of the sixties would begin to divorce en masse—and call those divorces "friendly." Something, he thought, was wrong. She looked at him, her eyes wide with fear. Then she transferred her gaze to Geraldine Duerbeck leaving the morgue, walking, her back straight, her gray head held high, toward the police car. The older woman's dignity was inviolate. There would be no talk of other marriages in front of her. The ordeal was over. Over twenty years later, John Vining would still be claiming Ruth Bullock could have been broken that night if the nice young cop had asked more questions about her first marriage—and insisted she go into the morgue.

Dr. Glennon Engleman was photographed by the press entering the Newstead Avenue Station early the morning after Bullock's murder. Stockily built and attractive in spite of his round face, he was wearing a dark topcoat and hat. The photos suggested a hint of swagger in his attitude. Mrs. Bullock was also photographed leaving the station, a tissue held to her nose, her swollen eyes overflowing with tears.

The investigators, led by Sergeant Frank O'Neill, a burly Irish cop who would go to his grave obsessed by the Bullock case, were interested in the $64,000 worth of insurance the widow would collect—and in proving whether or not the dentist had really spent the night of the murder in the prosaic middle-American fashion he described. He said he'd taken the bus downtown to Stix, Bear, & Fuller to buy his second wife's Christmas gift, met a patient and friend at the office, picked up his wife Eda at her job at the public library, and finished the evening with a late dinner at home, his mother's house where he and his wife also lived, a leisurely late dinner attended by two of the young men who worked on his odd jobs, as Nick Miranda did. Eda, Annora, and the boys backed the story. For some reason, O'Neill wasn't convinced.

While the feature writers were gathering the data on James Bullock—orphan, member of the Immanuel Lutheran Church choir, veteran, "a fine chap"—the hard-news reporters and the cops were getting a different story on his bride and her former spouse. The juiciest parts of that story didn't make the papers. In those conservative times, when even the newspapers conspired to make sure things appeared to be more or less the way they were supposed to be, readers had to be content with the elements of scandal they were served, such as the news the young couple were mortgaged to the hilt, more shocking then than now, and more interestingly, how they had met. Mrs. Bullock claimed a friend, a member of a loose-knit social organization she called "The Guys and Dolls Club," had given her James Bullock's name and number; and she had then called him suggesting a date. But she couldn't remember the friend's name. Nor could she put the authorities in touch with any other club members. Could that friend *really* have been Union Electric's part-time dentist, the man who fixed James's teeth, Glennon Engleman? the papers asked. *Was* the marriage arranged by the dentist as a murder-for-profit scheme? The papers asked. The public gasped.

Either James Bullock was exactly what he appeared to be, an ordinary, nice, young married man, made interesting only by virtue of death, or he was leading a secret other life as a homosexual man. Newspaper stories only hinted at the latter by reminding readers of the area's unsavory reputation and asking the question, "What *was* James Bullock doing at the Art Museum?" The hints were enough for many.

Whatever doubts the authorities may have had about Bullock's sexual inclinations, they were beginning to get a very clear picture of Ruth's. She was obviously much more, or perhaps much less, than a perky kindergarten teacher who insisted she really had thought she was pregnant the night of her husband's murder and was surprised when it turned out she was not. Before her marriage, she had frequented the bars in the DeBaliviere Strip area, bars where women who entered alone really didn't expect to leave that way. Some said she was a B-girl. John Vining, who took a lascivious pleasure in the tales he was hearing, goaded O'Neill. His Irish sensibility offended, O'Neill threw up his hands after talking to the dozens, literally dozens, of men who claimed to have known her in the biblical sense. She was a "nympho-maniac"—and he was determined to "get" her.

The stories grew wilder as the days went by. Rumors about a secret black book were circulated among cops and reporters. Supposedly she was sexually involved with people in high places; and so the truth of her husband's death would be squashed. The typescripts of interviews with men she'd known were passed around like illegal porn. A married riverboat man claimed he and Ruth had broken her bed in one wild night of sex. His narrative picked up steam with the telling: "She was so hot; she wanted it hard too. And she never could get enough. I've got a pretty big rod, and she wanted me to ram that thing in her as hard and as long and as often as I could. I've never seen anything hotter than her little body twisting under me, her legs wrapped around my waist, pulling me into her cunt, her little tits hard while I pumped away. I had a new bedroom set delivered to her the day after we broke the bed."

Some of the cops were beginning to call Ruth and her collection of men "The Doll and Guys Club."

As if that weren't enough, the kindly neighborhood dentist she'd first married was allegedly an abortionist whose alibi for the time of the murder wasn't exactly unshakable. Another patient claimed she'd tried to reach him at the office during the time period he was supposedly working on the teeth of his good friend Joe. The pressure was put on Joe, who finally said the Doc had been aborting his wife's pregnancy that night; and of course they had lied, because the truth was illegal, wasn't it? Furthermore, Engleman had purchased a .22 at a Belleville, Illinois, hardware store, but the gun couldn't be found. He'd given it to his father-in-law, he said, who'd reported it stolen from his car.

Meanwhile Ruth hired Marty Rosecan, a good lawyer who spirited her away following her dramatic near-collapse at the funeral to her mother's home in Kansas City, where she couldn't be extradited for mere questioning. It would take an arrest warrant to get her back, and the evidence didn't support a warrant. Nor did the climate of public opinion in St. Louis. Readers had been titillated, but they really didn't want Beaver Cleaver's teacher to be a party to the murder of her husband. The zealous young Circuit Attorney Thomas Eagleton was soundly criticized in a Catholic paper for harshly questioning the sweet young widow, whose indiscretions were only given glancing recognition in the press, about her sex life at the coroner's inquest. The *Globe*, ever mindful of conservative Catholic opinion, followed with an exclusive interview, done just before she left town, in which she tearfully detailed the emotional rough treatment she'd received from the police. No wonder she didn't want to come back for more. The Doc too had his supporters. Who could believe that a young dentist, married to a librarian, would be involved in such a thing?

Eagleton, a man with political ambitions, backed off. Some said he did so because an indictment would open Ruth's past, and the little black book full of secret names, to the public. Most, including the young attorneys who worked in his office, felt he had no choice, given the emotional climate of St. Louis in 1959. One of the young attorneys, Richard Dempsey, went into private practice and took Ruth as a client.

Whether coincidentally or not, after Joe's statement and Ruth's return to Kansas City, the hit-men theories were developed. Over the years many cops would journey to many prisons to interview men who claimed they had been hired by Engleman and Ruth to kill Bullock. Some of the cops would believe some of the alleged hit men, who, if they were telling the truth, may have been the only hit men in America working with birdshot—and stupid enough to follow a man shot four times to make sure he fell.

The only legal action resulting from the Bullock investigation was a warrant issued to search Engleman's house and office for proof of illegal abortions. His step-niece, Saundra Meredith, the step-daughter of his wife Eda's brother, answered the door at his home. He resisted arrest, punched John Vining, the arresting officer, in front of Sandy, Eda, Madre, and Melody, and was fined $100. Sergeant O'Neill thought he had a witness who would testify, a woman whose pregnancy had been aborted by the Doc and who suffered an infection. But the woman, Rita, was quickly married off to Donald Ray Horton by Engleman's sister Melody, who paid for the wedding. No testimony from the newlyweds. Case dismissed.

What impressed young Nick Miranda about the Bullock affair was the way Madre handled it. His mother would have cried and carried on, slapped his face, and got down on her knees to pray for his soul if she'd ever suspected he was involved in crime, any crime, much less murder. Not Madre. She was on Doc's side. Unlike his father, Frank, a passive man who worked for the railroad, drank beer, chewed tobacco, and seemed devoid of opinions, she had an opinion on every subject and knew everything about Glen's life. He said she knew everything he did because she could "astral-project," which meant, as Nick understood it, that her soul could leave her body and follow him around.

Doc said she knew everything and yet she never disapproved of anything within Nick's earshot—and Nick spent a lot of time with Madre, planting flowers, trimming shrubs, eating lunches, big ham sandwiches and hamburgers three inches thick, cooked with onions, the bun steamed on top to sop up the grease. She seemed to feel Glen was the most likely of her three sons to rise above the working class, and she didn't seem to care how he did it. He and Melody were her clear favorites. When the police came after him, she was mad at the police. Nick marveled at that. His mother would never get over it, the police coming to get him. She would be running behind him, smacking him, all the way to the police car.

Of course, the Doc didn't say to Nick, "I shot him," not yet, not until a few years later, but he let him think that he had.

"Bullock was a fag," Engleman confided in Nick the same day he had told the *Globe*, "I can't understand why the police are giving me all this trouble. Looks like they are grabbing at flies." They were talking in his private office while a dental patient waited in the chair for the shot of Novocain to take effect. Once the Doc had forgotten about a patient so long the painkiller had worn off while he and Nick made a trip to the hardware store. He'd started over with another shot, forgotten again while he and Nick drank sodas downstairs at the drugstore fountain, and finally drilled while the man held on to the chair until his knuckles turned from white to blue—because, hell, two shots of painkiller should be enough for a horse.

"If I had done it, I would have used Tom to lure him out there; Tom knows more than a thing or two about how to tease queers. For sport, he and his buddies roll perverts at the Torch Club in East St. Louis. Bullock didn't deserve to live, you know. He was no good for Ruth, a woman like that. She needs a real man."

Nick knew what he meant by Ruth needing a real man. He'd been on a camping trip with the Doc and Ruth years ago when they were married. He'd seen the looks they exchanged, the sex she suggested with her eyes. She had a way of running one finger, just one finger, down the side of Doc's face or up his leg. The way she did it, Nick could feel that finger running right up his leg and into his groin. He'd listened to their rhythmic humping and heavy breathing, the guttural animal-like noises she had made, and the sound of Doc's voice, droning on low most of the time, then crescendoing to a peak. It was his first exposure to sex outside the printed page.

"She couldn't make do with a part-time fag, you know. You do everybody a favor when you get rid of scum like Bullock."

"Right," he said, eyes shining with devotion. Young Nick Miranda saw the murder of James Bullock as the ultimate manifestation of Doc's power. Like God, he rewarded and he punished. The man's bravado with the press was incredible! He had actually called the *Globe-Democrat* to comment on a story they'd run about him and then held an impromptu press conference outside the station. The cops, the press—they were all fools beside him. "Right," he said again. "Right."

"You have to take care of women," Doc said. "Ruth's set now. She's better off."

Surely Doc knew how to take care of women, Nick thought. His second wife, Eda, was a little blonde, a pretty woman, with beautiful, high breasts; and his sister, Melody, who looked to Glen for leadership too, was also a beautiful blonde. Nick had been to her wedding when she married Bill Gonterman, a rich man, and she was the prettiest bride Nick had ever seen, or could imagine seeing. A princess. Nick had cut out the newspaper photo of Eda and Melody and Glen coming out of the Bullock inquest together and taped it to the wall in his room. Doc knew women.

"You have to take care of women," the Doc repeated. Nick was listening; he always was. He didn't, after all, have anyone else. Why, who knows, without Doc, he might even have died. A few weeks after James Bullock was killed, Nick Miranda got very sick. He'd had a sore throat which he'd ignored, hoping it would go away, since his mother couldn't afford doctors; and he had been working at the Engleman house when suddenly his face felt

hot, his throat closed up, and his ears hurt, bad. Doc put Nick in his and Edie's bed and rushed out to get penicillin. For three days and nights, Nick slept in Doc and Edie's bed while they slept in the living room, Edie on the couch, Doc on the floor. For three days, Madre fed him soup and Jell-O and Doc called home, several times a day, asking. How's Nick? Is Nick getting any better?

Of course Nick listened to everything Doc said.

RUTH: *I don't remember any details about the Bullock murder, if I heard them. Glen said he was a fag, but I don't know if it's true or if he killed him behind the museum so it would look like he was a fag. Glen got some of the money. I know that. She, the widow I mean, didn't get the insurance money for two years after the murder. It was contested. And she had to come back here for a hearing. She was married and had a baby. She was a little fatter then, when she came back. There was something about hit men, and the gun was never found. Glen said he sawed it into pieces and threw them in the Des Pere River. She finally won the money and invested $20,000 of it in the drag strip Glen was running in Pacific, Missouri.*

McGarvey put down the text. The cigarette package on his desk was empty. He opened the bottom drawer, looking for another, and found one, half-filled, next to the toothpicks. When James Bullock was murdered, he had been a week away from turning twelve, living in Chicago with his family, oblivious to St. Louis. He looked at a *Globe* photo of Edna Ruth Ball Engleman Bullock that Alsup had pulled from the newspaper morgue and brought to him a few hours before. She was very pretty, unlike the second Ruth. Why did Engleman keep marrying women named Ruth? Sure, Ruth was a common name on the South Side, but two out of three wives seemed a bit much.

He picked up Ruth's testimony again. The pattern established in the Bullock murder apparently held in the Eric Frey case. The cast of characters was bigger, their lives more intertwined. Complicated. It was a fucking soap opera. He sighed. Had Ruth, the second Ruth, been jealous of all these women? Were the things she said wild accusations springing from a jealous female heart?

Had she started with tiny bits of truth and elaborated upon them to create these scenarios? It was possible, for instance, that the dentist knew more than he wanted to tell about Bullock's death, but that he hadn't actually killed him. If he had killed him, why had so many city cops failed to nail him? McGarvey picked up the text and read.

> BOBB: *Ruth, are you aware of the accidental explosion that took place in Pacific, Missouri, in 1963 in which a subject by the name of Eric Frey was killed?*
>
> RUTH: *Yes.*
>
> BOBB: *Can you tell us what you personally know about that incident?*
>
> RUTH: *Well, you will have to ask me some questions on that.*
>
> BOBB: *Were you married to Dr. Engleman at the time, or were you going with him, girlfriend, boyfriend, in 1963?*
>
> RUTH: *Yes, yes, we were together, not married, but seeing each other.*
>
> BOBB: *At any time during your relationship with Dr. Engleman has he ever mentioned the incident to you?*
>
> RUTH: *Yes. He said that, that he and Jack Carter arranged to have, through a dynamite explosion, to have Eric Frey killed, when they were building the drag strip.*

Murder Two: Eric Frey, September 26, 1963

Less than a year after James Bullock was murdered, on October 22, 1959, an ordinary brown-haired young St. Louis man entered the Air Force. Though interested in many things, Eric Frey hadn't been more than an average student, and sometimes he was less than average. His Air Force buddies regarded him as a guy who was too eager to be seen as knowledgeable. He would take a little information and promote that minimal knowledge into expertise—which was a dangerous way to behave in the Air Force. He was liked but not trusted, not the man you wanted at your side in an explosives class, for instance.

While in the service, Frey had three hundred ninety-three days lost in three years' time, attributed to "bad check" and AWOL charges. When he was discharged on February 12, 1962, an officer who had liked him warned, "You're going to keep running into trouble in life if you don't stop being so optimistic about your chances. Stop dreaming and start planning." He was, it seems, given to spending his cash on the proverbial soldier's downfalls— wine, women, and song—then writing checks on a zero balance, expecting to cover them with bets he would win or loans he would collect. Some of his AWOL days were spent in drunken stupor. Many more were devoted to the money chase: trying to find the cash to cover a check before it bounced. While he knew the officer was right, he also liked dancing and fast cars, and he had no idea what he was going to do with the rest of his life.

Back home in St. Louis, Frey began frequenting the bars and clubs in the Gaslight Square area, where nightlife was flourishing in the early '60s. The last of the beats, the pre-hippies, the gay, jazz aficionados, and the adventurously young made the area a chic oasis surrounded by a black ghetto momentarily held at bay, a sharp contrast to south St. Louis, where Saturday night meant *The Lawrence Welk Show* on television. At the Crystal Palace, he became friends with a male dancer named Ricky, who suggested that Eric too could be a dancer—or at least a dance instructor. Soon he was working at Ray Quinlan Dance Studio on the South Side, teaching middle-aged ladies how to tango, mambo, and fox-trot. Some of them also wanted to learn the twist.

He told them he'd done the twist at the Peppermint Lounge in New York City where it all began. Soon he found it easy to flatter the ladies as well as lie to them and, by treating them with the right mix of flirtatiousness and respect, get them to sign up for extra lessons, increasing his commission. One of the ladies he so charmed was blond and buxom, still pretty in spite of her spreading midriff and sometimes bloated face. Her name was Melody.

"What a beautiful name for a dancing lady," he said, winking at her. "Melody, Melody!" he crooned, waltzing her around the floor in south St. Louis. "Oh, Melody!"

She liked him so much, she said she wanted him to meet her family. Politely, he asked her questions about the family. She said she and her brothers were building a drag-strip operation in

Pacific, Missouri. They had purchased the land and were in the process of clearing it. But none of them really knew anything about the drag-racing business.

"I know about drag racing," he said.

"Really," she replied, a little breathless from the turns around the floor. "Then you must come take a look at our operation and give us some advice."

Nick Miranda might not have appreciated Melody's suggestion that advice was needed from another young man. He liked to think the idea for the drag strip was his—and that he was the crown prince in Doc's court, composed of Melody, his brothers Gene and Vernon and their wives, some male friends, and the young hired hands. He had already become the only one who could hold his own in verbal jousting with Doc. The strip got started because the previous autumn he and the Doc had been sitting around the house wondering what to do on a Sunday afternoon while Madre cooked dinner when Nick made the suggestion that instigated the whole enterprise.

"Let's go to the drags over in Alton," he said; and he'd made the suggestion in part because he wanted to get away from Edie, who was seething because she'd wanted to cook dinner and Madre had told her no again. "It's her kitchen, babe," Glen had said; and that was that. Edie couldn't cook anyway, but she pretended she could, pretended she would, collecting recipes Madre dismissed as "silly" from women's magazines. Madre was sweet to Edie mostly, dismissive of her really.

"She's not Glen's intellectual equal," Madre sniffed. "He always marries women who aren't his equals." Nick liked Edie, but he understood Madre was always in charge because Glen wanted it that way. Glen might yell at his mother if she disagreed with him, but he never spoke ill of her. Nick had never heard him say one small negative thing about her.

"My friends and I go over there sometimes," he prodded. "Let's go look at the races, get out of the house." So they got in Doc's car and drove across the bridge to Alton, Illinois. "Jeez, look at all the Missouri plates!" Nick said as they pulled into the lot; and he saw the unmistakable signs of interest bloom on Doc's face.

"Yeah," the Doc said. "It's the only strip in the area, isn't it?" Nick told him it was. He got out of the car and walked up and down a few rows rather than taking a direct route to the entrance gate. "At least half these cars, maybe sixty percent, have Missouri plates."

He was sizing up an opportunity. Excitedly he began to esti- mate the size of the crowd and the take at the entrance gate and concession stands. The more excited he got, the faster he talked; and he was talking fast that afternoon, talking and laughing at his own jokes, his elbows flapping crazily. Consuming popcorn, hot dogs, and soda, Nick, who already had a weight problem that sometimes made him the source of Doc's ridicule, followed be- hind, eating almost as fast as the Doc could talk, laughing along with him.

"I could bring the whole family in on this," Doc said. Family was important to Doc; he was always looking for ways to bring them into his schemes, for their profit, not his. "Gene and Fran- ces. Melody. Jack Carter too . . . hell, he's been friends so long, he feels like family. Since you gave me the idea, Nick, and you could bring in a lot of kids, I'll make you the publicity man and give you some stock. Carmen and Nedra can work the concession stands. And Sandy. God knows we need to find something for her to do. We can get you invited to the meetings of those hotrod clubs, the membership is heavy in these, they've got to meet every week or month or whatever . . . we can get you invited to those meetings, there may be three thousand kids in the city of St. Louis alone . . . we can get you invited to these meetings and you can pump the club."

Excitedly he laid plans. He was feeling so good he apparently didn't notice he told his favorite joke three times, the joke Nick had already heard dozens of times. *There were these two black football teams, see. They scrimmaged; and one team got the ball. One guy ran with it and he was sacked hard, knocked out of the game. Some guy in the stands stood up and yelled. "Hey, put Elbow in! Let Elbow carry that ball." Well, they scrimmaged again; and the same team got the ball. Another player got sacked; and that same guy in the stands stood up and yelled, "Hey, put Elbow in! Let Elbow carry that ball, I say!" Well, they scrimmaged again; and the same team, Elbow's team, got that ball.*

*Another player got sacked; and that same guy in the stands is yelling,
"Hey, put Elbow in! Let Elbow carry that ball!" All of a sudden one
player stepped out of the huddle and yelled at that guy in the stands.
"Elbow say he don't wanna carry that ball."*

Doc laughed and laughed, elbows flapping; and Nick laughed
too. He hadn't yet admitted to himself the Elbow story wasn't
even funny.

Doc began looking for property that week. The drag strip was
supposed to be good for Sandy. A beautiful girl with a well-
proportioned body and long thick hair the color of honey, Sandy
didn't look like she should have problems. Her mother, Eda
Engleman's sister-in-law, was beautiful; her father, Eda's
brother, could have been cast as an F. Scott Fitzgerald hero:
handsome, accomplished, decent but vacuous. She had, however, attempted suicide at age sixteen in Houston where she'd
been sent to live with her grandmother when ostensibly she failed
to adjust to her family's move from Missouri to North Carolina.
Following the suicide attempt, she spent six days in the hospital.
Then it was decided she would live for a while with Eda and
Glennon in St. Louis. Eda, who dimly perceived the rivalry between mother and daughter that had really sent Sandy to Texas
and furthermore could smell sex in the air between her husband
and her nubile stepniece, was ready to ship her back to North
Carolina by the time the drag strip project got under way.

"It will take a year to clear that ground, Glennon," she said.
"Sandy could go home and come back if she really wants to work.
What help is a girl with hard labor?"

His eyes blazing, he shouted, "She isn't going home! Your own
family, and you don't want to look after her when she needs our
help! If she bothers you so much, I'll make sure she spends more
time out of the house. She can come down to the office if she
likes. I can find things for her to do there."

Sometimes Sandy, supposedly on clerical duty, pulled down
the cot from the office rafters and napped in the last cubicle while
he was seeing patients. When he had a break he would come to
her. Sandy's arrival in his life was convenient, because his blond
lover, Barbara Varney, was marrying an acquaintance, another
dentist, James Boyle. Besides, Sandy was less trouble. The preg-

nant Barbara could easily be more trouble than he needed. He started things faster with Sandy than usual with women, perhaps because he was feeling the void Barbara had left. Or maybe Sandy's extreme youth coupled with her emotional instability left her more vulnerable, making her in a sense the blankest of slates. He was scaling the height of his power then, comparing himself in his own mind to Svengali, the fictional character who transformed women through his hypnotic powers. Yes, he believed he was Svengali.

On hot days Sandy wore short shorts, usually white ones, and a halter top, no panties. He wakened her by sliding his hand under the cuff of her shorts and working his finger into her vagina, stroking the side of the little hard nub he told her was her clitoris. He gave her words for the parts of her body she hadn't known existed, and he insisted she use the words, sooner than he had insisted with other women. Saying them left her breathless. He licked her there in places she didn't know mouths could go. She liked that best, she told him, the long strokes of his tongue, followed by faster ones; and the noises he made—"umm, umm, umm" as she was coming—and finally, "Sweet pussy, that's a sweet pussy, *yeees*." He would draw out the "yeees" so long that she would have laughed if his face had been anywhere but where it was. When he first said that word, "pussy," she'd told him it reminded her of the nursery tale, *I like little pussy, her coat is so warm, and if I don't hurt her, she'll do me no harm;* and he had laughed. She can never do me any harm, he had said, not pussy, not pussy, not her.

"Now suck it, suck me," he told her, unzipping his black trousers, releasing a penis she didn't yet realize was remarkable for its endurance. "That's it, yes. Put your hands around it here and hold it while you suck me. Suck me like a baby suckles its mama's breasts, that's it, honey, *yees*."

Sometimes he pulled a condom over the top of his penis before he entered her, and sometimes he didn't. In her innocence, she thought he was wise enough to know exactly when the condom was needed—and when it wasn't. Often after they were finished, he held her while patients shot full of Novocain waited in chairs, afraid to close their drying mouths; and he talked to her about his plan. He could help her get enough money to get an apartment of her own, so she wouldn't have to go back to North Carolina or live with Aunt Eda either. It was a simple plan, he said. There was no other way a girl so young and totally unprepared to earn a living could ever get ahead on her own. He could give her a start, he promised, a start, the way he'd given her special knowledge about her clitoris. She was such a beautiful girl; she should have no trouble carrying out her part of the plan. All she had to do was pick the right man, and the rest was up to him.

"I won't know how to pick," she said; and he told her he would help. He put his finger there, next to her clitoris again, and she squirmed. "I won't know how," she whispered. "Will I?"

"I'll help you, baby. Your part will be easy," he said. "The rest is up to me." She was sweating, holding on to him, grinding her hip into his, grinding against the pressure of his finger. "Sweet pussy," he whispered. The shock of the words he used had the same effect on her skin as running through a cold sprinkler on a hot summer day. "Easy, baby, easy."

When he wasn't talking to her about his plan, he was telling her about the drag strip. It was, he said, the perfect investment, because interest in drag racing hadn't even peaked yet. Thousands of young people poured their money into the Alton strip, he said. It was surefire. And Sandy could believe that. She'd lived in plenty of places, but she'd never lived anywhere for cars like south St. Louis. She wrote her mother: "People here are crazy about cars. Everybody has a souped-up engine on jacked-up wheels." She didn't realize how neatly the enterprises would dovetail: the drag strip and his plan for her.

The Pacific Dragstrip Inc., which was going to keep Sandy busy and make them all rich, was really nothing more than a stretch of trees and weeds in Franklin County. On weekends and summer evenings, Engleman, his brother Gene, his lifelong friend Jack Carter, Nick, and Donald Horton, who had claimed to be one of his dinner companions the night Bullock was murdered, chopped down trees and burned underbrush. Occasionally Eric Frey came out to lend a hand. Melody had introduced him to the men as "someone who has little tidbits of knowledge on everything"; and Engleman had flattered him by listening to the tidbits he contributed on drag racing. A respected professional man had never listened to him before.

Most of the manual labor was performed by the principals; little was contracted out. Engleman was proud of his prowess as a handyman and laborer. He liked to joke at the poker parties he hosted for essentially the same group that he knew how to use *all* his tools. More than once he reminded them they were true Americans because they were building something "from the ground up" and "by the sweat of the brow." The work went smoothly as long as everyone did what he thought they should. He had to be in control. If anyone argued, even disagreed with him, he grew hostile. The heaviest cash investment, $20,000, came from Ruth Ball Engleman Bullock, whose insurance suit had finally been settled. She was listed with the others as a shareholder in the corporation. In the evenings, the women, Melody, Eda, Frances Engleman, and often Sandy brought a picnic dinner to their men working on the strip. At one of those picnic dinners Melody introduced Sandy, wearing short shorts and a man's shirt unbuttoned, knotted, and tied under her breasts, to Eric Frey.

The first time he kissed her, she inserted her tongue in his mouth as the doctor had instructed her to do and pressed her crotch against his. The courtship was hot and brief, conducted at the drag strip where they passionately petted in full view of everyone—and in the bars on Gaslight Square. With the doctor's encouragement, they were married on September 28, 1962. Sandy was eighteen. Though they didn't share an apartment until January, shortly after their marriage, the young couple purchased insurance policies on his life. The premium on one policy was ninety-nine dollars a month, so high the insurance agent had tried to talk them out of it. They bounced the first payment check, and that company dropped their policy. Pacific Dragstrip Inc., through its secretary Melody Gonterman, also applied for group life insurance, covering, among others, Eric Frey, who worked full-time as a general mechanic for Remmert-Werner Aircraft.

Marked by financial and health problems, theirs did not appear to be a happy marriage. Eric was in therapy for a brief period in February 1963 and was hospitalized by his psychiatrist. After the insurance-check incident, they bounced more checks. Then, in need of money, they resorted to the increasingly common con: Sandy filed an insurance claim against the Crystal Palace for bruises and a miscarriage arising from an alleged fall on the premises. The Doc told Nick the suit was bogus. He had aborted her pregnancy, he said, and the bruises had come from Eric, who pushed her around. "He's no good to her! He's a mean son of a bitch!" the Doc railed. "I don't know if I should shoot him or blow him up."

His diatribes against Eric—"Killing him would be doing society a favor, ridding it of some vermin . . . People don't have the guts and so forth to do that . . ."—became more lengthy and vehement as the plan developed. They were going to kill Eric Frey at the drag strip, kill him because he deserved to die. Kill him because the strip needed the money. Kill him because killing him was the way to join the punishment he deserved with the money they needed in one violent act. He and Jack Carter were going to do it, and Nick was going to help. This was the first time Nick had been drawn into planning sessions; and the planning, he thought, would never end. Over and over again, the Doc repeated his orders as though they were slow learners in school. His original horror at the thought of being involved in murder gave way to numbness. They talked so long Nick was crushed, worn down to an agreeable cipher, by the words.

Sometimes they talked around the kitchen table at Doc's house, with Madre preparing a meal behind them. With a sharp cleaver, she chopped chickens into parts, dipped them into milk and flour, as her favorite son planned a murder. Her presence anesthetized Nick. She put the chicken in the pan, and while it sizzled, she turned around and told them her husband Frank paid the utility bills within two days because he thought they had to be paid the day after you got them, as if he thought someone was waiting for his money and would give him a gold star for being on time, as if he thought they'd come after him if he waited a week. Doc ignored her and kept on talking. They talked so long Nick never really believed it would happen at all; and in his mind, the instructions were punctuated with Annora's complaints about the utility bills.

By summer, Sandy was spending a lot of time at the dental office, where she shared cot privileges with the doctor's new girlfriend, Ruth Jolley. Doc told Nick that Ruth was avid for adventure; he was certainly avid for her. His lust for Ruth was already greater than it had been for any other woman, and Nick really couldn't see why. When Doc wasn't planning Eric's murder, he was planning a robbery of the Red Roof Inn with her, but he was adamant that she not be told about the murder yet. He understood the principles of escalation very well. By the time he told Ruth he'd committed murder, she would be able to accept it as the next logical step, the complete extension of the power he deservedly held.

"Never tell them what they're not ready to know," he said to Nick, who realized with a shock he'd been handled the same way as Ruth. The robbery was meant to be their first date; and Nick, who didn't like Ruth, was supposed to go along. Since his own dates were dependent on the use of Doc's car, he agreed, but he was happy when the plan fell apart. Ruth's information about the safe had been all wrong.

The drag strip opened on Labor Day, for Sundays only. Sandy and Eric worked at the strip, earning $1.25 an hour for running the concession stand, the time clocks, working at the pit, the gate, or wherever they were needed. In addition to their meager wage, they were also promised stock in exchange for labor. One Sunday afternoon Nick watched them together and almost believed they were happy. The Red Roof Inn caper had fallen through, hadn't it? So might this.

"Are you really going to kill him?" Nick asked. The Doc stopped painting a sign in mid brush stroke to look at him as if he was crazy. The rest of the day Doc rode his ass, calling him a "fat, lazy, good-for-nothing Mexican." As Nick was leaving, he called out to him: "You'll marry a fat Mexican bitch and have eight, ten, a dozen fat little kids and live in poverty all your life!"

Nick's eyes smarted. It was the worst thing Doc could say to him, and when the punishment was over the next day and Doc spoke to him kindly again, his relief was palpable.

On Thursday, September 26, 1963, Eric Frey drove home from work, picked up his wife, and went straight to the drag strip to help with a dynamite project. Jack Carter, Doc, Gene, and Nick needed his help in blasting shut an old, unused well, he told Sandy. Since Doc had discovered the kids were playing in the well, he was anxious to cave it in and fill it with dirt and rock. Eric thought this was a good idea, and he was pleased when Doc particularly asked for his opinion on how the job should be done.

The children, Engleman's three nieces and a nephew, were all between five and seven years of age, typically curious, active little kids. They had bragged about having a secret hiding place where they sailed their boats. Doc thought their hiding place was a shallow stream until he discovered their boats, aluminum pie tins, in one of the abandoned wells.

"They could hurt themselves bad," he'd told Eric, holding the little tins in his hands. "That well is ten or fifteen feet deep, rocks all around it. We have to close their little secret place before they get hurt."

Eric had agreed. He knew exactly how to do the job, and Doc had gratefully put him in charge. Since Thursday was Doc's day off, he'd been out there early with Nick and the others clearing tree stumps and brush along the entrance road. Nick put down his shovel and waved when Eric and Sandy drove in. He spoke to Eric briefly, then walked with Sandy further down the road as Eric conferred with Doc on the dynamite job. He had no intentions of being near the blast sight. Let Doc and Carter work that out with him. Eric said he knew exactly what to do because he'd worked in munitions in the service. Anything anyone else had done, Eric had done it too, only better. He was that kind of guy, well-meaning but always getting in his own way. Nick convinced himself that if anything was really going to happen, then Eric had put himself in the way of it happening—and probably nothing was going to happen anyway.

"I don't want to be anywhere near this stuff," Nick said, putting his arm across Sandy's shoulder. She looked at him quickly, then away. They both stood tensely, their bodies stiffened, waiting for the sound of the charge. He kept talking to Sandy near the edge of the road, too far down to see what was happening.

"The fumes from this stuff make me ill," he said. "I don't

want to be too close. When we used dynamite to blow the post holes out, I set it off with a battery.''

"Do you really think it's going to happen?" she asked softly.

He looked back then. The charge should have gone off, but it hadn't. Maybe it wouldn't. He looked just in time to see Doc come up behind Eric and hit him over the head with a rock. The blow stunned him, but Eric wasn't unconscious, so Doc pushed him down into the well.

"Why do you want to kill me?" Eric cried. "Why?"

There was screaming and gurgling, like the sound of an animal furiously drowning, and silence. Doc climbed out of the well. Then Jack Carter finally got the charge to ignite. After the explosion, Doc yelled, "Eric!" That, of course, was part of the plan, the feigned shock and horror after Eric Frey had dynamited himself in the well. "Eric!" Doc yelled, playing his part so well. "Eric!"

Nick looked down the road and saw Gene Engleman, who had been working on post holes, come toward him. They ran to the explosion together, with Sandy behind them. Through the smoke and dust, Nick saw rocks caved in around the well. He heard the Doc's voice coming from inside the well. For a minute, because the cries of "Eric!" had been so convincing, he thought Doc had been hurt in the blast while trying to save Eric, but then he heard the voice again, commanding, strong. Doc was in the well now, calling up to them that Eric had been caught in the blast. Nick looked into Jack Carter's stricken face and thought he was going to be sick, so he turned away.

If Jack Carter had been less conscientious, he wouldn't have been close enough to know what had really happened to Eric Frey. Like Gene Engleman, he could have gone for years believing what he wanted to believe—telling himself Doc really hadn't done what he set out to do, telling himself it had been an accident after all. Instead, screwing his narrow, weathered face into a schoolmarm's expression of distaste, he'd said he would stay when Glen had encouraged him to walk further down the road.

"Don't be such a pussy," he'd said when Jack opened his

mouth to articulate doubts, an admonition that usually had the desired effect on him. He had always liked Glen because the dentist was bolder than he was—and willing to bend the law when he saw the unfairness of it, not take the injustice like the average working-class stiff. All his life he'd packed his sack lunch and gone to work on time, no matter how bad he felt or what the weather, collected his paycheck, which had been shot full of holes by deductions, and not complained to anyone. All his life he'd taken things; and Glen had not. Whatever little windfalls had come his way had come through Glen—through Glen, who had the guts to get around the rules that usually worked against the little guys like him. "Go on," he'd said. "If you're going to be a pussy, help Gene down the road. I'll do it."

This time Jack wouldn't meekly walk in the direction Glen pointed. Some sense of duty compelled him to stay close. Maybe he just didn't want to be a pussy. He watched Glen hit the kid over the head, push him still-conscious into the well, and hold his head under water until he drowned. Standing out of danger, he watched the charge go off so the blast would cover the kid's body with rocks, making it look like he'd died in the blast, the victim of his own stupidity. He stood there and watched.

"Jesus, God, Glen, what have we done?" he said, putting his hands in front of his face like a child who didn't want to see the scary part of the movie he'd insisted he wanted to watch. My God, they'd run a few scams before, but murder? This was murder. He had stood there and listened while Glen held that kid's head under water. "What have we done?"

Before the smoke had cleared, Glen replied, "We killed him, Jack. You know that. You know what we've done."

Carter took his hands from his face and looked at Nick and Sandy, who had just come up to the well. Sandy's expression was blank, but Nick's face was registering emotions faster than the pieces of a kaleidoscope dissolved into new formations. They had all been in on this, but Nick and Jack hadn't really believed it would happen. The two men looked away from each other, and Nick walked toward the road. For seventeen years, Jack Carter would carry this secret inside his body. When he finally died of cancer, he would believe the cancer had been blasted into him at the drag strip by the same piece of Primacord that blasted the rocks over Eric Frey's dead body.

"Someone get to a phone and call an ambulance!" Engleman called, playing his part. "It looks like Eric's dead."

"We have to talk." Frey's body was still in the well when Doc took Nick Miranda and Jack Carter aside. "We have to agree on a story which we'll repeat without deviation to the authorities. You're in this with me. I've taken care of both of you when you needed taking care of," he said. "You're accessories to murder if the truth comes out."

They sat with their heads down, looking up only when Doc commanded, listening, accepting every word. He would kill them too, if not today then another day, if they didn't listen and accept. The threat was implicit in his voice. He would kill them too. Nick did, and did not, believe that. Some distance away, Gene was trying to comfort Sandy Frey, who had thrown herself on the ground and was kicking up dust with her pounding heels and flailing fists. Her shirt had come open; and dirt and sweat were mixed on her breasts, forming a mud slick. Nick was shattered, but he would put the pieces of his adoration together again. Like an heirloom vase mended with Elmer's glue, it would show the cracks, but the Doc would accept the container, pretending it was good as new, recognizing without admitting his responsibility for the damage. For Glennon Engleman's oldest friend, however, the façade would be preserved out of fear, but it would never hold water. The feelings would never be the same; and the dentist would disdain him for this. Carter cried quietly while Eric Frey's body was placed in the ambulance.

The Franklin County sheriff's department ruled the death accidental and didn't file a report. No autopsy was performed on the body. Sandy Frey called her insurance agent that night to report Eric's accidental death and ask when she could pick up her $25,000 check. She had her husband's body cremated the next day, the eve of their first anniversary, so there could be no autopsy at some later date to prove the cause of death.

Her insurance agent, who was shocked by her request coming on the very day of her husband's death, tried to convince her a monthly check from the company would be a preferable form of settlement, especially since she was pregnant, but she insisted on receiving a lump payment. She immediately gave Engleman a check for $16,000, an "investment" in Pacific Dragstrip Inc., which filed for bankruptcy the following year. Sandy got her apartment, a cramped place on Chippewa, not far from Engleman's office. In January 1964, she went back to Houston to her grandmother's house, where she gave birth to Melissa Ann Frey, the baby she and Doc both claimed was his. And as Melissa Ann grew from baby to toddler, the chubby little girl came to look exactly like the doctor, whose mother baby-sat for her from January through October of 1965 while Sandy restlessly roamed the country with a girlfriend. "My son Glen," she told Nick, "has every right to procreate as he sees fit; he is an intelligent man and that intelligence should be passed on."

Connecticut General Life Insurance Company, which held the drag strip's policy on Eric Frey, refused to pay; and Sandy had to sue them to get her money. The lawyer who investigated the case, John Emde, developed an impressive file on both the Frey and Bullock murders, but nothing happened with the information he showed to various law-enforcement agencies. Jack Carter, Nick Miranda, Sandy Frey, and Glennon Engleman told their stories in deposition form. Dick Dempsey, the lawyer Engleman had hired to help Ruth Bullock get her money, represented Sandy. The company paid her claim.

Around that time, Nick Miranda began having nightmares. He dreamed about Eric Frey crying, "Why are you trying to kill me? Why?" Frequently he woke screaming in his bed, drenched with sweat. Quietly, he began to pray; he knew he couldn't be part of something like this without paying a price, either here or beyond. Sometimes he envied Glen his sure atheism. Like Annora, he was convinced there was no god. How could he admit to God and do what he did?

BOBB: *The incident happened in 1963. Approximately how long after that did he tell you this?*

RUTH: *A couple of years anyway. I can't really remember for sure.*

BOBB: *Did Dr. Engleman state the reason that he and Mr. Carter did this?*
RUTH: *Yes, it was for insurance money.*

McGarvey put down the text and got up to stretch his legs. He checked his watch. It was after one A.M. Too late to call Diana, his wife, and tell her he was still working. She'd probably gone to sleep by now. He rubbed his eyes and thought he should go home, get some sleep too. But they had started electronic surveillance, and he wanted to be as familiar with Ruth's story as she was. The more he read, the more he doubted. Maybe Engleman had felt responsible for the accident causing Frey's death and had taken the blame on his shoulders by saying, "I killed him," to Ruth and others. Maybe he never meant, "I killed him on purpose"—just, "I killed him." And maybe they had blown it out of proportion because of his violent temper.

He looked at the pictures on his desk of Diana, pregnant with their second child, and his son. His son was the same age as Ruth's son David, but she talked about the boy as though he were a baby. She was overprotective, as any mother standing between her child and a father who was a murderer might be. They were playing with David's life too, not just Ruth's. If this went all the way, that kid—almost without warning—would be picked up and relocated someday. He would have time only to throw his favorite toys in a bag, if that; then he would be out of there. And it would be up to McGarvey to get him out. He felt the responsibility of David sitting heavily on his shoulders. He wanted his own son, Louis, named after his great-grandfather, to be a boxer, and he'd set up a punching bag in the basement for the kid to practice, though he used it too. He wanted his own son to be tough, maybe because he'd grown up in a tough Chicago neighborhood. In a sense he could understand how Ruth's husband might not be entirely happy with the way she raised their only child.

He paced the room a few minutes, went back to his desk, and picked up the pages. Bullock and Frey. Now Halm. Jesus, these guys weren't too smart, were they? If Ruth had the story down right, these guys were about as naive as you could get.

RUTH: *The particular one [murder] that I am referring to was the man named Peter. I can't recall his last name at this moment, but it's an unusual name. It started with H.*

MCGARVEY: *What do you recall about Peter?*

RUTH: *Glen told me that he was going to kill Carmen Miranda's husband, that he was planning this and there was nothing I could do about it.*

MCGARVEY: *How did he say he killed him?*

RUTH: *He told me that he shot him.*

Murder Three: Peter Halm, September 5, 1976

Only two females remained constant figures in the doctor's life from the murder of James Bullock in 1958 until he shot Peter Halm in 1976: Carmen Miranda, Nick's little sister, and Melody, his own sister.

His marriage to the sweet and quiet Eda ended violently in 1965 when he literally threw her out of the house, hitting her on the back with a hat box as she fled. She went to her brother's house in North Carolina and told them Glennon had tried to kill her with an overdose of barbiturates—which made her brother recall a strange incident his father had shared with him. In 1959, Glennon had sat for hours, until three one morning, at his father-in-law's table slicing a .22-caliber gun into pieces, announcing his intention to throw the pieces into the Des Pere River. They had thought it was unusual behavior at the time, but then Edie's husband was given to extremes.

Eda told a partically incoherent story about her husband's activities. Glen told her, she said, he'd either killed someone while he was in the service, or had knowledge of a murder committed in the service by his friend Joe—a murder that involved covering up Joe's homosexual liaisons. Maybe he'd told the story both ways, so she was confused as to which was the truth, but she was sure he and Joe were in on the Bullock murder. "Glennon pulled the trigger," she insisted, *"I know he did."* No matter how he'd told the story or she'd remembered it being told, she'd insisted he'd pulled the trigger.

His relationship with Sandy, who returned to St. Louis in October 1965 to reclaim her baby, also ended angrily. Doing what he told her to do had made her a young widow and mother; suddenly she wasn't so docile anymore. He didn't like the change in her. When she appeared to be moving beyond his control, he accused her of stealing his coin collection and called her mother in North Carolina, where Eda was staying, screaming wildly about her "misdeeds." She was "hanging around with St. Louis's most notorious lesbian Big Betty," he raved. "Don't be surprised if something happens to her." By this time Eda had told the Van Nests that "the gruesome foursome: Glennon, Nick, Jack Carter, and Sandy" had killed Eric Frey too.

Sandy's mother was convinced the doctor meant to kill her daughter if she didn't get out of town as Eda had. She wrote Sandy: "I just want to warn you that you're playing with fire as long as you are in the same town with Glen. I guess he hates you with a passion and will probably go to no ends to get rid of you one way or another. He can't stand you being around and you know too much on him. I think that's why he wanted Eda out of the way . . ."

Sandy took her mother's advice, scooped up her baby, and got out of town. And shortly after his second divorce was final, in April 1967 Engleman married his girlfriend for several years, Ruth Jolley, a woman with intelligence and courage, capable of playing Bonnie to his Clyde. She was involved in a counterfeiting scheme that sent his friend Bob Handy to jail, and the Doc would later say she'd proposed other schemes, including bank robberies, that didn't come off. Ruth gave him his only son, David, his one legitimate child. If she was not the most beautiful of his many women, she was, or at least he thought she was, his ideal mate.

He also had a new best friend, Bob Handy, whom he'd met before the Frey murder when Handy shared an apartment with Donald Horton. Unlike Jack Carter, who was, as he'd said many times to Ruth, "afraid of his shadow," Handy had "the courage of a lion." Privately, Ruth visualized the characters in *The Wizard of Oz* when Doc compared Handy to a lion. Wrong animal, she thought. Handy was the one who went out looking for a brain—or he would be if he were smart enough to know his was missing.

Handy was merely stupid, Ruth thought, but Nick Miranda was a lowlife not worthy of trust. Nick thought he was smarter than the rest of them because he knew so many big words. When Nick married Barbara in 1965, Ruth, who wasn't married herself yet, had rushed forward to sign their marriage license as a witness. She meant the gesture in goodwill, but later she heard him tell Barbara the sight of her name on the paper made him sick. "She's desecrated our marriage," he complained. That was her last attempt to befriend him.

Nick was in California most of the time during the summer of 1976. Ruth didn't understand what he was doing, some kind of movie business, mostly big talk, she was sure. Anyway, Nick was gone. Maybe that explained why Glen seemed so preoccupied with Carmen's welfare. He told her Peter beat Carmen—and that someone had to stop him. She wasn't sure if she believed this or not, but she told him it was Nick's problem to do something about his sister's husband. What Glen might do was too frightening to contemplate.

The marriage had only been briefly happy for Ruth. She'd tried to divorce Engleman unsuccessfully several times. He wouldn't agree to a divorce and withheld money whenever she tried to get him to talk about one. They'd recently moved into a new condominium in south county, where upwardly mobile South Siders relocate, a place she loved. Annora had died, and for the first time, she was living with her husband and son alone. She was "going to give it a try again," she told her sister Jeannie. When she used the phrase "trying to make it work," she was conscious of the way other women were describing the effort they were putting into a relationship in which the romantic games were no longer played or the sex had died. In her marriage, it was people who had died—and by her husband's hand.

In spite of that, they led a superficially ordinary family life. In the summer of 1976, they had her nieces and nephews up from Texas and Jeannie's two children from Memphis; Engleman had promised her he would help entertain them. It was going to be a family summer, he'd promised, before Carmen became his chief concern. She reminded him of that one Saturday morning in late July, when her patience was exhausted.

"You're supposed to be there with these kids," she said, working to keep her voice soft and wheedling. They were still in bed. "You're always making yourself scarce on Saturdays and Sundays, and you promised me you'd be here with the kids." She half-turned toward him, making a promise she wouldn't mind keeping if he would promise something in return. "You said you'd be here with us."

"Babe," he said, sliding his hand under the covers to rest between her legs. "I'm working on something."

"*Carmen!*" she snapped. "That's what you're working on."

"Are you jealous of Carmen, babe? She's married now. You know I think of her as a daughter." He put one finger inside her vagina. "Pussy's warm. Come on, babe, give me a kiss. Put your head down here and kiss it." He threw off the cover. "It's hard. Rock hard."

She allowed him to put her hand around his penis. It wasn't rock hard yet, but she knew it would be. He could talk it into standing up any time he wanted; and sometimes she thought he wouldn't even be able to perform if he couldn't talk, and talk dirty, while he was doing it. Tape his mouth shut and he would be impotent.

"I've got four kids here and my own little son," she told him. "I want you to be here with us."

"Babe, you have to stop harassing me about that. I've got something to do, something that I'm going to do, and you just have to accept it."

"What?" she persisted. "What do you have to do that can't wait until these kids are gone?"

"Suck me," he told her. He shifted their bodies so that she was straddling his knees, and he lowered her head to his cock. She complied; and she had one ball in her mouth when he told her what he had to do: kill Carmen's husband, Peter Halm. He took great satisfaction in having her just where she was when he told her his plan. The shock of what he said made her behave in a sexually subservient way. To his mind, it turned her on as much as it did him.

The attempt to murder Carmen's husband failed that day, though he didn't tell Ruth so for weeks. He and Handy had laid in wait near a covered bridge in Pacific, Missouri, at a place they believed was in the jurisdiction of Franklin County, the same police force which had labeled Eric Frey's death accidental without an investigation. They were Glen's favorite cops. As Carmen was leading Peter to the covered bridge, a group of little kids appeared out of nowhere—and scared Glen and Handy away. It was poetic justice, she thought. He should have been home with his own group of little kids.

She didn't know they'd tried and failed to kill Peter Halm when Glen and Handy came in that afternoon. They said they didn't do it, no explanation. They just didn't do it. Since it hadn't happened, she convinced herself it wouldn't.

> RUTH: *So I thought, what is going on here? Is he involved with somebody else and he's telling me this as an excuse to see somebody else? You know how you think when you are a woman and you think, how do you know guys? So anyway I never really expected it, the murder, to occur after that. But it did.*
>
> MCGARVEY: *Did he ever mention the reason for killing Peter?*
>
> RUTH: *Money, insurance. She was going to give him $20,000 for doing this.*

As the years had passed, apparently Engleman's compulsive need to control the people around him had grown. The hostility and racial bias of the South Side nurtured him, while dentistry gave him the respectable cover he needed to put himself above the law. If he'd been less than a professional man, lived elsewhere than the South Side, and surrounded himself with people who had more education, years, and life experience than the young and poor he attracted like a magnet, he wouldn't have been the demigod he was. This man, whose self-conception was heroic, exhibited the same primitive emotions of any antisocial punk: spite, vanity, sentimental affections, and hot flashes of violent anger.

But the more he considered Ruth's statements, the more doubtful McGarvey was. It was possible Ruth told the truth as she believed it, but the Doc could have been lying to her for years. A man with a violent temper . . . a man who had probably been involved in petty insurance and tax schemes . . . a man like that could convince his wife he was capable of killing and had in fact killed. Maybe he kept her in line by telling her those stories. Or maybe he got off sexually that way. Maybe she was right in her fleeting suspicion that he used the stories to cover up affairs with other women. Anything was possible. Including jealousy on Ruth's part. These stories all involved women—women and the doctor, beautiful women and the doctor, who appeared to be horny as hell. On the other hand, she had little pieces of information she couldn't have gotten any way he could imagine unless she was telling the truth. He had the Halm report on his desk, and the details of the crime scene matched her description.

Murders Four, Five and Six: the Gusewelle Family

BOBB: *Okay, you said that a couple of single girls lived upstairs when you and Dr. Engleman lived in the house on Compton. Can you tell us approximately what year that was—and what were their names?*

RUTH: *Barbara's, I don't know Barbara's maiden name or her roommate's name. It had to be sometime in the '60s. Barbara married Ron Griswell and his parents were killed. I don't know who killed his parents. I don't remember that part clearly. At a later time Ron was killed.*

BOBB: *What did Dr. Engleman say to you about Ronald Griswell being killed?*

RUTH: *He told me that, in colusion with Barbara, he was going to kill Ron Griswell.*

McGarvey put down the typescript. The story got wild beyond belief here. They had stopped the tape before she could go on with it. He was afraid this stuff was pure bullshit, if not Ruth's, then the Doc's. Surely Ruth was playing square with them; they had made her understand they couldn't protect her if she wasn't. There was, however, plenty of room for doubt.

PART THREE:
The Wiring of Ruth

"You know, David had a story about the snakes and the
porcupine. The snakes lived in this little cave, and the
porcupine knocked on the door and asked if he could come in.
The snakes were very amicable, and they said yes. The
porcupine came in and asked if he could take a nap. He took
up a lot of room, and every time the snake moved, the
porcupine stuck him. Finally, the snake said, 'You are going
to have to leave.' But the porcupine said, 'No, I think I am
going to stay.' The snake had to leave. What's the moral of
that story? Know your guests before inviting them in."
—Ruth Jolley Engleman

Sunday, January 20, 1980

Doc glanced over his shoulder at David sleeping in the backseat.
In the front, Handy looked like he might nod off too, his hand
going slack, wrapped around the thermos of hot chocolate he'd
brought along for the boy, his eyes heavy, hypnotized by the
rolling Missouri countryside. It was a beautiful day for the trip,
nippy but not too cold. Ruth would worry it was too cold because
she coddled the boy. She would turn him into a faggot if she had
her way. He meant to get David away from her before it was too
late. After a certain age, a mother like Ruth was no good for a boy.
David was fast nearing that age.

"Should get there about the right time, don't you think?" Handy said, leaning back.

"I think so," Doc replied. Handy, who liked animals better than people, was almost as excited about the trip as David. You had to tell Handy a lot of things two or three times and then take him by the hand and walk him through it, but where animals were concerned he had a rat-trap mind. Handy definitely loved animals. He would have made an excellent biologist or conservationist. Hell, he could get gophers to eat Bit-O-Honey candy bars out of his hand. Ruth was wrong to write him off as a big dumb mug. Well, she was wrong about a lot of things. He thought about her face, frozen in the mask of maternal disapproval she'd worn that morning, and he laughed. Ruth had a way of getting uppity, forgetting just where it was she'd come from.

The sun was coming up behind the clouds, and the light shone, diffuse, melting through the bare trees in an otherworldly way. It made him think of his mother, dead now for several years. Nick had mentioned Madre just the other day when they were having lunch at Grone's Cafeteria. They were talking about something obscure. Out of the blue, Nick had said, "Madre would probably know something about it. I never knew a woman like her for knowing about so many things." Probably some dish on the menu had brought Madre to his mind because he'd enjoyed her cooking so much. "She had a better vocabulary than any woman I've ever known."

That was true about Madre. She had drawn on a wealth of information from her past lives, which was why she constantly surprised people by what she knew. A woman who read incessantly, she was a mental and spiritual giant who only appeared to be a charming South Side housewife. Not a candy-ass mother like Ruth had become, she would approve of taking David to watch the eagles fly south. Hadn't she always encouraged Glen to read and study on his own? His grade-school teachers had shuffled him into a vocational high school because he came from the loins of a working-class man, a clerk for the Wabash Railroad. His family on both sides were country folks, his father's family from Texas and his mother's people, part Cherokee, from Oklahoma. From her Cherokee heritage, she'd drawn her spiritual strength. His background was why his teachers thought he'd be better with his hands than his head. They thought he'd be like his father, content to work an eight-hour shift plus overtime, the grease permanently under his nails, content to reward himself by drinking beer each night until he fell asleep, to live his life afraid of breaking any rule. Why, the man wouldn't even jaywalk. His mother had often disparaged him to her sons. Actually Glen's teachers didn't care what became of him. He exasperated them by not paying attention, and they were too stupid to know how smart he was. Only Madre had known.

Madre had said, "Never mind. You'll show them you're good with both your hands and your brain. You'll turn this to your advantage."

He looked again at the delicate blond boy sleeping soundly in the back. David was almost as pretty as Melody had been, a male version of Little Miss Pretty Two Shoes. While he loved the boy fiercely, he was sometimes disappointed in him, though he admitted that to no one, not even Melody. He'd been a young rascal, suspended from school numerous times—stories of which he was still proud—while David was a regular brownnose, a teacher's pet. When he married Ruth, he had expected more of her than this, what she had done to this child. She'd had the potential, he thought, to be his true mate. What had happened to her he didn't understand. Perhaps it was motherhood, the hormones mellowing her brain, or perhaps it had something to do with a conflict she hadn't worked through in a previous life.

Handy, not quite asleep, caught Doc's eye and grinned. "He's a good kid," Handy said, as usual getting the general idea of what was going on in his head, yet somehow missing the key point. "He's a good kid, Glen, like his old man."

"I broke the strap on Mom's binoculars, Dad," David whined. They were in an observation booth overlooking the dam and locks at Clarksville, the eagles flying six to fifteen feet above them. Handy was studying the birds in the trees through the telescope on a tripod. "She's going to be mad at me. Don't tell her I broke it, will you?"

"It's all right," he said. "She won't be mad. Here, I'll trade you binoculars. Look straight up. We got here at just the right time. They're leaving now."

David looked up just as an eagle took off. Gasping, he reached his hand out. "I can almost touch it!" he cried. Then, behind the first, another eagle took to wing. Mesmerized, they watched until seven eagles, only two mature enough to have the fully white heads that earned their species the name "bald," had flown away.

"Let's go back down and look at the stuffed eagles in the sporting-goods store," Doc said.

"Oooh, are they dead?" David asked. "Will they be messy? Dad, do you think Mom's going to be mad about her binoculars?"

"Do you know why birdshit is always wet, David?" he asked. Like his mother, Doc took every opportunity to educate, not only David, but anyone, especially the young people. "Because they have a common carcass for the urine and fecal matter. Whenever they have a bowel movement, they also urinate. So it's always stringy."

"Yuck," the boy said, hurrying along, clutching at his father's hand. He didn't like anything messy. Sometimes Doc had an urge to take his little nose and rub it in the mess of life, but there was plenty of time for that.

One of the stuffed birds was a golden eagle. Doc watched Handy, unable to take his eyes off the golden bird, while a biologist explained how they were artificially inseminating the eagles. While he talked, his assistant came forward with a live bird, a female, sitting on her hand. Suddenly Handy's attention jerked to the live bird; his eyes filled briefly with tears. David saw the bird at the same time and started. He moved closer to his father, so close the smell of his Johnson's baby shampoo filled Doc's nostrils with regret. He wished the boy had responded to the bird the way he and Handy had; with pride and kinship. Wasn't the good old American, the guys like him and Handy, an endangered species too?

They stopped for hamburgers, french fries, and Pepsis on the way home; playing the alphabet game as they drove. Doc got the first one, A for ash, a tree Handy failed to recognize and David hadn't heard of. Handy and Doc got six apiece, and David got four, grabbing the R for rocks as soon as it came up and coming on strong at the end, seeing the Zephyr filling station before they did. Doc dropped Handy off at his house in Mehlville and drove toward the condo a few blocks away to where Ruth paced the floor waiting for them. It had been, he thought, a very successful, educational trip.

The first thing she asked David was, "Did you get cold?" They talked about the eagles and the recurring fungus infection on David's feet. The boy danced around them, interrupting their conversation to find out when his friend Stephen had last called, when his friend Stephen might come home from wherever he had gone, and when he could go over to his friend Stephen's to play. Impatient, he went across the street to play with another child. Ruth wanted to stop him, but she let him go so they could talk more freely. She wasn't supposed to say anything to draw Glen out this time. "Just be natural," McGarvey had told her. "Get comfortable with the idea of being recorded." But she would have said something about Sophie's death anyway, she told herself. *That* was natural.

"The other night at ten-thirty there was a call," she told him. "And then yesterday morning at eight-thirty. A woman, the same woman; she has a voice like my sister. All she says is 'Murderer,' and hangs up the phone."

"Babe, I'm sorry," he said, his voice soft, sincere, momentarily embarrassed. "It's no longer in the news. Basically it's over, babe. They didn't have much in the way of clues, so they wanted to know my whereabouts. Of course I had a whole appointment book full. And the boys, three of them, Kevin, Michael, and Ron, came out to say they'd been there, working for me. Sister Rose Catherine called me that day at four-thirty and again at five-thirty. And she can testify I was there each time she called. It's over, babe. You saw the papers today? The headlines, babe . . . It's Iran. Seems Iran is fragmenting now, just breaking up. Russia, she'll go in there, babe, and turn those machine guns loose on that bunch of homosexual paraders and that will be that."

"I'm going to call Annette," she said, "to make sure David got over there okay."

When she hung up the phone, he started talking about inflation and the coming recession. He had to raise his filling price five dollars, he said, but fortunately the new filling material, a type of plastic, was cheaper than silver, only eight cents a filling. She wanted to ask him why he needed to raise the price five dollars, but she knew what he would say. Look around you, babe, look around you, and you'll see why: money. She looked around her and she saw a very modest American lifestyle, a toaster oven in the kitchen, a nineteen-inch color TV in the living room. Was that so much? He was a dentist. What did he do with his money anyway? She knew part of the answer to that: he put it into Melody's house.

"I am twenty thousand dollars ahead. Fortuitous event, with Berrera dying," he said; and the back of her neck tensed and prickled. Was he going to say something now? Say it anyway, even if she didn't ask him? "They asked for thirty percent court costs on top of fifteen thousand dollars, remember—and that's twenty thousand. Maric was a lousy person. This arrogant young fellow working for the government, the Alcohol, Firearms, and Explosives crew, is a kid out of college with a nigger supervisor. That's the end of that, shit."

"Will you stay for dinner?" she asked. The longer he stayed, the more likely he would talk. She had to keep the steady stream of words coming. "Are you hungry?"

"We had hamburgers, but I could eat again in a while. Maybe we'll go get something, babe. What would you like?"

"Pizza," she said. "Probably David would like pizza."

"Bill Gonterman was out of town this week, so Melody is saving the newspaper clippings. She's sending them to Willy Boy. It turns out he's suddenly sold a tremendous amount of timber."

"Uhm," Ruth said. She busied herself tidying the kitchen while he talked, because that would look natural. He particularly hated his brother-in-law and said he'd tried to kill him more than once. He and Bill couldn't be more opposite. Bill supported civil rights before it was fashionable, hired a black secretary, and gave fund-raisers for the N.A.A.C.P., which made Glen furious. She remembered a spectacular fight he'd had with Melody at Lake Tishamingo over one of those fund-raisers, "nigger kissing parties," he had called them. When Melody had defended Bill, Glen had unleashed an abusive tirade against her, throwing her off the property and tossing her picnic basket downhill at her. As much as he revered Melody and even more so Madre, she had watched them both catch his unholy wrath. She could still see Melody stomping jerkily down the hill in high wedge shoes, the basket bumping her heels for a good one hundred feet.

"Sold a stand of walnut he'd forgotten he had," Glen said, "forgotten he'd had! Sherrill was telling her mother about his windfall. And babe, I got Mrs. Gooch, and Gooch, that lying bastard. Sorry I took that old hoosier broad's tooth out, lower right first molar broken off, never had a filling in her head. I'm going to send them the clippings too. They're suing me for fifty thousand dollars. They've got a faggot attorney, dresses in red ties, plaid pants, and alligator shoes." The chair scraped as he moved it slightly out from the table to cross his legs. She wondered what those noises sounded like on tape. "She's claiming I left part of the tooth in there and she got infected. Well, I'm going to send her a newspaper clipping. Might as well make use of it. Dip it in thinner, delete all the prints on it, throw it in an envelope, and mail it to her. Pretty picture. Pretty picture.

"Babe, I don't like my fellow man."

She hoped McGarvey was listening good to that.

Tuesday, January 22, 1980

Marie was a greedy, avaricious bitch . . . I got an airtight alibi. Of course, they know just as sure as you and I are standing here, I could have had somebody to plant the bomb after I built it.

Doc's voice on the tape was shockingly soft. He spat out the most vicious words in a voice that, in its lowest register, was almost feminine. McGarvey pushed the fast-forward button on the little Sony recorder. He'd played the tape made Sunday afternoon, January 20, so many times he could pick up the next line from memory wherever he stopped. John Bobb, the "arrogant young fellow," had finally called it a day, and McGarvey was the last one in the office. He thought about Diana, and he was glad he never had to worry about her. She was seven months pregnant; she'd just quit her nursing job in anticipation of the birth. This

time she wanted to stay home for a while, which was fine with
him. They could afford it, and he didn't have strong feelings
about women working anyway, one way or the other. He was
extremely lucky to have a wife who didn't get upset when he
worked late and who would never, he was sure, get fat. Diana was
a happy woman.

Ruth, on the other hand . . . He tried to imagine what it must
be like in Ruth's shoes. She was financially dependent on a man
she feared, a man she believed had killed several people and
would kill her too when he thought she'd fulfilled her purpose.
Yet she'd borne his child. Wouldn't it pull a woman both ways to
love the son and fear the father? Her voice on the first tape was
almost natural. What little tension she displayed could be written
off as the reaction to publicity linking Doc's name to the Berrera
murder. If he'd sensed her uneasiness, he would have blamed it
on the phone calls, the female voice whispering, "Murderer." He
wouldn't have guessed the voice was Ruth's invention, a ruse to
draw Doc out. A good invention. No one would have guessed
from listening to the tape that she knew she was being recorded as
she played out the domestic scene common to many families:
killing time with an ex-husband who still wants you after he's
brought the kid back from the Sunday outing.

Doc clearly still wanted her. What was less clear was whether or
not he'd actually murdered Sophie Berrera. In his mind, Ruth's
story was far more credible now that he'd heard the Doc raving on
tape, but the dentist hadn't implicated himself in seven murders
either. He and Bobb had agreed she'd done well, better than they
hoped, on her first try. They hadn't expected to get anything they
could use in court. Murderers didn't usually admit to murder
anyway. They were always hiding behind lies, dodging the truth
with rationalizations. Perhaps they were always afraid of being
overheard, recorded, entrapped. Or maybe even they regarded
their deeds as too heinous to admit. Whatever the reason, they
rarely said, "I killed." They weren't expecting the Doc to hand
them anything either, especially on the first day. But they had
learned from listening to the tape that Ruth still had a great deal
of power in their relationship. He wanted her. *She* decided when
he would take them out to dinner and when he would spend the

night. They'd needed to know exactly where she stood with him, so they could gauge her ability to draw him out. And now they knew.

McGarvey lit a cigarette and told himself he'd play the tape one more time, then go home.

> DOC: *Well, you know the minute the federal government comes in on anything, they are going to immediately seek a wiretap, anytime an explosive is used.*
> RUTH: *Well, I am going to call the phone company and find out if they have it tapped.*
> DOC: *Oh, honey, they don't tap you there. They tap the house here . . .*

He went into a long explanation of how wiretaps are accomplished. Basically he knew how it was done. McGarvey thought they probably wouldn't get much on Nagra recorders and transmitters planted in the house. His knowledge of wiretap procedures and his expertise in electricity had made wiring his apartment a more difficult job; he knew what every wire was for, and if he had reason to check the wiring they were in trouble. Doc was already wary of "the federal government," if not of Ruth. He might talk more freely away from the house, where Ruth would wear a wire on her body.

"What if he finds it?" she had asked. They had reassured her that the wire couldn't be seen under clothing and that they'd be monitoring the transmissions closely in a nearby van, and would get to her within minutes if he did find what they promised he wouldn't. Privately McGarvey thought there wasn't much likelihood he'd grab her ankle in the middle of Ground Round and discover the wire taped to her anyway. He was surely beyond the age of public groping; and, as extra insurance, they took David with them when they went out.

He put out his cigarette, pushed the rewind button. He hit PLAY at an arbitrary point.

> DOC: *I had this drunken fag for a patient, had to take his tooth out, a wisdom tooth is all. And, oh, boy, he was something*

else . . . Sherrill has had it up to here with niggers working for her. She said, "I used to think you were bad being so down on them, but you're right. You can't teach those people anything." I said, "Well, honey, being unfair about people with intelligence hasn't been one of my bad traits. That's the whole trouble with niggers."

McGarvey rewound the tape. While it spun back to the beginning, he could hear the rest of Doc's story in his head. He had told Ruth about his sister Melody intervening to aid her daughter, Doc's niece Sherrill, in firing a gay black cook. Jesus, if the cook had been gay, black, *and* Jewish, would the story have gone on longer? The Doc certainly liked to hear himself talk. He got particularly wound up when he was educating Ruth in some esoteric area of knowledge, like how eagles were sexed and artificially inseminated, or how private homes were bugged, or when he was railing against homosexuals, blacks, and Jews. McGarvey put the tape recorder in his top right-hand desk drawer, stood, and stretched. At this point, Doc was an enigma. How could an educated man be such an avowed racist? Would someone who got up at the crack of dawn to take his son to Clarksville to watch the eagles fly kill another man's son for a cut of a modest insurance policy? It was a hard thing to believe.

If Doc had murdered Sophie—and several others—then *why*? Would he kill in cold blood for an amount of money probably not comparable to what he could have earned if he'd taken his dentistry more seriously? You had to know people's motives before you knew anything about what they had or could have done. He picked up the phone and dialed Dennis McCarthy, the *Globe* reporter who had been calling him since ATF had gotten involved in the Berrera bombing. If he could encourage McCarthy to run a story reviving the Bullock murder and hinting at Doc's involvement in the Berrera and Frey murders, he might be able to draw him out in conversations with Ruth. At least it would give her a new opening. He wanted to give Ruth every break possible. He'd never worked so closely with a woman informant before. How much could he expect? How far could he trust her emotionally?

Thursday, January 24, 1980

"Have the police called you?" Doc asked.

Rosie Sutterfield, one of his patients from the fourteenth, the day of Sophie's murder, was sitting in the chair, her little fingers, like red-tipped bird talons, digging into the Leatherette. His dental degree from Washington University hung in this room; she'd commented on it last time. "The real Washington University in St. Louis? The fancy, expensive one?" Her eyes flew to it again. Women like her were really impressed with that Wash U. degree, and they especially liked to hear how you'd gone on the G.I. Bill. Yes, ma'am, he'd been selected to be a cadet in the Army Air Corps on the basis of his high test scores. He'd shown his teachers at last, so that when he was ready no one questioned his right to Wash U.

Rosie's mouth, stretched open like a bloody gash, matched her nails. Not a bad-looking woman, he thought, but old. She *smelled* old. It was probably the fragrance she wore. Women dated themselves by the perfumes they wore—scents associated with other times. The makeup sat in the cracks of her face; her lipstick was comic. She looked like Lucille Ball, that old broad. Her eyes popped at the question, bulged out of her head when he asked if the police had called. Her tension sent a surge of power through his fingertips, and he wanted to laugh. Vigorously, she shook her head no.

"They've called some of my patients," he said, packing the indentation in her molar with plastic filling, "to verify my whereabouts on a certain day in question. I gave them that page from my appointment book. I suppose you saw the papers?" She nodded yes and tried to spit out her disbelief. "I know," he said, reassuringly, "it's awful what they can do to you. They haven't got a clue, so they persecute a law-abiding citizen. You know, they're afraid to go after the real criminals, the nigger thugs and the mafia"—he pronounced the word *ma-FEE-aah*—"element. They might get their suits wrinkled. So they have to do something to justify their paychecks and so forth." She nodded in agreement. The woman, he thought, really liked him. He warmed to his topic, the lousy stupid cops, until she was grasping the chair arm so hard she nearly slit the Leatherette.

The publicity hadn't hurt his business. He moved from Rosie to another hoosier broad who needed a tooth yanked. They kept on coming. Some of them said they'd seen the papers, and they were shocked, outraged, that anyone could even hint he'd do such a thing. Most of them didn't say a word, rightly behaving as if it were none of their business, which it wasn't. A few had been his patients since the time of the Bullock investigation. He was gratified by their support, the continued flow of mouths acrid from coffee and beer, cheap whiskey and more rarely, cheap mouthwash, mouths open and vulnerable beneath his fingers, trusting mouths. Yes, they trusted him, put themselves totally in his power whenever they sat in that chair.

Toward the end of the day, Ruth called. "Want to come over for dinner tonight?" she asked, her voice light, flirtatious. "David would like a pizza, and I thought you might want to come over and join us."

Apparently she'd gotten off her high horse about the mysterious phone calls, which she of course blamed on him. It was his name in the paper, wasn't it? she implied. She gave him a pain when she acted so put upon. David and I are suffering embarrassment over this. And why did you do it? She knew why he did everything he did: *money*. Ruth certainly knew about money. She'd spent enough of it over the years—and been a willing participant in laundering it. In fact, she'd been as enthusiastic over the counterfeiting scheme as anyone. She hadn't distanced herself from it until Handy blew it, and then Handy had taken the rap. He could remember her fuming because Handy had flushed the counterfeit down their toilet when he was told to get rid of it. She'd really been hot when Nick Miranda's younger brother, Charlie, the slow one, had found the stuff floating in the drainage ditch and shown it to a cop.

"I'll be there by six," he told her, matching her tone for tone. If she could flirt, so could he. She was a hot piece in the sack, for all her posturing outside it. "Bye, now, babe."

"Dad, will you come down with me to Magic Market—and can we get a pizza?" David asked as soon as he got there. "Buck

Rogers is playing on the television set at seven o'clock, and I want to be right here to see it."

He wasn't surprised that the plan included his buying the pizza and the junk David wanted. Ruth could still ask, *Why, Glen, why do you do these things?* She liked to distance herself from the realities, Ruth did.

"Do you need anything else from the market?" he asked her; and of course she did. This time he didn't mind. He handed her a sack of coins. He didn't need to tell her where they belonged, in the secret hiding place he'd built into the living-room bookshelves. What he liked best about being with Ruth was that he didn't have to tell her so many things. True, she still rubbed him uncomfortably in places, but in other places she fit against him the way his ass fit right into the hollow of their sofa, comfortably.

After they'd gone, she said into the transmitter, "Well, guys, I guess you heard that. They have gone down to the Magic Market. Keep your fingers crossed. He brought in a whole pile of change, and I'm just putting it away. He is acting kind of funny. I don't know what to make of that. But he brought in some coins."

McGarvey was monitoring the transmission in the van, disguised as a department store repair truck, parked in the adjoining lot. Right before Doc had arrived that night, a little old lady had rapped on the van, calling, "Is anyone in there? You've been out here a long time," but Doc didn't even glance in that direction as he left the building while Ruth talked. His hand rested lightly on David's head. The boy told him how handsome Buck Rogers was. *Handsome.* His son admired pretty boys; and that worried Doc. The only thing he had on his mind was showing that boy someday what real men did—and it wasn't shoot toy guns like a pretty-boy TV star. Ninety-nine percent of the general public didn't have what it takes to kill in cold blood, to take aim at something warm and breathing, squeeze the trigger, and shoot.

Friday, January 25, 1980

McGarvey shut off the tape. The quality was poor. In the clearest part, they had argued over the John's frozen pizza Doc had brought home. She insisted only Tortino's was *barely* worth buying and asked why he hadn't picked up a take-out pizza from a pizzeria. The cat, Fluffy, had been gnawing at the carpet covering one of the hidden microphones; and they'd had to call and tell her, *Get that cat away from there.* Then Doc had helped David build a wooden airplane from a kit. Jesus, they could have stayed married for an evening like that.

"You're doing okay," McGarvey said. She was on top of the relationship. That was even clearer than it had been. He looked across the conference table at Ruth, hunched forward eagerly, like a student who hadn't made the grade yet but was determined she would. She was still working at her job, but she'd taken the day off. Soon she would quit her job and would become the agency's dependent for a time, not Doc's. He felt the weight of her as if she were already his own personal dependent. "You sound relaxed. You handle it well."

"He didn't say anything," she fretted. "He really didn't say anything at all."

"We didn't expect an out-and-out admission." He lit a cigarette and told her about his conversation with McCarthy. "A newspaper story will give you something to hook onto when you talk to him, a reason for bringing up these things." He paused. They'd been beating around the bush on this one, and he thought it was time to ask the question outright. They had told her she was the best person to know how to get to him and encouraged her to share her ideas. Reluctant at first, she had gained confidence—and control of the situation. Finding a way to gain control with Doc was exhilarating to her. Now it was time to ask outright: "When does he do his talking usually? I mean, when is he most likely to open up to you?"

"In the bedroom, usually after sex," she said with no shyness. It was, of course, what they figured, but no one had wanted to bring it up. "He told me he was going to kill Peter Halm when we were in bed. I think he likes that, talking about murder in bed. It makes him feel more powerful." She picked up the Styrofoam cup of coffee in front of her, took a sip, leaving the rosy imprint of her lipstick behind. "Why don't we bug the bedroom?"

He liked it that she was beginning to say "we." She considered herself part of the team now. He had already upgraded his original estimation of her intelligence: She was bright, very bright, and bold. Already she was far less scared than she'd been in the beginning. Ruth was certainly more than a pawn in their hands; she was the key. Today, she'd made an important step: She'd said *"we."*

A few years back, Nick had overheard Doc tell Handy: "Nick knows I let him live." Driving on Route 40 into downtown to meet the two men for lunch, Nick thought suddenly about that remark. Their lunches seemed ludicrous to him now. Doc had said he was having a problem and alluded to reporters. Christ, he'd been such a kid when he'd admired Doc for "handling" the *Globe* like he did when Bullock was killed. Once he'd thought participating in Doc's social life made him part of something big and powerful. He'd thought Doc was a god. Now, he wished he were home with his wife Barbara and the kids. Doc had always told him he would end up fat and lazy married to an ignorant Mexican woman, eight kids hanging on her, at least one clinging to the teat. Well, he had two kids, one boy, one girl, and a beautiful wife, a woman of quality, perhaps better than he deserved. He had proved Doc wrong. He didn't want Doc to have power over him anymore, but he did. The hold now was largely, but not entirely, fear.

He didn't want to meet them for lunch, but he went where Doc told him to go and when. Long ago, he'd tried to distance himself from his former mentor, but he'd learned getting away from Doc was like pulling yourself out of tar baby's clutches. He wouldn't get free without leaving some skin behind. More than skin, flesh and blood. Only weeks ago over another lunch Doc and Handy had told him phase two of their plan with the other Barbara, the "golden girl," had been completed. Then he'd read about the discovery of Ron Gusewelle's body in an abandoned car in East St. Louis. And quickly after that one, Sophie. Each time he read about the deaths he knew were tied to Doc, he felt his stomach turn the way it had when Eric Frey was killed.

The feds were into the investigation this time because of the car bomb; he'd read that much in the paper. He didn't believe this crime could have been planned any better than the other ones Doc had masterminded; and so he knew there had been mistakes. Doc handled murder the way he handled remodeling jobs: He would decide he could beat a contractor's estimate by doing the work himself. Then he would invest more, maybe two or three times more, in supplies and new tools—which didn't even take into consideration the hours he lost from dentistry. And he'd end up building something that was a little bit off, like the murders, which were far from perfect crimes. Christ, Nick thought, he was scared not to show up for lunch when he was told. He was also scared to be associated with Doc right now, especially if the papers were sniffing him up again. He slapped his open palm on the steering wheel. For a moment he wished life were as simple as it had been when he adored Doc and the only thing he had to wonder about was where they would go for lunch.

Doc didn't like to eat too often at the same places, but he still had his favorites: Carnegie's in the Soulard area where Sherrill cooked and Grone's Cafeteria and the Broadway Oyster Bar, both on South Broadway. He talked more freely in restaurants than he did at the office, and he said it was a bad idea to talk a lot in the same places. But he liked Broadway, gritty and saturated with the smells of industry, the aroma of Switzer's licorice blended with the stench of a rubber-tire plant. The Oyster Bar, with old oak floors, a hammered cooper bar, exposed brick walls, and a fireplace, would have been taken over by young lawyers, entrepreneurs, and TV announcers if it had been located anywhere else— and would have appealed to Nick more if it had been taken over by such a crowd, the people he emulated now. Doc had settled on the Oyster Bar, then at the last minute picked Carnegie's for lunch with Nick and Handy. He wondered if the plan had been changed at the last minute because Doc didn't trust someone, maybe him. They were waiting in the parking lot when he pulled in, standing beside Handy's car talking. The talking stopped when he opened his car door; and, after acknowledging him, they walked into the restaurant ahead of him in silence.

"I put my foot on that damn reporter's ass and kicked him out of the office," Doc said softly from behind his menu, "the photographer right behind him. There were two reporters, but the other one was timid. Smart. He stayed out of reach. You should have seen that photographer, cradling his camera like it was a football, running out of there."

"Assholes," Handy said. He was laughing, not laughing hard, yet there were tears forming in the corners of his eyes. Nick, who wasn't saying much, watched those tears form, like warning flashes of lightning, then disappear. Was Handy, the "courageous lion," finally scared? "They haven't got anything on you, Glen. Where do they get off?"

"Rehashing old stuff, that's all they're doing. The Bullock murder." He closed the menu, signaled the waitress, as usual assuming when he was ready they were ready. He never failed to pick up the tab either. "You know what that young detective from the explosives crew asked me. He said, 'Doc, I'm not blowing smoke at you but you are quite an intelligent man.' I said, 'I can see the smoke now.' He said, 'Let's get away from this.' He said, 'Tell me, what do you think of the international situation?' They haven't got anything. That's pretty clear. I quoted Marx. I said, 'Thrust the bayonet in. If it hits steel, pull it out.' Then he says, 'We're too weak to do anything.' I said, 'Well, that's the reason they are doing it.' He said, 'What do you think is gonna happen?' I said, 'They'll get half of us.' I said, 'The Metropolitan St. Louis Police Force will cease to exist.'"

Handy laughed harder then; and Nick laughed too. The waitress brought Handy a beer, and coffee for the other two. Nick took a sip from his, put it down, and said, "What do you think is gonna happen now?"

"They haven't got anything. If the papers come out with another story, I'll sue. I've already talked to Dempsey. I'll sue!"

"Have you heard from the golden girl?" Nick asked. He knew Doc still had the hots for Barbara; he'd been drilling her regularly. He had to miss the sex now that they were being careful and staying apart. "The money might come in handy. Maybe you could take a trip, get away for a while." Christ, he wished Doc would take a trip, just disappear. Maybe he could breathe free then. "Hasn't she gotten anything yet?"

"I haven't heard from her and don't expect to for a while," Doc said. "It's too soon. She isn't supposed to get in touch with me until things have cooled down. I don't have anything to get away from. It will all die down—or I'll sue their asses. I'll build my retirement fund on their faggot butts. Crummy-ass little bunch of pissants."

"How much does Ruth know?" Nick asked. He certainly didn't trust Ruth; and if Doc did, he was more the fool. Ruth would sell her own mother out to save her ass. She prided herself on her brains, but she couldn't carry their lunch. "Do you think it's a good idea for her to know what's going on now that you're divorced?"

"A lot of men are in prison because of their ex-wives," Handy said, jumping more vigorously into the conversation than he normally did. "Plenty of them, Glen. They're sorry afterwards they didn't keep their mouths shut."

"Ruthie knows enough to keep *her* mouth shut," Doc said. "Don't worry about Ruth."

Nick wasn't so sure Ruth could be trusted to keep her mouth shut if she were amply rewarded for opening it. He wouldn't have been surprised to learn Ruth had begun meeting her ATF contacts in a room at the Ramada Inn on South Lindbergh, not far from the condo. It was, McGarvey had told her, safer than risking being seen by one of Doc's associates as she was coming in and out of the federal courts building on Market Street. She was sitting in that room, sipping coffee, talking strategy, even as Doc lifted a triple-decker turkey club sandwich to his mouth and Nick and Handy watched him, frowning, lost momentarily in their own thoughts of Ruth's potential to betray. Ruth, Nick thought, could be the key to the man's undoing, but he wasn't going to issue any more warnings. There was always the chance Doc would turn on her suddenly and kill her. He wouldn't want to feel he'd had any part in instigating that. Besides, he had worries enough of his own. What if, after all this time, they came back at Carmen for Peter's death? Christ, if anything happened to Carmen now, after she'd finally pulled herself back together, *he* might kill the Doc.

Saturday, January 26, 1980

"Doctor Engleman, you are at your office!" Sister Catherine said. She usually spoke too loudly into the phone, and she was doing so today. He held the receiver a little away from his ear. Why would a goddamn nun speak so loud? "I was worried about you."

"Where should I be on Saturday, Catherine?" he asked reasonably.

"I just saw it in the paper, Dr. Engleman . . . how awful!" Her voice went up even higher on the word "awful."

"You mean my retirement fund?"

"Retirement fund?"

"Catherine, when I get through suing them, I can retire."

"Oh, good for you. Well, then I can come in Monday?"

"Yes, I'm going to be here working."

And she said, "Oh, good. I'm happy to hear you're in such good spirits. God bless you."

Sister Catherine was good people. She was garrulous and had unpleasant breath, but in spite of both he liked her. He picked up the weekend *Globe* and looked at the 1958 file photo of himself on the front page, the very picture that she had seen. It was a flattering photo, and he didn't mind seeing himself again as he'd been. Had that pissant photographer really thought he'd let him take a new picture? Was there no limit to their audacity? The headline read, DENTIST, FIRM BENEFITED FINANCIALLY AFTER 3 DEATHS. What particularly galled him was the contents of a tiny box under the headline, "This story was written by Bill Bryan, Dennis J. McCarthy, and John C. Shelton." They were proud of themselves, weren't they? He'd tried to call his lawyer, Dick Dempsey, but he wasn't in the office. When Dempsey finished with them, they'd be looking for jobs. The *Globe* would have to fire their asses. They couldn't hurt him, not when he had good people like Sister Catherine rallying around him. Who did they think they were?

Ruth had called first thing that morning too, as soon as he'd gotten to the office. *Oh, Glen, did you see the paper?* Everybody acted like the world was ending. It would all blow over. *Oh, Glen, oh, Glen.* Ruth couldn't take the pressure; she wasn't as tough as she thought she was.

He'd told her, "Well, Ruth, I'm what's known as a hardened criminal. Everybody always thinks a criminal's got his jaw clenched, blood oozing out of the corner of his mouth. The hard-

ened criminal, these people like Richard Nixon, like Jimmy Carter, Jimmy Hoffa, right out there in front of the public's eye,
pulling their shit off and getting by with it. Selling out our country
like fucking ignorant Ford is going to sacrifice our cruise missiles
for the good of SALT. And so the *Globe* worried about a pissant
local affair. I just hope I'm alive to collect the money when I sue
them, Ruthie. I've never lost contact with reality." And she had
said, "Well, Glen."

He read the story again:

> Dr. Glennon E. Engleman or a corporation in which he had an
> interest benefited financially after two unsolved murders and a
> mysterious accidental death, an investigation by the Globe-Demo-
> crat has revealed.
>
> Records show these links among the three deaths:
>
> —A lawsuit claiming $14,504 in unpaid bills to Engleman from
> Sophie Marie Berrera, who was killed when her car was dynamited
> January 14, will be dropped, her heirs said.
>
> —The widow of James S. Bullock, whose murder near the St.
> Louis Art Museum December 17, 1958, is one of the city's most
> famous unsolved slayings, invested $15,000 on a car drag strip in
> which Engleman was a shareholder and director. The investment
> was made after Bullock's widow received proceeds from his life
> insurance policies.
>
> —The widow of a drag strip employee who was killed Sep-
> tember 26, 1963, in what was ruled an accidental explosion,
> loaned $16,000 to the drag strip after receiving proceeds from her
> husband's life insurance.
>
> Engleman, a 52-year-old south St. Louis dentist, refused to be
> interviewed Friday and ordered two reporters to leave the recep-
> tion room at his office at 4630 Gravois Avenue.

That was enough. He slammed the paper down on the desk.
What did they expect him to do—ask them in for coffee? He
picked up the paper again and scanned the rest of the long story
continued on page 9A. It rehashed the Bullock case, what little
the reporters knew of it, and printed testimony from the insurance hearing which Sandy Frey had won. It hinted they knew
where Sandy Frey was but he doubted that. She'd pulled the hole
in after her all right. They probably thought they were clever by

ending the piece with the exchange that had taken place in his office on Friday.

> Engleman opened the door of his office when a reporter rang a buzzer. When reporters identified themselves, Engleman declined to be interviewed. He then tried to physically push the reporters out of his reception room.
> Engleman then said, "Get the hell outta here. Get out! Get out! Get outta here."
> "Doctor?"
> "Get out!"
> "It's important to you."
> "Get the hell out of here! Get the hell out of here! Go on, get out of here!"
> "Doctor . . ."
> "Get your . . . ass outta here."

He threw the paper back down on the desk and walked into a treatment room. An old hoosier broad was sitting there with her rancid mouth open. She'd been waiting so long, some of the pain-killer might have worn off. He picked up the pliers. She gripped the chair arms, but she didn't flinch. She probably had enough alcohol in her bloodstream to deaden any pain he could inflict upon her. Even if she didn't, she was tough enough to take it.

"You guys had supper?" he asked as soon as he walked in the door that evening.

"No," Ruth told him. She knew the tape was running, but she was used to the way her voice sounded on tape now, so she didn't think about it anymore. Okay, she had a slight country twang. It wasn't that bad, really. Would he ever be surprised to know what he sounded like! "We are starving to death. Why don't you take us out?"

"Dad, we finished the town! We finished the town!" David yelled as he ran into the room. They had been building a town, an old time western city, from a kit. The plastic logs and all the other pieces had littered his bedroom for weeks. "It's upstairs. Go on upstairs and see it."

"Okay," he said, looking at Ruth, raising one eyebrow. "Let's see how the jail came out."

She looked at him and did not flinch. While David showed him the town, she powdered her nose, checked the wire to the microphone hidden on her body. She wasn't nervous about that anymore either. Like she'd told McGarvey, she knew she could handle it. He'd told her it took eight to ten men, sometimes twelve, to keep a rolling surveillance of them when they went out to eat. They had to follow loosely, he said, or they ran the risk of being made. She imagined those men following her and Glen and David in an intricate rolling ballet of cars, one taking over when another turned off so he wouldn't ever get suspicious of one particular car behind him. They did it exactly like she'd seen it done on television. That pleased her—because so much of television was junk—and also made her feel safe.

"Oh, please, Dad, can't you go get something so we don't have to go out?" David said as they came back down the stairs. "I don't want to go out."

"No, David," she told him. "We're going out to have a good dinner. I'm hungry." She was meant to be the lead in this auto ballet, and she would not let them down.

She had wanted Chinese food at Leong's, but Leong's was crowded. It was too long to wait with an irritable ten-year-old, she'd said. Really, her body transmitter only had power for three hours. She didn't want to waste time while they stood in a crowded vestibule, unable to talk.

McGarvey had explained she could turn it off to conserve power now and then, but she shouldn't do that unless it was necessary. When it was, he would come inside the restaurant and signal her by removing his hat, and she would shut it off. They did this, he said, so he could swear he'd told her to shut it off and protect the integrity of the tape. Otherwise some lawyer for the defense might accuse her of playing with the tape.

They ended up at the Ground Round, on Lindbergh, which David liked better anyway because the restaurant specialized in hamburgers and electronic games.

"Oh, Glen, the whole thing, I want you to know, has me sick," she said. David was busy across the room putting quarters in slots. She wondered if the clanging of the games and the noise of the jukebox on the loudspeaker interfered with the transmission; she supposed it did. Fortunately, Glen had opened the subject himself by saying again he would send today's newspaper story to the old hoosier broad who was suing him. "Absolutely sick. I am concerned about David. I don't want him to have any problems at school as a result of it."

"He won't," Doc said as he munched on a handful of popcorn. "It will all pass, be over and done with. That's exactly what will happen."

"Have you heard anything from Barbara?" she asked. McGarvey had told her to mention Barbara, the golden girl Ruth claimed was involved with Engleman in other murders, but if he didn't bite, drop it. Don't lead him into a denial, he'd said. If he denies it, we're stuck with the denial. She could tell McGarvey was doubtful about that whole part of the story, and she would love to draw Glen into a discussion of Barbara and her dead in-laws and husband. "Shouldn't you be getting something out of her?"

"No, I don't think I will for a while." The waitress put his steak and baked potato in front of him, smiling hugely. It irritated Ruth that those girls—not two steps removed from their hoosier mothers just because they were working in south County, not South Side—would pay attention to him and not her. Even if she asked them a question, they would look at him while they answered. "That will be all for now," he told the little thing.

"I wanted steak sauce," Ruth said irritably. "Well, I guess I'll see how it tastes first. Maybe I won't need any." They chewed silently on their steaks until David came back. She'd allowed her irritation with the waitress to distract her from managing their conversation, and she was berating herself for that. "Hi, David," she said. "Don't you think you should take the time to eat?"

He would talk in cryptic terms as long as David sat there. She knew that. The trick was to go back to the subjects he touched and make him talk more fully about whatever he'd said as soon as David got up to play the games again.

"I want more popcorn," David said. Then a waitress announced the birthday of a little girl named Jennifer. The jukebox stopped while people sang "Happy Birthday," started up again. "I want dessert, Mama. I would like some dessert!"

"Okay," she told him, looking around for that little blond snit. "How do you figure Marie?" she said to Glen. "Why didn't she just desist after she knew?"

"She was under surveillance by the Bomb and Arson Squad for thirty days," he told her, finishing the last of his steak while David played with the ketchup bottle.

"How do you know?" Ruth asked. She looked the waitress straight in the eye, but the snit turned away before she could signal.

"Because I had somebody watch, some people that waited on Arsenal for a bus to come. There was only one bus. He sat there reading the paper. The bus came and the bus split. Everybody boarded; he never got aboard the bus. She was under surveillance. But after thirty days they give up."

"David, why don't you go and play now?" she said. "We'll have dessert when we're all finished eating. Take this change and play some more games."

"I offered to pay her five thousand dollars . . . five thousand dollars lump sum. That stinkin'-ass Jew baby of hers said, 'No, we want it lump sum, all of it.' This broad, she just thinks she is going to break it off in me, Ruth. Today I do business with Fine Laboratory. You know what Fine costs per tooth? Ten dollars and tax. She had it up to eighteen dollars. Charged me two percent interest on the unpaid balance."

"Why didn't you handle it with a lawyer is all I'm saying."

"Babe, I should let this Jew baby and her have twenty, twenty-one thousand of my money? After all those years of her screwing Fred, then screwing me? Hey, babe, you said it yourself, you don't owe her anything. She gouges."

"She did, but you could have handled it in a different way."

"Oh, no, I couldn't have handled it in a different way. I got this Jew, this arrogant Jew son of a bitch, this Gartenberg. Dempsey said he was one real son of a bitch, babe. I couldn't have handled it different, babe."

"Was it all past history they were talking about in the paper? Was Melody contacted?"

"All past history, babe. Past history. Those arrogant fucks."

"Dad, I need another quarter," David said, materializing at his elbow. "No, another dollar."

"Dollars don't grow on trees. That's the last you get," he said, handing him four quarters.

"Well, I still think," Ruth began. The waitress approached their table, looked at Glen and asked if anyone wanted dessert. He ordered David's hot fudge sundae. "Spend your quarters," she told him. "Go on. Your dessert will be here when you get back." Then she said to Glen, "I didn't know you were such an explosives expert like the paper said you were." McGarvey had told her they'd planted this in the paper. It was a gamble, he said, but they needed it for court.

"Now isn't that awful, how they come up with that crap," he said, the satisfaction in his voice belying his words, guaranteeing he would pick up on the chance to display his expertise, as she'd known he would. "Now they laid that on me. There's no reason for them to lay that one on me. But I am an expert." Gamble, hell. She'd known the expert tag was irresistible to him. "I learned under one of the very best, Tex, an old demolition powder monkey from World War II," he bragged. "Handy, when I was making it up, says to me, 'That makes me nervous.' He says, 'You put the wrong wires together, we got it.' I said, 'Well, why don't you wait out back then?'"

"Can you get me a pack of cigarettes?" she asked the waitress.

"Well, you'll have to wait until I deliver this order. I don't have change in my pocket right now. You'll have to wait."

"I got the nicest card from Sister Celeste," he told her.

"I'll have to go get my own cigarettes, won't I?" she said to Glen, not the waitress, who was putting David's sundae on the table.

"Would you believe Channel Four reading the Bible verse read at Marie's funeral, 'Let the angel of God pursue those who would do me harm'? They said her Bible was worn with that verse underscored. All the times I talked to that bitch, she never talked Bible. See what happened to her, the Jew needed money, five thousand dollars, he probably got half of it, but he wanted it all at once. He couldn't see five hundred dollars a month for months.

There's as much blood on his hands as someone else's. I was up against the wall. A seizure notice was pasted on my door. I was paying eighteen dollars a tooth to Marie plus two percent interest. Well, I'll tell you one thing, Marie did know I wasn't anybody to shit with. When she found that first love potion in her backyard, boy, she knew. She said, 'I know who did it. Bingo, I know who did it.'"

"She was a fool," Ruth said. The tape around her ankle was irritating her. She wanted to scratch it, pull it loose. Had he said enough to arrest him? Had he made it as clear to McGarvey listening in the van as it was to her? "Marie was a fool," she repeated.

"A fool," he agreed. "Ruth, nobody had ever better tell me, 'I'm gonna get you.' Oh, boy, I would never tell anybody that. Never, boy. People get hot."

"Nice to be a little boy, isn't it?" she said, looking at David, pulling back on the lever of the video games. Would it still be nice for him in a few more weeks, after he was snatched away from his father?

"Oh, God, yes. Mom and Dad are seated at a table. He's got money in his pocket; place is full of excitement. He's on the wander . . . as long as he can check in. That's what kids need. As long as they can look up and see you there. Maybe there will come a day when he will make inquiries. Well, hey, I don't know. He will reach that point in life when he has some pangs of conscience about it, but if he is mature enough and involved enough with me, he'll be okay. Babe, you just have to resign yourself to the fact that, like Melody says, you have a few years with him before his peers get him. That's the period now, your period. It won't last."

"Yes, it is," she said, "and I love it." David came back to the table. "I have to run back to the rest room," she said. He wanted to be sure she had that message, didn't he? *Your time is now, babe; and then it's my time.* Well, her life and David's future depended on her stopping him now. She wasn't going to let him kill her; she wouldn't let him have David either.

RUTH: *We are going to be leaving this place in a few minutes. I sure hope you got some of that. He admitted he did it. I am back in*

the rest room, so if you excuse me, please. I do need a little bit of privacy.
    TRANSMITTER GOES OFF FOR A LITTLE WHILE.
    RUTH: *Oh, boy, I hope you got some of this.*

"Wasn't that enough?" she asked anxiously. She had been so excited about this tape; and now he was telling her they needed more. "He admitted it, didn't he?"

"You always want to get as much as possible, make as good a case as you can before you quit," he said. After the taping sessions they met in the downstairs bathroom of Ruth's condo. It was a small room, and the proximity to her made him uncomfortable. But it was the only place in the house they felt certain of carrying on a conversation that couldn't be overheard by David if he happened to wake up. "Look, I know how you feel, but I think we have to go on. You did good, Ruth; you did real good. Let's don't quit now. Maybe we can get a stronger admission, something Dempsey can't distort. There are many more things he could admit to, more murders. As long as you still have his confidence and you're in good shape, it's just a matter of time before he gives us what we want."

"And he hasn't talked about the other murders on tape, has he? I asked him about Barbara, did you hear that?" She was sitting on the toilet seat, rubbing her ankle where the adhesive had been, coming around to his position. "I'd hoped to get him to say something about Barbara and that deal, but he just dropped it."

"You did good, Ruth," he repeated, "but we can't stop yet." He felt like he should clap her on the shoulder, but in the confines of that little bathroom, he couldn't bring himself to do it. Jesus, it smelled like lilac bathroom freshener, overpoweringly sweet. And he kept thinking about the kid asleep upstairs. "A little while longer. If it looks like you're in danger, we'll move in. We'll end it and pull you out right there, whether we've got a case or not. You know that. Someone's on his tail constantly." He didn't tell her that Doc had almost walked in on them when they were setting up equipment the other day. The agent who had been following him had lost him, and they just made it out the back door before he'd come in the front. "Hey, you don't want to quit now, Ruth. I know you better than that. And you know we aren't going to let anything happen to you."

She looked up at him and smiled. He knew her well enough to know how much she'd come to value her place on the team. Surprisingly, he valued it too.

Tuesday, January 29, 1980

"Where are you calling from, Barbara? I told you not to call unless it was an emergency." He'd been getting ready to leave the office when his golden girl called. It was good to hear her voice, but the phone might be tapped. "Is it an emergency?"

"I'm calling from a phone booth in Illinois, exactly what you told me to do if I had to call," she said, sounding frightened. "You tell me if it's an emergency. I saw the *Globe* and I'm scared. What's going to happen?"

"What's going to happen, Barbara, is that I'm going to sue their asses off. I've already talked to Dick Dempsey. They haven't got anything, nothing. I wouldn't be surprised if my ex-wife sues them too, for bringing all this up again."

"You mean the first Ruth?" she sighed. "Are you sure, Glennon, are you sure it's going to be all right?"

"Honey, just don't do anything foolish. It's all going to blow over."

"What if they come to question me?"

"Why should they, honey? That dumb-fuck nigger confessed to killing your husband. He did us a big favor, baby. That was a break we couldn't have counted on. Why should they bother you?"

He finally calmed her down. It was unlike her to get so upset. In fact, he couldn't remember when Barbara had been upset. Everybody was acting like the world had ended. He pulled on his coat and opened the door. The wind felt chillier than it had in the morning. Maybe they were going to get snow.

"I got a hundred on my spelling test, Dad," David told him as he walked in the door. The boy was usually waiting inside the door when he came in, which made him happy. Ruth had cooked a pork roast, and the aroma was delicious. This was how families were supposed to be, he thought, and if it weren't for Ruth, this would be a family. "And I saw one of those toy birds today, Daddy, at school. One of the birds we saw. And we're studying the sun in school. In millions more years, it's going out."

"Kimberly bought you one of those birds, didn't she?" his father said, referring to his sister Melody's daughter.

"She did, but it didn't work," Ruth told him. "I bought some bakery bread to go with the roast."

"Umm, sounds good," he said appreciatively. While she put dinner on the table, he talked to David about the sun. "We don't know enough about what has transpired at the core of the sun or the planets. The trouble is we get inaccurate theories because we don't know. Big inaccuracies. In the course of your life you will hear a hypothesis like this advance considerably. The advance will be made on the basis of knowledge which isn't known now. My God, ten years later, it's amazing what they'll know they didn't know now." They sat down to the meal and he told her warmly, "Oh, babe, this looks nice."

After dinner, Ruth wanted to wax philosophical in front of the television set. That always amused him because he was the one who introduced her to the Rosicrucians, who taught her about reincarnation and past lives. And now she talked about it like she was teaching him. Who did she think she was showing off for?

"Here we are, just inhabiting the body, but we'll remain, always remain, as a form of energy. We'll always exist," she said. He agreed with her, of course. He let her ramble on about why some people are seekers and others, you hand them the truth and they reject it.

"Some who go and seek sometimes take on more than their personalities can handle," he said. She nodded her head, and he continued. "In all the years I've dealt with Bob Handy, he was just not able to accept. But he didn't reject it, babe. He doesn't understand and he hasn't advanced, but he didn't reject. Maybe he couldn't handle it."

"He doesn't know anything about it or he would."

"Jack Carter is another person who rejected it."

"There are kinds of people who have no control over it once

they get involved in it," she said, hinting she was thinking of him. His forays into the occult had only put him more closely in touch with his darker side, she'd told him. "Once the door is open . . ."

"Then they are controlled, babe, they aren't in control. My mother told me that nobody ever laid it on me, that there is a small segment of people who are drawn to it without anyone laying it on them. There is no other rationale for myself. I remember when I did my first big climb, astral-projected out of my body and so forth. I felt like I could pee on society."

"Yes, but there are other influences. What about the sun signs?"

"Babe, I don't want to get into that."

"What does Melody see in your stars?" she persisted. "What does she see in your future? Or isn't she telling you now that all this is going on?"

"She sees debris and decay, babe—and betrayal."

"Well, ask her to be more specific if you really believe she knows."

"She knows, babe. My mother knew. She's told me about the tribulations as far as money. That humbling aspect has been there for years. She told me it will bring you down, Glen, shake you, rattle you up. It has done that. Melody knows what will happen to Kimberly and Sherrill too, that they will lose mates. And Handy. Oh, babe, Melody's got Handy's future. That guy has the courage of a lion."

"Maybe he just doesn't understand danger. Maybe he's just stupid, not courageous."

"No, babe, he just has courage. Goddamn he has courage." It angered him that she always had to knock on Handy. "You've never been in a position with him where you saw it."

"It's going to snow," David said, interrupting them. "Look on the TV. It's going to snow, two to four inches."

David went upstairs, and Doc switched the conversation to sex talk. He could usually get her in the mood by telling her stories he'd heard in a bar or from one of his patients. This time he told her about Handy's new woman, who lived in Edwardsville, Illinois, a good-looking woman, empty in the head and hot between the legs. She said they were a match, and how did he meet someone in Edwardsville, anyway? When David said he was hungry again, she told him to eat a Ritz cracker. She cleaned up the mess in the kitchen and then turned to him with the invitation he'd already read in her arched hip. "Would you like to share a blanket and watch the rest of that program in bed?"

"You feel nice, babe," he said appreciatively, wriggling against her under the blanket. It was easy to get her hot. He didn't know if she had any idea how hot she was, how good she was in bed. Like his first wife, Ruthie, she was a hellcat. But Ruthie had known she was. Ruth, on the other hand, was demure in public, especially since David began to grow up; in bed, she seemed perpetually to surprise herself. When it was over, she straightened herself in a way that said, Oh, my, that won't happen again; but it always did. "Pussy's warm, babe. Pussy wants to play."

He put his hand between her legs, a familiar move, priming the pump. It was easy with Ruth. He was pretty sure she didn't fully appreciate the ease with which her juices flowed. In all the years she'd been married to him, and even now, he thought she was faithful to him. In other lives, he was sure she'd been a courtesan, a love slave, a harlot; and her body still remembered those tricks. She moved into the center of the bed, toward him, and moaned softly. Her legs gripped his hand.

"You miss me, babe," he said, pulling her on top of him. "Fuck me," he insisted, easing her over him, moving her fleshy hips with his hands. She had put on weight over the years, but it didn't matter. Under his hands, she moved rhythmically, their breathing accelerating at the same pace. As usual, he came right away. "Oh, babe, oh, babe," he gasped. "Let me catch my breath."

He rolled her over, so they were facing each other, side by side, and so his hand could continue to pleasure her. When he could breathe easily again, he lowered his face, whispering over and over again, "Sweet pussy, sweet pussy." He kept up sex talk the way amateur ball players chatter in the field. Even with his head between her legs, his mouth attending to the clitoris, the part of the female anatomy he had named and courted long before it was fashionable to do so, even then, he chattered. The sounds were guttural, slapping against her vaginal walls like echoes of explosions underwater. The echoes, as much as his tongue, set off her own vibrations.

"Suck me," he finally said. He was ready to get it up again, very proud of himself that, at fifty-two, he still could. "Suck me." He usually came twice. At his age, *twice.* He would proudly tell any man that.

"What do you make out of this newspaper business? I don't know what to think about it. It's been such a freaky thing," she said. They were lying side by side in the dark, the room illuminated by the light of the TV. "What do you make of it?"

"What bothers me is when I think about Kimberly and how that story hurts her. Kimberly reads that and she doesn't know that Nick Miranda, Jack Carter, and Sandra Frey were present when Eric dynamited himself in the well. He got killed in front of seven people. Is that an accidental death, babe? And Sophie, babe . . . hey, we were prepared to prove she wouldn't have won that lawsuit . . ."

"Yes, but Glen, you said yourself you would have lost," she interrupted. She couldn't let him start rambling in that lying, defensive manner or she'd lose him. After she'd told McGarvey this was the time he'd talk, she couldn't let him get away with bullshit. "What right did you have to kill her anyway, Glen? Do you see what I mean?"

"Oh, babe, let's not get back to that point. I'm talking about it from a lawyer's standpoint, not from that bullshit guilty-or-innocent standpoint," he said irritably. "Those three dumbass kids from the *Globe*—not one of them is over twenty-seven, babe— were given license to rum amok by the paper. Dick will tear them apart. What did they do, Babe, but go back into the archives of the *Globe* to pull that crap out? They're making me out to be a mass murderer, three murders by their account. Christ, Charlie Manson only killed five in the Sharon Tate murder."

"Okay, Glen," she said wearily. "They may be completely wrong. But my question to you is still why. What made you do such a thing? Maybe she would have won the suit or not won it. Why did you have to settle it this way?"

"Oh, babe, that whole issue is over and done with. I'm only concerned with making some money off the fact now." He began to ramble again about how he should have sued the *Globe* back in 1958 and wished he had. She wanted to put her hands over her ears and shut him out, but she had to go on. "They tied these other two into the drag strip, babe, but there was no connection with Berrera and the drag strip. The drag strip isn't here anymore, so how do they tie it together now, babe?"

"What I'm trying to solve in my mind is why you felt that murder was a necessary thing to do. If you could have just let this thing with Marie drag out through the courts . . ."

"Babe, in a year, just by working at my practice I'll clear up my debts now."

"Okay, in a year's time you would have been in better situation than you are now." She felt the tension rising in his body. The sex was already undone. Still, she persisted. "So why couldn't you have stalled for a year?"

"Why, babe? To pay her off? Hey, babe, I'll be perfectly frank with you. I disliked the bitch."

Ignoring the increasing warning notes in his voice, she said, "Why couldn't it have been settled differently?"

"Ruth, Ruth . . ." he began, his voice rising, threatenly.

"Outside of killing her," she persisted. "That's just so horrible."

"Goddamn, Ruth! You think I'm a son of a bitch! Well, that bitch deserved killing. She was a mean enough bitch. I disliked her enough. Now that's all. There was a simple solution to it. She was fuckin' mean when she was young, and she didn't do nothing but get lousier as she grew older, lousier."

"But, Glen, the thing of it is that you just can't go around killing people, just murdering them because you don't like them."

"Hey, babe!" he said, his voice finally rising out of control. "You can't tell me to handle things, let things work out. You can't think I'm going to let an arrogant Jew and that lousy bitch fuck me!"

He stopped. They had both heard the sound of footsteps at the same time. Damn, she thought, he was rolling.

"Here he comes," she whispered; and he responded softly, "Yeah."

"Well, don't look now, but here he is," Glen said.

"You okay, David?" she asked. "Oh, you little fellow."

"Mama," he whimpered.

"What's happened to him?" Glen asked, reaching out to pat the little back, as she pulled him under their covers.

"He's had a bad dream, that's all."

"Kids have bad dreams," he said. "I used to have them. I used to have them. I'd go in and sleep with my mom and dad."

"Let me give you a kiss," she said to David. "Such a big boy. My sugie."

"Mama," he said, already falling asleep between them, his voice rising and falling like breath, "I have those dreams that everything's really hard . . . and so I just . . . and something just gets bigger and bigger and bigger . . ." Then he opened his eyes, struggled to sit up. "We got everybody in this bed but Fluffy."

"Fluffy is not allowed," Ruth said, easing him back down between them.

"I hope not," Glen said. "You know what would really sound pretty? If we put a little bell collar on Fluffy. Then as she was making her fast path around here, she'd ring that bell."

Within minutes, they were all asleep. Over eight inches of snow fell that night, trapping McGarvey and Bobb in the van. They couldn't get out and leave footprints.

"Did you listen to that tape yet?" she asked McGarvey, the phone clutched nervously in her hand. Her cheeks were hot. She could feel them. She felt like a teenage girl calling some boy. "Did you get a chance to listen yet?" she repeated, filling the space he'd left empty. "Well. Then when are you going to listen to it?"

"Yeah, Ruth, I listened to it," he said. It was the second time she'd called that morning. Admitting he'd listened to the tape embarrassed him. He wasn't proud of this. But she was bent on forcing him to acknowledge what had happened in the bed. She'd switched the recorder on before their sexual interlude, apparently knowing it would happen, and apparently wanting him to hear it. "I heard it."

"Well," she persisted. "What did you think?"

"Ruth, I think you're pretty good." He waited. Fortunately she laughed, which is what he'd hoped she would do. "Listen we need to go over the things he said. I'll meet you this afternoon at the motel, okay?"

She agreed. He hung up the phone, relieved to have that moment behind them. Jesus, he'd listened to them fucking on tape. And she wanted to know what he thought about it? Was she embarrassed too? Or was she rubbing his nose in it, reminding him of what they'd done together as part of this team?

He lit a cigarette and turned on the tape recorder again. It was set to play at the point where they'd begun talking postcoitus. He didn't want to hear the Doc whisper his own brand of terms of endearment again. In fact, he'd already made it clear around the office there would be no other copies of this tape made, ever. It would be played for the people who had to hear it, and none of them would get the chance to make a copy and play it at cocktail parties in the future.

When he pushed the PLAY button, Ruth's voice, more girlish than usual, was asking, "What do you make out of this newspaper business?" She sounded entirely credible, as if she hadn't known about the planting of that story since the idea had been conceived. Ruth *was* good, damn good.

He played the entire conversation again, listening to it the way a lawyer would listen. Would it hold up in court? Perhaps he'd said enough about the Berrera murder, but he'd skimmed right across Eric Frey's death, admitting nothing. The growing anger in Doc's voice as Ruth persisted in asking him, "Why . . . But why did you have to murder?" worried McGarvey. Could he have reached across the bed, placed his hands around her neck, and strangled her to death before they could have gotten inside to save her?

He knew the hardest decision he'd ever have to make was when to stop the taping and pull Ruth out of there. Each time he told her they'd like to get a little more, he saw the fear in her eyes. He knew she liked him, trusted him; and knowing that made it harder to ask for more. She quelled the fears and gamely agreed, throwing herself more enthusiastically into the planning. Sometimes he watched her plump little figure marching determinedly out of that motel room, armed with the strategies they'd just developed—and he felt like the worst bastard in the world. Well, not the worst—but he did feel almost as low as Doc.

Still, he felt they needed her to get the Doc to say the word "kill." He would tell her to push a little harder. The more trusting Doc was, the harder they could push.

Thursday, January 31, 1980

McGarvey was in the van monitoring the transmission from Ruth's condo. Clearly Doc was planning to spend the night. He had settled into the bed, but nothing was going on. He'd been complaining to Ruth about the high cost of renting dental equipment and somehow she had pulled the conversation back to the *Globe*'s story. Irritably, Doc kept trying to change the subject, swatting her off like the proverbial fly. If McGarvey had been able to talk to her, he would have told her to back off. The tone of Doc's voice was scaring him. She, however, seemed impervious to it.

"Jesus, why does she keep bringing it up?" he asked John Bobb, who was drinking coffee and watching a little portable television. "She's hitting him too hard for the mood he's in, and she's just getting him hot."

"Turn it up," Bobb said, shutting off the TV.

McGarvey pushed up the volume. The transmission was coming in more clearly than usual that night, for which he was grateful. If the Doc turned nasty, he wanted to know it right away, not have his snarls lost in static.

> DOC: *Ruth, hey, what's done is done. Now please let's not get into an argument. What's done is done. You are not going to change me. I'd like to finish the night out in this bed, babe. I don't want to make that long trip home. I know every goddamn pothole, chuckhole, manhole cover, everything else between here and Washington Terrace by heart. Ruth, what you're doing is known as*

nagging, babe! There's not a thing you or I or anyone else could do to undo it. It's done.

RUTH: *Did you have to take the absolute, ultimate step?*

DOC: *Babe, can't you understanding something? I asked you to quit! You don't know what it is, the absolute ultimate. You're giving me a bunch of rhetoric. You . . .*

RUTH: *Are there never any alternatives for you?*

DOC: *Ruth, I told you . . . I just got through beseeching you to stop it. And you come right back to it, Ruth?*

RUTH: *There are never any alternatives with you, Glen.*

DOC: *Ruth, there is never any shutting your big fucking mouth up. Ruth, you just won't quit. You are like a needle stuck in a groove. You . . .*

RUTH: *I'm trying to understand it.*

DOC: *Oh, Ruth. I told you there was nothing you could do. Nothing I could do. It's over. It is done with.*

RUTH: *Glen, you have absolutely no compunction at all about killing people. Why don't you . . .*

DOC: *Ruth, I don't kill people. When you start accusing me of killing people, I start wondering if I am in a bugged room. You are no longer my wife. You can testify in court against me, Ruth. That makes me a little bit edgy, Ruth. You think about that. . . . You dwell on it for a little while.*

McGarvey tensed. He could hear the sounds of Doc throwing back the blankets, getting out of bed. Bobb moved toward the van door, and McGarvey was ready to follow him when he heard the unmistakable sound of a zipper being zipped up. Goddamn, he was putting on his pants; he was getting out of there.

"Wait," McGarvey whispered. "He's getting dressed. If she shuts up, I think he'll just walk out."

RUTH: *Dwell on what?*

DOC: *The fact that you are continuously discussing something in the quietness of a bedroom. You are not my wife. You tell the reporters and the police that. Now you want me to acknowledge a murder so you can go in and testify.*

RUTH: *Oh, Glen, be serious.*

DOC: *Yes, Ruth, get serious. I know, Ruth, people can get hot. They can slash out at one another. They can talk too much about things. But, Ruth, why can't I get you to drop this one thing? Why don't you drop it, Ruth? I am not about to stay here in this room with you when you want me to acknowledge a murder. Why do you think the police came here in the first place?*

RUTH: *Why did they?*

DOC: *Because you're the ex-wife, Ruth. They wanted you to spill your guts, Ruth. And you didn't. And the reporters, Ruth. Why are they out there?*

RUTH: *I'm just on the list, Glen. That's all.*

DOC: *No, Ruth. They're waiting for you to spill your guts, Ruth, because you're the ex-wife. Handy didn't have to tell me. It's a known fact. He said there are all kinds of guys in the penitentiary because of their ex-wives.*

RUTH: *He didn't have to tell you what?*

DOC: *That there are guys in the penitentiary because of their ex-wives. Handy told me that. Tactfully. I said, I know, Bob. He said a lot of them are sorry afterwards.*

RUTH: *There's probably a whole pile of dead ex-wives, huh?*

DOC: *What, babe?*

RUTH: *I said there's probably a whole pile of dead ex-wives.*

DOC: *Oh, babe, why can't we be amenable? Shit, you got your mind stuck on this one aspect now. You've been harping on this every time we've been together.*

RUTH: *Glen. . . .*

DOC: *Let's just drop it, Ruth.*

RUTH: *I'm sorry, Glen.*

DOC: *Ruth, there is nothing I can do to change it. Why do you just keep harping on it? . . . You are not going to change me. Can't you understand that, Ruth? You are not going to change me, Ruth . . . It's like asking me not to be me.*

The door slammed. The relief inside the van was palpable. McGarvey wiped the sweat from his forehead, looked over at Bobb.

"Jesus," he said. "Why the hell did she do that?"

Then Ruth was speaking to him over the transmitter: "Bill, he is just leaving now. So after he is gone, give me a call, okay? Bill, he is just getting ready to leave now. He is out in the car, so give me a call whenever he is gone. You know it might not be a bad idea if you came by and picked up this tape tonight and you could be able to analyze it tomorrow."

She clicked the transmitter off. He waited for a report from the tailing agent saying Doc was on the road and headed toward Melody's before he went inside. Ruth was waiting for them in the downstairs bathroom. Visibly upset, she was trembling slightly. He thought he should hug her, but he clapped her on the shoulder instead. If they gave her any encouragement, she would fall apart.

"Jesus, Ruth," he said. "You really had us scared on that one. You really had us going. Maybe we'd better cool it for a few days. What do you think?"

Tuesday, February 12, 1980

They had pulled the recording equipment out of Ruth's condo on the first. Since then they'd been turning the tapes into rough transcripts with her help. Most days she had worked with them for eight or more hours, listening to the tapes and helping them fill in the inaudible spaces. She'd had only one meeting with the Doc since the thirty-first. They'd taken David to a sport show at the convention center. Hardly any of that tape was audible and nothing of importance had been said anyway.

They were stalled, and Ruth knew it. They had a weak case and Doc no longer trusted her. McGarvey had decided to pull her out. She'd quit her job; she was ready to go. He had one last trick, and then he would go with what they had, get Ruth out of there, and call it quits.

He picked up the phone and dialed Detective Sergeant John McCrady in the St. Louis County Police Department. He'd gotten the Halm murder report from McCrady on January 19, after the first session with Ruth. Until this point, he had confided nothing in other police agencies. He knew they distrusted feds for just that reason—withholding information—but he'd done it to protect Ruth. The fewer people who knew about her, the safer her life was. When he got McCrady on the line, he told him about

Ruth's information on the Halm murder and set up a meeting between them at the Ramada.

Then he called Dennis McCarthy, who had been digging on his own and bugging the hell out of him with the facts he was putting together, linking another murder, Halm's, with financial gain to Engleman. He had convinced McCarthy that *if* he had a hypothetical witness and *if* that witness's life might be endangered by a premature telling of the story, he should wait before printing it. McCarthy had understood the "ifs" meant someone's life did hang in the balance and had waited, though not patiently.

"Go with the Halm story," McGarvey told the reporter when he got him on the line.

Thursday, February 14, 1980

FORMER ENGLEMAN AIDE BENEFITED AFTER SLAYING OF HUS-BAND, the *Globe* headline read. Once again, Bryan, McCarthy, and Shelton were named in the black-bordered byline box. Doc read the paper with mounting fury. They named Carmen—and Nick too, "a stockholder with Engleman in the now-defunct dragstrip." Those arrogant pissants had done it again! He'd told them when they called yesterday he was going to sue them so they'd better not run another story—and damned if they hadn't quoted him threatening to sue them again.

He called Nick, waking him up, but Nick was so groggy with sleep during the conversation he didn't get much satisfaction. Nick had been running a concert hall in north St. Louis featuring bluegrass and other music. Well, Nick, as a businessman whose reputation could be damaged by this kind of publicity, would have plenty of cause to sue, and he surely would too.

Twenty minutes later Ruth called. Her phone had been set up to record their conversation.

"Glen? Did you see the paper?" she said. Her voice sounded genuinely frightened, but he was certainly going to be careful what he said to her over the phone anyway. "Did you see it, Glen?"

"Oh, yes, I've already been talking to Nick this morning on the phone about it. I don't know if he retained anything. He was groggy with sleep. But I imagine Dick Dempsey will just be ecstatic about this when I talk to him. Nick says he's going to sue them. He was in California at the time. I remember Nedra saying he was flying in that night when I was at the mortuary. They called me yesterday. Someone from a TV station called me too, but they backed off. Did you see that business about 'I'll sue you' and so forth? They knew that and they just went ahead with it. Well, I'll tell you, Ruth, I don't see where they can prove Carmen gave me any money."

"Well, what did Nick say? Is he here or in California?"

"No, he's here, Ruth. He's been back here for over two years now. Carmen's in California. The *Globe* reporters went out there and attempted to talk to her out there, and she said she wouldn't talk to them. She refuses to talk to them and they get back on the plane and go home. They're just pissants, making a little junket." He kept talking for several minutes, rambling about Carmen and all he had done for the Mirandas from the day she was born. Then he said, "Well, Dick Dempsey, the cautious attorney, said after the last article, 'Let's wait a couple of weeks and see if they turn up anything else.' Well, it's been what, a month since Marie got dynamited, and they can't come up with anything else, so they dig Carmen out of the woodwork. Probably someone dropped a nickle in the box and put a bug in their ear on that one."

He talked for fifteen minutes and finally asked Ruth, "Well, are you guys going to be home tonight?"

"We are if you're going to take us out to dinner."

"Yes, yes, yes."

"For Valentine's Day."

"I know. Melody got one of those big Hershey's Kisses for David. So . . ."

"Okay, why don't we go early. Avoid the crowd. David will be hungry as soon as he gets home from school anyway, so let's plan on five."

"Okay, bye now."

He put down the phone and picked up the paper again. With growing fury, he read the lead one more time.

A former dental assistant to Dr. Glennon E. Engleman, who is the sister of a former fellow stockholder with Engleman in a business venture, received more than $37,500 in cash and life insurance payments after the 1976 unsolved slaying of her husband, records show.

The incident is the fourth violent death of a St. Louisan, including three unsolved killings, after which Engleman or a person associated with Engleman received financial benefit, a Globe-Democrat investigation has revealed.

They recapped what they'd said in the last article about the Bullock, Frey, and Berrera killings, then said they'd been unable to get a comment from Carmen. Fucking pissants were getting themselves in deeper and deeper!

David was watching out the window for him. As soon as his car pulled into the parking lot, the boy shot out the door. She knew it could be the last time David would ever stand at that window, watching for his father's arrival. She felt the wire against her leg, its presence burning. Would her son understand someday?

"I wondered where you were going, bub," she said, the lightness in her voice surprising her as they came in the door together.

"Aunt Melody made these little cookies," David said. "Oh, I love these cookies!" He turned to Glen and said, "Okay, give me a hint on what you are going to give me on Saturday, Dad, huh?"

"No hints," he teased; and to Ruth, he said, "My attorney is ecstatic. He said he hopes they dig up a couple more in the next few weeks." McGarvey was right: He was primed, dying to talk.

"Did you go see Dempsey?"

"No, we got together on the telephone today. He's busy."

"When is he going to start?"

"Well, he's waiting for a couple more weeks." He said to David then, "You want to go to the Ground Round, is that right?"

"You can guess why," Ruth laughed, and they bundled into their coats, went out the door like any other middle-American family celebrating Valentine's Day. She heard the quarters for the electronic games jangling in Glen's pocket as he climbed into the car. "I hear you're ready for him," she said.

After they had ordered and David was playing a game, she asked him about the large red abrasion on his nose. He said it had been a large pimple and proceeded to tell her how Melody had popped it. "Diabetes, babe. I'm suffering. It's making its in-roads. I don't heal." And she asked if he needed ointment. She thought this time she would be smart and not direct the conversation immediately to the topic of murder. He was the one who should need to talk this time.

"McCarthy, that reporter who called last night, he said he had Steve Schiff on the line, that reporter from Channel Four," he said. "He told me Steve Schiff was on the line and did I want to say anything. I told him about my plans to sue, and that was enough for the TV people. They dropped it." David ran back to the table and collected more change. "Melody said, 'You know, Glen, you're really something. Here you do all this stuff, and you're still gonna turn around and sue and try to make money.' I said, 'Yeah, Melody, I'm pretty bad.'"

"Well, you do have a way of using the law for your own purposes," she said carefully.

"That's right."

"You don't believe in it, but you do use it."

"That's exactly it. Hey, babe, here you are at the beautiful age of thirty-nine, and our government is sitting around while the goddamn Russians might be getting ready to turn loose on us. What should I believe in babe?" David came back, and he said to him, "Why don't you get us some popcorn, David? Why don't you show a little initiative? Do you know what initiative is? Initiative is doing something without being asked. See if you can run us up a bowl of popcorn."

"I hope Melody was laughing when she told you that. Was she?" Ruth asked. She was watching as her son located a basket and filled it from the popcorn machine. Initiative. If he stayed within his father's sphere of influence much longer, he would learn the same meaning of the word initiative that Glen had taught the Mirandas. "Well, was she?"

"She was bemused." He signaled the waitress and ordered a Michelob beer. Then he began talking about money problems again, and she thought she was going to lose him.

"Look, Glen, at that couple over there," she said, pointing to a youthful pair who were exchanging a kiss over a heart-shaped dessert. "Aren't they cuties?"

"They are cute . . . people planning a future, babe. Hey, in twenty years, Ruth, what the hell has happened to the American race, poor American schmucks. Look at Bob. Give it a second thought, Ruth."

"Give what a second thought, Glen?

"Babe, we're in the middle class and we can't send our kid to college. They came along and perpetrated injustice on us with niggers. Our society is spoiled. Our cities . . . they have deliberately destroyed our cities." He launched on a tirade about blacks and welfare, which the waitress interrupted by asking him, "Excuse me, honey, what do you want the little one to drink?"

"Coke will be fine," she spoke up. "Glen, are you sure you don't want a salad to go with that Reuben sandwich? It doesn't seem like enough."

He insisted he wasn't very hungry and moved back into his tirade. She thought she was losing him. He wouldn't ever trust her enough to say anything again. She would leave St. Louis sometime in the next few days. This could be her last chance, and she was going to blow it. Over the loudspeaker a girl with an Ozark voice announced another birthday in the house. His name was Edward.

"Happy birthday, Edward," Ruth said. "Well, Glen . . ." The music in the background started up again. David ran back to the table. Glen handed him quarters, complaining to her he'd paid twenty-five dollars on his electric bill and fifteen dollars on gas because he couldn't afford to pay the whole bills. "Did you get a chance to discuss this article with Nick again?"

"Yes, uh-huh."

"About the money? Did Carmen get a lot of it?"

"Yeah, Carmen got a lot of dough. I sure didn't want to discuss this with you over the telephone, babe. We figured Carmen for a hundred thousand. I would get twenty thousand. Well, it turned out . . . a large policy from the phone company was not switched over from the parents to Carmen and so I agreed to settle for ten thousand."

"You mean Nick was in this thing?" she asked, her heart racing.

"No. Carmen and I. We just roughly figured a hundred thousand, but we were wrong."

"Why do you think she hasn't paid you the rest of it? Is she all right mentally?"

"Nick says she's doing just fine."

"You don't think maybe she gave Nick the money to give to you and Nick didn't give it to you?" she said, using the approach she and McGarvey had agreed upon. Nick would be the main thrust. She would cook him up by planting the idea that Nick had ripped him off. "Nothing would surprise me about him."

"Babe, the time will come when I'll go out to California to talk to Carmen. If she tells me that, well, the specter of death is never far from Nick."

"Does he know that?"

"Oh, Jesus, babe, hell yes he knows that."

"Yes, but he's such a sneaky thing," she hissed, allowing the bitch in her to come out. "How would you ever know about it? Look how long it's been. Did you know that the reporters were out to see Carmen before you read it in the newspapers? Did he call you up to tell you that? Well, did he, Glen?"

"No."

"Well, why not, Glen?" She suddenly felt she had an advantage and she was pressing it. "Why?"

"We don't know that he knew it. We don't even know the paper called her. They're doing a lot of lying right now."

"They say she worked for you for eighteen months. And they say Nick was the one who got you involved in the drag strip business. That's true, isn't it, Glen?"

"Babe, you're so biased about Nick. And you know we're as guilty as hell, but still and all we're looking at the legal question of this. Three of them, three of them, Babe . . ."

"Go, play," she told David, who was picking at his food. She pushed the quarters in front of him. "Glen, why don't you have a little meeting with Nick and just tell him that, tell him that you are thinking about going out to see Carmen. Just tell him you know he still owes you money—and see what his reaction is. Wouldn't it be just ducky if she had given him the money and he didn't give it to you? The first ten thousand dollars he gave you he didn't have a choice, but what if there was more?"

"Nick came out of the bank, right? He had the money in an

envelope, all hundred-dollar bills that I brought and gave to you and Handy. Peter never changed the beneficiary on that other insurance policy from his mom, babe. He brought it home from the office, pretended to sign it—but he never did it. Nick didn't cheat. His mother never liked Carmen very much. She came to Nedra's house after the funeral and wanted Carmen to sign over all the insurance, everything to her. That kooky mother. She wanted everything her sonny boy had."

"You know, Melody's right, Glen."

"What the shit. I'm an average American, that's all."

"Glen, was this an afterthought, after the marriage with you and Carmen—or was it your idea before?"

"He mistreated her, babe. He berated her because she came from a poor family. Do you know he almost got her killed driving that bike on the midline stripes?" He signaled for another beer, then switched the subject again to money.

Her pulse racing, she risked his anger by pulling him back. "Was Nick receptive? He didn't give you the brush-off, did he?"

"Nick never gives me the brush-off, babe. Last fall Handy and I had a stiff talk with Nick. We simply told him we were gonna let him live. He'd better get his ass on the ball. Get after Spinks. That time it wasn't Nick's fault. The nigger wanted a ninety-thousand-dollar gate up in New York."

"You don't think he absconded with the five thousand dollars?" She dimly remembered this story: Nick, who managed Michael Spinks, the boxer, had bought an insurance policy on Spinks's life, with someone else's money, of course; and Glen and Handy were supposed to kill him. Well, the two hit men had made two trips out of state, one to Philadelphia, one to New York City, only to discover their quarry wasn't where he was supposed to be. "Glen, don't you think he might have? I've never trusted him."

"I know, babe. Handy was just for getting rid of him over this deal. 'I'll shoot the big dumb shit,' he said. I said, 'Look, he's got two kids.' Handy deferred to me that time. Handy won't let me forget that he acquiesced on something that was a major decision. But you can rest assured I'll find out about that money, babe. How would you like to have somebody like me on your shit list? Be pretty bad, huh?"

"Nick figures time has passed and he doesn't have to worry." She paused. She recognized the threat implied in "How would you like to have somebody like me on your shit list." He was reminding her he'd killed Sophie and that he could kill her too. "Doesn't he say anything about Carmen? Don't you ever ask him?"

"He says she's fine. Well, babe, Nick knows Handy and I— plus we've got a third person very much in the background who does simple little killings for a thousand bucks . . ."

"What kind of kook is that?" she asked, the hairs on the back of her neck standing up. Would she be dead now if Glen had had a spare thousand dollars this week? "Does he like killing or is he just desperate?"

"I'd say he picks it up for extra money."

"He's got to be nuts, Glen."

"I think he has confidence in himself. I do know one thing, babe, there's no driving urgency on my part to keep getting rid of my fellow man. That's the last thing I'm interested in now. I just want to settle down quietly, practice a little dentistry, get into some business venture."

"Bob Handy wouldn't say anything to anyone, would he? I mean, Glen, don't you wonder why it's in the papers now? I am worried about Carmen's mental stability with all this publicity."

"She's stable, babe. Hey, when I saw Carmen the last time, she was over it. She was over the trauma . . . and, hey, do you know what, Ruth? I'm going to tell you something, Ruth. You can be sexually intimate with another person, but when you're homicidally intimate with another person and all . . ."

"Were you sexually intimate with Carmen?"

"Aw, no, honey. And I'm telling you this for this point. When you've had to keep a secret to yourself for weeks and months and all at once when you finally get back to your partner, wow, it's who knows what an outpouring, what a relief. I had that with Carmen, babe. And with Handy. Handy and I, we never talk in the car, the office, or the phone, ever. Handy and I, we go to lunch, we go to a different place all the time. When we're getting out of our car, walking back to where we are going to eat lunch, we say everything we have to say. The possibility always exists the cops will set up a trap and bug us if we come to the same place too often. Everything we have to say, we say between our car and the door of the restaurant. I had that same homicidal intimacy with Carmen, babe. When she came back from California for her mother's funeral—hardworking old woman she was—I had a moment alone with Carmen. She said, 'Hello, Glen, how are you?' I said, 'Fine.' That intimacy was still there between us, babe. You could feel it."

"Glen, not a one of them has worked out. Wouldn't you agree?"

"No, babe, that isn't so. Where would I be, babe . . . I wouldn't even have that office where it is today if I hadn't gotten that ten thousand dollars from Carmen. Goddamn, honey, take that ten thousand away from me, I wouldn't have the money to buy two-by-fours. Ruth, all that crap those little piss-ass bastards sling, I just have to live with that in this town. Do you think you can run our waitress down, David?"

"But why, Glen?" she said; and she wasn't really saying it for the tape.

"Why, Ruth? Why? You're experiencing it, babe, right here," he said, pointing at the quarters left on the table beside David's plate. "Money, money, money."

She didn't respond, and abruptly he started talking about women working at men's jobs and being too selfish to have babies. Melody, he said, had gotten further than most girls, and she'd still had babies. Ruth excused herself and went to the ladies' room. Inside the stall, she said into the transmitter, "I am in the rest room, Bill, excuse me." She shut off the transmitter and shut her eyes. She wanted to cry, but she knew she couldn't. He would see the tears on her face and ask why.

The transmitter clicked back on in less than two minutes, and she said, "Okay, Bill, I will try to question him a bit more about Carmen. But we are getting ready to leave now. I'll just have to play it by ear." Her voice was shaky but triumphant. She knew she'd done well. Very soon it would be over. She would have second thoughts and self-recriminations, but for now she just knew she'd done a good job.

They had him. They had him good and clean now. He had

said, "I have no desire to keep on killing my fellow man." He had admitted taking money from Carmen following Peter's death. They had done it. *Ruth* had done it. They had him! That little woman had earned whatever peace of mind they could give her in a new life.

"It's worth being stuck in the van on my anniversary for this," John Bobb said, interrupting his thoughts. He'd forgotten it was Bobb's anniversary. "What a night! I can't believe it. I can't *fucking* believe it!"

"Yeah, we didn't fucking believe her the first night we heard this story," McGarvey responded, lighting a cigarette. He was still tense and he wouldn't relax until Doc was out of the condo that night. The pleasure he felt in making the case was still tempered by concern for Ruth. "We've got the Halm case made." Privately, McGarvey thought the Berrera case would hang together, but Bullock and Frey, especially Bullock, would probably never be made. "What do you think about the Illinois story?" he asked suddenly.

Bobb shook his head. No opinion. At that moment he didn't care. What could you want for one night? McGarvey still had his doubts about the Illinois murders. Because of the need for secrecy, he hadn't made any real inquiries over there. Madison County, at that point in time, had a terrible reputation for leaks, and a leak could kill Ruth. He had been able to learn that one of the insurance policies that paid off the widow on Ron Gusewelle's death was a $40,000 policy with J.C. Penney, exactly as Ruth had said it was. A toll call to Illinois on her phone bill was made to the Amoco Refinery in Wood River. McGarvey didn't quite believe the story of three murders—but, on the other hand, were those facts pure coincidence? Or had Barbara, the golden girl, planned and executed three murders herself perhaps, then told Doc the details?

He turned his attention back to Doc and Ruth and David. They were leaving the Ground Round, heading for the condo. Jesus, he hoped she didn't let him stay the night.

Glennon Engleman leaned back in his ex-wife's bathtub and sighed. The water was as hot as he could stand it, and the heat felt good. In the bedroom, David was acting silly, playing with that stupid cat, Fluffy. Why did Ruth encourage him. *Fluffy, I love you. I love you. Will you marry me? Marry us, Mom, will you?* And Ruth, going along with his nonsense. David, you and Fluffy are married, okay. *Forever?* Forever.

"Don't use all the hot water," Ruth called into him.

"I hear you," he shouted. "I'm already on cold. Come in here and sit a spell."

"Well, don't get too comfortable here, mister, because you are not staying the night. Don't get too cozy and comfy in the bathtub," she said from the doorway.

"Well, will you let me have a fifteen-minute bath?"

"Since you took us out for Valentine Dinner, you can have a bath," she said, smiling to soften the words, but she meant them.

"Oh, thank you, that's big of you." He looked up at her. Christ, her hair really did look awful. That reminded him of her suit against the beauty parlor. "Have you heard anything regarding your hair?"

"I really should follow that thing through, I guess. Maybe it's too late. I haven't heard a thing."

"Honey, you're on the docket. When your number comes up, you'll hear."

"Glen, all you ever think about is lawsuits. I'm not going to worry about it anymore." She changed the subject by asking him about his nose again. "W. C. Fields," she teased him.

"The diabetes, babe." He really didn't want to talk about his nose. "You know, babe," he sighed, settling back deeper into the tub, "dentistry really is a good living. I should be doing better. I don't know if I've got my priorities wrong or what."

"Your priorities have been messed up all the time," she snapped.

"Steve Schiff, you know, did me a big favor by backing off."

"Do you think Steve Schiff wants his car blown up? No. That's why he didn't do the story."

"Ruth, you have to be a goddamn fool to be a cop or a nosy-ass reporter. You think I would take on somebody like me? Steve Schiff didn't. The reporters are dumbasses."

"We made our commercials today in school, Dad!" David burst into the room. "Teacher said I was especially good."

"Okay, David, shut that door. Shut that door, son. It's cold in here."

Engleman was sitting on the edge of Ruth's bed putting his clothes back on while she talked to someone, her sister, he thought, on the phone. Christ, if the phone hadn't rung, she might be sitting beside him, maybe receptive to a move in spite of what she had said earlier. Anyway, he was tired. Maybe this weekend if she stayed as pleasant as she'd been tonight. There was always another night. Or so he thought at the time.

Tuesday, February 19, 1980

"Mama, are they policemen?" David whispered to Ruth in the backseat. "Are they, Mama? Where are they taking us?"

Ruth was shushing him, promising him she would explain later. They were, she said in a typically maternal fashion, going somewhere nice, somewhere he would like. *But why can't we take Fluffy? he whined. Will Fluffy be okay when we get back?*

McGarvey glanced across at Steve Alsup. They were taking Ruth and David to the airport, to a safe location where they would stay for six weeks before being permanently relocated. Ruth would be back for the trials—and whenever else they needed her. She and David would not return to the condo, or Fluffy. "Why can't they take the damn cat?" Alsup had asked him earlier. Because they can't, that's all. The Federal Relocation Program has its rules; and one of those rules is no pets. Relocated witnesses spend time in motels and hotels, places where pets aren't welcome. And pets might draw attention to them, blowing their cover.

"Mama," David repeated. "Mama." His voice sounded young, fragile. He was clutching the canvas bag of toys she'd hastily packed for him before they'd picked him up at school. "Mama," he said, his voice snagging them like kitten's claws.

He felt for Ruth. This was the hardest thing she'd ever have to do. Jesus, it was the hardest thing he'd ever had to do, and he wasn't the adult who'd sit on the edge of a strange bed that night explaining to a boy that his father was a murderer, that his mother had helped the police catch him and that they had to leave town to protect her life. Christ.

He glanced in the mirror at Ruth. Her mouth was set firmly, she was holding up well today. She had seen Doc one last time the day before. That meeting had netted nothing, and they'd decided abruptly to pull her out. They were pushing their luck, and he disliked pushing it with her nose. Her sister called him regularly in the middle of the night to yell at him for what he was doing to Ruth, and he didn't blame the woman. Since the fourteenth, Ruth had been on an emotional roller coaster, and he'd been trapped in the speeding car with her, going along reluctantly for the ride. When they'd met in the bathroom after Doc had gone, she'd been jubilant. Then her jubilation gave way to doubt. *Have I done the right thing? What about David? What will David think of me when he gets older?*

"Mama, where are we going on the plane?" David whispered. "Are the policemen making us go away, Mama? Why? Where's Daddy? Mama, I want my Daddy."

"Hush, David, hush. The policeman are helping us. I'll explain it to you later. For now, you just have to trust me. Trust them. They want to help us, David. They aren't going to hurt us." She had her arm around him, stroking his blond head as she spoke.

"Why couldn't we take Fluffy?" he repeated.

"Because we're going someplace where cats can't stay," she said, catching McGarvey's eye in the mirror.

Someone was supposed to pick up Fluffy that day and take him to an animal shelter. For the past few days, when they weren't transcribing tapes or meeting with someone, he had taken Ruth around to settle her affairs. Knowing she would be pulled out within days even if she'd had another successful meeting with Doc, they'd sold her car through a dealer someone in the office knew. They had made arrangements for the disposal of everything, and Fluffy was the last detail.

"Mama," David said, as they pulled into the airport, "why are these policemen taking us away? What did we do wrong?" But he got out of the car when they opened the door for him. "I wish I could take Fluffy," he said, for the first time looking McGarvey in the eye.

It was McGarvey who had to look away.

PART FOUR:
The Arrests

*"To friends and neighbors, he is a nice, pleasant man,
always helpful, often retiring and protective of his privacy."*
—*St. Louis Globe-Democrat,*
Monday, February 25, 1980

Friday, February 22, 1980

George R. "Buzz" Westfall, County Prosecutor, had just returned from lunch with Robert Kingsland, U.S. Attorney. They had eaten at The Coal Hole, a Clayton restaurant near Westfall's office favored by power brokers for its dark interior and heavily padded chairs placed around generous tables spaced a good distance from each other—an ambience that courted secrecy. The meeting place was Kingsland's choice. Westfall, a hardworking law-and-order prosecutor, well under forty and prematurely graying, usually lunched at Powers, a dark and crowded bar noted for its spicy chicken wings and wall decor, nonfunctional clocks, and its clientele, Clayton attorneys, especially prosecutors. Perhaps he ate his lunch elbow-to-elbow with his own companions and whoever sat at the adjoining tables to let those people who believed that eventually any elected official would surrender to the onslaught of temptations know his integrity was unassailable. Certainly he was an astute politician, always mindful of what the "citizens" in this predominantly white and upwardly mobile county enclave would think. On the other hand, he liked chicken wings and his fellow prosecutors.

"Get Gordon Ankney on the phone, will you, please?" he said to his secretary as he walked past her. She had him before Westfall could hang up his coat. He glanced up at the painting above his desk, the one he usually ignored, of a figure from some shadowy olden war standing before a firing squad holding the last cigarette in one hand, stretching out the other plaintively in his direction. Then he sat down and picked up the phone. "Gordo, have I got one for you."

He and Ankney, who prosecuted special cases for the city and county, had the kind of friendship they described as "going way back." Coming from diverse St. Louis backgrounds, Westfall from the projects, Ankney from the comfortable middle class, they'd worked together as young prosecutors in the city. Both loyal to the Cardinal home teams and the deep friendships they had formed in their youth, they had spacious homes in the county and attractive wives who bore babies and planned dinner parties. Their courtroom styles were different—Ankney performing like a slightly laid-back Boston lawyer, Westfall behaving as though he personified the Superman code of truth, justice, and the American way—but their bedrock beliefs were the same. No one found a murderer as morally loathsome as Buzz Westfall did. Gordon Ankney, however, came closest. Even given his strong beliefs, the first time he'd asked for the death penalty as a prosecutor Westfall went through an agonizing period in which he doubted any man's right to ask for another man's death.

"What's up, Buzzard?" Ankney asked. He was one of a select circle of friends who knew Westfall's nickname Buzz came not from his propensity for short haircuts but from the honorary name Great White Buzzard, bestowed upon him at birth by an Indian friend of his father's.

"I had lunch with Bob Kingsland. He called yesterday and told me he had a special case to discuss. Then he asked me if I remembered Glennon Engleman's name from the Bullock murder."

"Before my time," Ankney responded. "That's the Art Hill murder, isn't it?"

"Right. Kingsland was in the circuit attorney's office under Eagleton then. Anyway, Bob said they had good reason to believe Engleman, the South Side dentist who was the prime suspect in the Bullock murder, was also responsible for several other murders. He described him as crazy in the Hitler sense, and he said he needed our cooperation to get him."

"In other words, they think they might be onto something, but they want us to get involved so they won't fall on their faces if they're wrong," Ankney said wryly. His distaste for the feds was even greater than Westfall's. A former football hero at Washington University and naval officer during the Vietnam War, he disdained the overly cautious approach of federal prosecutors and distrusted the FBI. "Is it an FBI case?" It was an article of faith with local cops and prosecutors that the feds, particularly the FBI, expected one-way cooperation: They wanted everything you had and were willing to give you everything they thought you needed to know in exchange. "If they want us involved, they want someone to do the shit work."

"No," Westfall laughed. "It's ATF's. Apparently this has been Bill McGarvey's baby, which goes a long way toward convincing me to give it a fair hearing. He's always been square with us."

"What have they got?" Ankney asked. He had told Westfall he liked ATF, an organization he regarded as more gutsy and daring than the FBI, and he particularly admired McGarvey, who was his idea of what a good investigator should be and usually wasn't. "I suppose it doesn't hurt to listen."

"He says they've got a *fiend*," Westfall repeated, playing with the word in a guttural growl, his voice registering a healthy degree of skepticism. "They've been working with a secret informant and they seem to believe the informant's life is in danger. Bob's calling Washington to try to get special dispensation to prosecute on federal and local charges so it will be impossible for Engleman to make bail. But they can't get warrants as quickly as we can get them. Bob knows my style. He knows I'll issue the warrant if I think it's justified."

"How are they going to convince you it's justified?"

"They have tapes. Engleman's been under electronic surveillance for three weeks. We've been invited to a meeting tomorrow morning at nine A.M. at ATF."

After agreeing there were better things to do on Saturday morning, they also agreed to meet. Then Westfall called his wife Lau-
rie. He tried to keep the weekends free for her and the kids
because he put in such long hours during the week. She wasn't
going to be thrilled about this. While he was talking to her, his
mind kept drifting back to the conversation he'd had with Kingsland. "Look," Kingsland had said, "we've got a fiend running
loose in St. Louis. We've got to get him off the streets and keep
him off the streets." It wasn't like Bob Kingsland to be so melo-
dramatic.

Saturday, February 23, 1980

It was slightly before eight A.M. when McGarvey began setting up
the conference room down the hall from his office. He was expecting thirteen other people, including Kingsland and his own
boss, ATF Special Agent in Charge Jim Elder. Other than Elder,
who had worked through every move with him from the beginning, and Rick Buckles, the Assistant U.S. Attorney who had
been begun laying the groundwork for legal cases, the others had
minimal information about the tapes they were about to hear—
and just listening to the tapes was hard work. Restaurant clatter
and the drone of the television, the heating system, and David's
chatter all but drowned Doc's soft voice in some sections of the
tapes. The soothing backdrop of domestic noises might also make
it more difficult for some people to hear the hard meaning of the
man's words. Glennon Engleman, like many other murderers,
combined a diminished capacity for true human empathy with an
overblown sentimentality in his personal affections. His sentimental regard for his son, Melody, Bob Handy, even for Ruth,
came through in his voice on the tapes. Would the men listening
to those tapes be influenced by sentimentality?

Jesus, McGarvey thought, he would never go into one of those
family restaurants again and hear the clang of electronic games

and the hostess announcing another kid's birthday without thinking of Ruth, Doc, and David. Even he was touched on some level
by the Doc's affections.

He checked the headphones placed at each seat one more time to
make sure they were functional and aligned the pads of paper and
pencils. The door opened, and he was relieved to see Buckles walk
in first. A smiling man, his body already giving the suggestion of
rotundness, Buckles was the epitome of the good midwestern man.
He was also regarded as the best prosecutor in the office.

"We've got him," Buckles said encouragingly. "There's no
way a group of law enforcement people with intelligence and
goodwill can walk out of this room today without doing something
about Glennon Engleman."

"Jeez, I hope you're right," he said, filling two coffee cups.
"What worries me is they'll get bogged down in the territorial
stuff. You know the guys from the city and the county have been
badly treated by federal agencies before. Why should they walk in
here eager to cooperate?"

"Agreed," Buckles said. "But I think they feel more favorably
toward ATF than other agencies. Besides, you've got the evidence. A lot is riding on Westfall since the Halm murder took
place in the county. You know Westfall's reputation. He won't let
territorial considerations or politics stop him. He'll move fast if
he's convinced the man's guilty."

"*If* he's convinced. We've got the best chance of making the
Halm case on murder, but Westfall has to do it." They both knew
the only federal charge they could make in the Halm murder was
mail fraud, good for eighty-five years at the maximum, and not as
good as murder. They had the Berrera bombing case, which carried a maximum of life, but since Engleman had apparently paid
someone else to plant the bomb, that case might be harder to try.
"He's good as gold for Halm on murder, but we were skeptical at
first too. It's a lot to swallow," McGarvey said, sipping his coffee,
burning his tongue. He tried to imagine being in their position
and having to absorb the whole incredible tale, on tape no less, in
one sitting. He had come to the story in chapters and he remembered his own doubts at each new chapter. And wasn't he still
skeptical about the Gusewelle material—material he meant to

downplay today for the very reason he was afraid it might turn out to be so much bullshit? "I wish the tapes were easier to listen to . . ."

The door opened again. Jim Elder came in, followed by Terry Adelman. They needed Westfall so they could get Doc off the streets immediately and keep him in jail until trial. There was no bond on capital murder in the county. Ironically, it had come down to the point where they needed one good white hat against the Doc.

McGarvey had watched their faces turn while they listened to the tapes; with them, he waded through those three and a half weeks' worth of tapes, trying to imagine how it must sound for the first time. Phrases stood out: *The lousy bitch deserved to die . . . Handle it another way, Ruth? . . . And pay that lousy bitch and her Jew lawyer.* Each man had moved from skepticism to a reaction varying from stoic acceptance to moral outrage by the time the Doc had said over Valentine's Day dinner, *Carmen and I . . . we just roughly figured [him for] a hundred thousand.* And, *You're experiencing it right here, Ruth. Money, money, money.* Yes, he had particularly watched Westfall, who, he knew, would be the key man; and Wastfall, he felt, was convinced.

They were hung up on one phrase, the critical phrase, garbled by background noise. Again and again, they listened to it. Had Engleman said, "There's no driving urgency on my part to *keep* getting rid of my fellow man," or had he said, "There's no driving urgency on my part to get rid of my fellow man"? The difference would be crucial in court.

McGarvey watched their faces, seeing his own struggle with the phrase relived in their features. By now, they believed he was guilty. But would they have a case that held up in court? Again, they played the phrase. Ten, twelve, fourteen times. One by one, they said, "I hear it; yes, I hear it. He said, '*keep* getting rid of . . .' He said it!"

Finally, Westfall took off his earphones. It was late in the afternoon. He looked wearily around the table at the other faces, settling on Ankney's.

"I've heard enough," he said. "Let's issue the warrants. He's good for the Halm murder. We know he's good for that."

"We can probably turn Nick and possibly Handy," McGarvey said, smashing another half-smoked cigarette into the ashtray in front of him. "If we arrest all four at the same time—Carmen in California and the other three here—we can keep them from alerting the others and minimize the chance of someone taking off. The surprise element will prevent them from collaborating on a story, and if one decides to cooperate, we can check their story against the others."

"We'll need to turn someone," Westfall said. "We've got a pretty weak case if we don't." Then he looked hard at McGarvey. "What about Ruth? Will her credibility hold up?"

"I've told her we don't need any surprises and I don't think we'll get them. She's admitted to helping launder the money." He lit another cigarette. Jesus, he knew exactly what a good defense lawyer would do with Ruth: paint her as a manipulating and greedy ex-wife who had reaped her share of the rewards from his crimes and now wanted to get her son's father out of their lives for good. "We told her in the beginning one lie could blow the whole deal. I think she's been square with us. Everything she's told us has checked out."

They developed the plans for four separate arrests: Glennon Engleman, Robert Handy, Nick Miranda, and Carmen Miranda Halm would each be arrested the following day. The arresting officers would include representation from ATF, the city, and the county. No one questioned McGarvey's right to arrest the Doc.

Sunday, February 24, 1980

It was nearing one in the morning when Engleman knocked on Wayne Woodruft's door on Goethe Street in the deep South Side. He heard the dogs barking immediately. Those damned dogs. How did Wayne, Ruth's cousin, and his wife stand their constant barking, their stench? It was several minutes before Woodruft peered through the parted curtains and finally opened the door.

"Glen," he said. The air from his house was hot and dog-scented. Engleman stood back. "What on earth are you doing here in the middle of the night?"

"I'm looking for Ruth. Have you seen her or heard from her?" He looked past Woodruft to see his skinny wife hanging back in the doorway to the dining room, clutching a flannel wrapper around her body. Ruth didn't like her; she was too much like the past, and this was probably the last place she would go if she were trying to get away from him, but he'd looked everywhere else. "I can't get her on the phone."

"Glen, I haven't heard from her in a few weeks," Wayne said, shaking his head, rubbing his whiskered chin, enjoying his moment of importance. "What's going on? You two fight about something?"

"I need to get in touch with her," he said, looking down at the dogs clustered around the man. "I think she's trying to cause me some trouble."

"Glen, you and Ruth been fighting about something as long as I can remember," he said. "Did you call Jeannie? Has she talked to her? Maybe Ruthie went down there for a spell."

"I haven't called her," he said. He didn't think Ruth's sister would tell him anything if he had called her; she wasn't exactly in his corner. Ruth could be sitting right there and she'd say, 'Why, I haven't seen her Glen, I have no idea where she is.' Again, he looked past Woodruft into the house. Christ, the man and his wife seemed to be chronically depressed, not that they didn't have reason for being depressed. They couldn't rise above their beginnings as Ruth had, thanks to him. He remembered thinking when Wayne's and Ruth's Uncle Richard blew his brains out and Wayne had found the body that at last Wayne had something real to be depressed about, and he had made the most it. "If you hear from her, let me know, will you?"

"Sure, Glen. Sure. Anything you say." He was already backing away from the door into the house, the dogs closing around his knees. Christ, he hadn't changed since that day they'd had a big fight at a family barbecue out at Lake Tishamingo. Wayne had thrown down his fork and said, "Why do you always have to be on about the Jews or the niggers, Glen, the Jews or the niggers. Why can't we ever get through one meal without you going on about something?" Pathetic. The guy was a pussy, first time he speaks up about something and he defends the goddamn niggers. He'd thrown Ruth's little cousin out and pitched the six-pack of Bud he'd brought behind him. If Wayne'd thought the two years he refused to speak had bothered him he was crazy. "Sure, Glen, sure," he kept repeating as he backed away and closed the door.

Engleman heard the chain snap into place as he walked down the porch steps.

"Goddamn pissant," he muttered to himself, slamming the car door, starting the engine, heading again toward Ruth's condo. *Pissant.* Ruth and her brothers and sister had been determined not to turn out like that, and for the most part they'd succeeded. Jeannie and one of the brothers had married well, and so had Ruth. It could have been a lot better if Ruth had lived up to his expectations. He was sure she'd talked to the police now. There was no other explanation for it. If she thought they'd hang him on her say-so, she was a fool.

He pulled into the parking lot and tried his key in the condo door. It didn't work. The locks had been changed, and the place was dark. Had she been back since he'd been there a few days ago and changed the locks? What the hell was she planning to do? Sell the place and get out of town? Where did she think she could go that he couldn't find her? At least he had some satisfaction in knowing that if she'd been back, she'd seen the message he'd left her on the bed: the Ouija board open, the pointer aimed at the tarot cards for death and betrayal that he had placed on the board.

As he drove back to Melody's he figured he was being followed, but escape was not on his mind. It was not in his nature to run from anyone, especially the cops. He would rather beat them at their own game. Saturday afternoon Melody had walked right up to the surveillance car parked down from her house and asked the cop what he was doing there. Just doing my job, lady, he'd said, just doing my job. Well, they could follow him as long as they wanted. They were wasting the taxpayers money, they weren't going to catch him in the act of doing anything, they weren't going to beat him.

Engleman wasn't surprised to see the two cops at the door at 12:50 Sunday afternoon, but he wasn't particularly worried either. For the murder of Peter Halm, not Sophie Berrera! It was Ruth's doing, then, of course. It was Ruth. Nick and Carmen would be arrested too, but he could count on them. They wouldn't dare talk. He smiled. At the time of his arrest, he had $2.36, one comb, a Chap Stick, and an aspirin in his pockets. He turned to Melody and said, "Don't worry. They can put my body in prison, but they can't keep me there. We both know I can astral-project."

When Handy heard the doorbell ring, he thought it might be Annie, the young Edwardsville woman he'd been dating. Though his mug shots and newspaper photos would never do him justice, Robert Handy was a modestly attractive man. Dressed in jeans and a flannel shirt, he had large dark eyes and thick dark hair, graying but still luxuriant, though it was beginning to recede. His ex-wife had been a bunny at the St. Louis Playboy Club, and he looked as if he could have been, in better times, married to a bunny or perhaps been a prizefighter now gone slack in the jaw. Engleman called him "that beautiful specimen, that fine figure of a man," which was an exaggeration, an aggrandizement, but Handy did have the appearance of someone who had been *better*. Smoothing back his hair, he opened the door expecting to see Annie and imagining her the way she'd looked the night he met her, stripping at an East Side club.

"Robert Handy?" one of them asked. Of course they were cops. His heart raced, but he knew his face betrayed no emotion. "We have a warrant for your arrest for the capital murder of Peter Joseph Halm, Jr." Fucking Christ, after all these years, *Halm*! "You have the right . . ."

He sighed. Yeah, he knew all about those rights. He would have to call his sister Millie again and ask her to find a lawyer and listen to her crap about Glen. One more time. Good old Millie, she would always come through even if she couldn't stop talking. She would tell him again how she loved him better than their other siblings, always had, always would, in spite of how he made her hurt; and he would have to listen. The cuffs came out, and he put his wrists behind his back, assuming the position for cuffing, politely, though not meekly. Nothing would come of this, he was sure. Nothing would really come of this. He was also sure who had turned on them: Ruth. Goddamn, he'd warned Glen about Ruth.

"Glennon Engleman has also been arrested," one of them said as the other snapped on the cuffs.

"I don't believe it," Handy told him. "Not Glen." He looked at the arrogant young cop—Glen said they were all arrogant, nothing but pissants who thought they were somebody because they had a little bit of power—and realized slowly the guy was telling the truth even before he pulled a copy of the arrest order from his pocket. "I don't believe it," he repeated, but he was already beginning to believe it. Nothing else but Glen's arrest would have made those pissants smile like that. "Not, Glen," he said, his voice catching in a sob. He would kill Ruth; he would do it himself. "Not Glen." That goddamn Ruth, he would kill her.

When they led Handy to the St. Louis County police car, he was openly crying. He didn't pay any attention to the radio message concerning Carmen Miranda. The agents who'd been sent to California had said there was "no sign" of her. That made no difference to Handy, who was consumed with grief at the thought of Glennon Engleman in jail.

Carmen knew she had to come home when the *Globe-Democrat* reporter traveled to California to talk to her about Peter's death. She shouted at him through the door, telling him to go away, and her boyfriend Rex Robinson, who was a backup musician for Frankie Valli, went outside and politely asked him to leave. The next day she woke in California and picked up the paper from her lawn to discover the story the *Globe-Democrat* had written reviving interest in Peter's death tucked inside her own paper, and suddenly she was reading about herself instead of the quieter news in Simi Valley. The sunshine couldn't protect her anymore. She called her sister Sandy and said, I have to come home, but I don't have any money, please get a ticket for me, can you? And Sandy had called TWA and got her home that night while Nick was telling St. Louis reporters who called him, "My sister has suffered a tremendous, traumatic shock and I just don't want her to go through this again. She's still not back to the Carmen we knew before this happened." Nick was still acting like he could talk everyone away, but she was already thinking he couldn't this time.

Carmen was sitting on the sofa in the family room talking to Barbara Miranda when the knock came on Nick's door. He had been expecting that knock since 1963 when Eric Frey cried, "Why are you trying to kill me?" It had finally come. He squared his shoulders. If it involved Carmen, he would do everything he could to save her, but he was scared.

"Nicholas Ralph Miranda? We have a warrant for your arrest."

If they wanted only him, and not Carmen, perhaps she would be left out of it after all. But he didn't see how she could be. Whatever the cops had, they'd surely gotten from Ruth. He had probably always known Ruth would turn as soon as she felt her own neck was on the line. Probably the only thing he and Melody and Handy had ever agreed on was Ruth. The question in his mind had always been: Which one will do the other in first? Will Doc kill Ruth before Ruth turns in Doc?

He put his hands behind his back for the cuffs as Barbara and Carmen watched from the doorway. His kids, Chip and Mandy, were playing upstairs, and he wanted to get out of there before they came down and saw him cuffed. Barbara was crying. He wanted to cry himself, but he had to keep his head together.

In the police car he heard the same radioed message that Handy had not heard through his tears. They were looking for Carmen Miranda and she was not in California. He said to one of the cops, "Carmen's at my house. You just left her back there." The car turned around, heading back to his house, and he began to pray, harder than he'd ever prayed in his life. *Let me have a moment alone with Carmen. Only a few seconds. That's all I need, and I can save her. If I talk to her before they do . . . God, she's suffered enough. Let me take care of her.*

As the car pulled back into his drive, he suddenly remembered something the Doc had told him long ago, shortly after the Bullock murder: "Nick, you have to take care of women." Funny he should think of that now. Doc had put her in this mess, and now he would have to get her out.

Her liquid brown eyes congealed in fright, Carmen was led into the car. Nick had his moment alone. He told her, "Don't say anything unless I tell you to say it. If they tell you I said you should talk, don't believe it unless you hear it from me. Don't say anything unless I'm there with you, telling you to say it."

Unable to speak, she nodded.

McGarvey paced rapidly back and forth in a corridor at the St. Louis County jail. Engleman and Handy had been booked separately. Doc was cool, amused and condescending, treating everything as a game, a game he expected to win. His eyes glittered with excitement. He was enjoying the game and anticipated beating the cops again. And maybe he would. They'd thought they could get Handy to flip, but he was proving very stubborn. Privately, McGarvey didn't think he was going to talk. When he'd heard that Handy had cried over Doc's arrest, his heart had sunk. Doc was really into that guy, really in good.

And now Nick and Carmen were arriving together. Jeez, those two had been handed a break. Exactly what they'd sought to avoid had happened: Two of the conspirators had been given the opportunity to talk to each other. By keeping them separate, they had hoped to keep their stories straight. As soon as one had said something, they could take it to the other and say, "Look you're implicated; this is what we know. Now do you want to talk?" Without that game plan, it could be harder to get Nick to turn. At the very least he'd probably told Carmen to keep her mouth shut until she had an attorney. As soon as a defendant asks for an attorney, the police are required to stop asking questions. McGarvey stopped pacing and lit a cigarette. Most of the time he worked around that by not asking questions at first, by trying to say as much as he could and getting them to listen to his pitch before they could open their mouths and ask for an attorney. It was like selling vacuum cleaners door to door.

The federal case on mail fraud wasn't even close to being put together. They hadn't been able to subpoena bank statements and insurance records with Ruth still in town. Even when they made the case, as they would now that they had the time to pursue it, mail fraud wouldn't keep Doc off the streets. He had to be held without bond, and for that to happen, the county's murder case had to be good. Everyone at the meeting yesterday had agreed on this. He put out his cigarette and went back into the room to talk to Handy again.

"I want an attorney," Handy said before he could begin. McGarvey moved down the hall to the room where John McCrady was questioning Nick.

"Has *he* requested a lawyer yet?" Westfall asked as soon as McGarvey opened the door. The four lawyers, Westfall and Ankney, Buckles and Adelman, were sitting in a small room waiting for progress bulletins on the interrogations. Since Handy had refused to talk without counsel, McGarvey had transferred his attention, and his hopes, to Nick and Carmen. She wouldn't say anything at all unless her brother told her to do so; he kept requesting immunity for both of them in exchange for cooperation. Westfall had begun by offering a life sentence for her and immunity for him in exchange for cooperation. Jeez, she would have been an idiot to go for that.

"Nick doesn't waver. He rejects your offer and keeps asking for total immunity for both of them," McGarvey said. He had explained to Nick that while the state didn't have a case on him, he did have one through the broader federal conspiracy laws, which would allow the tapes to be used against him. It wasn't a strong case, but it was a case. "He's sweating buckets out there, but he's holding firm."

"If she asks for a lawyer, we haven't got anything on her either," Ankney reminded them.

McGarvey nodded. They kept reminding each other of the facts they all knew, as if they hoped by repeating them often enough someone would find a way to change them. All they had on Carmen was Engleman's accusation on tape. While they were all convinced she'd married Peter Halm with the intention of conspiring in his murder, they couldn't prove it. No evidence linked her with the crime. A good lawyer would walk right in the door, lean on the table facing those four, ask what they had on his client—then go back in there and tell her she could walk as soon as they posted bond. There would never be an indictment unless a deal was made with Engleman. And *any* lawyer she called would know they weren't going to make a deal with Engleman when he was the one they wanted to get.

"Talk to him again," Westfall said. "If he still hasn't asked for a lawyer, he's only clicking on seven out of eight cylinders. I don't care how tough he's talking. If he were really smart, he would have realized he should talk to a lawyer. Give it another try."

"It might weaken our case to give them both a pass," Buckles said. "I don't think witnesses have as much credibility with a jury if they've been given a complete pass. These two don't deserve it."

"How long do you want to give him to figure it out?" McGarvey asked on his way back out the door. He was ready to give them both passes because he wanted Nick's cooperation. He'd known the pass was inevitable since he sat down across the table from Nick. The key to Carmen was Nick; and Nick would go down saving her neck. He sensed Ankney was with him, but Westfall, who would have to answer to the voting public when the newspapers announced a murderess had gotten a deal, was holding back. There was nothing the voting public hated more than deals with criminals. And there were few things Buckles hated more. McGarvey sympathized with his feelings, but . . .

McCrady had gone down the hall for more coffee; Nick didn't know where McGarvey was, probably with the lawyers. McGarvey was in and out of that room, bouncing back and forth between him and the lawyers like a drop of water skidding over hot grease. When he sat in a chair, his foot moved rhythmically back and forth. Nick pulled out a clean white handkerchief and mopped his brow. He wished he knew *everything* Ruth had told them. McGarvey had played a section of tape for him in which Ruth and Doc had discussed the disposition of Carmen's insurance money. Hell, that story was even worse than it sounded on the tape he'd heard. Had Handy turned over too? He thought it was unlikely. If Handy had flipped, they would have told him. They would have lorded it over him; they wouldn't need to make a deal with him and Carmen.

Their latest offer, a twenty-year sentence for conspiracy to murder for Carmen and a lesser charge with a lesser sentence for him was still not acceptable. He would hold out for immunity. Maybe he could survive in jail for a few years, but Carmen . . . Carmen could not. Couldn't they look at her and see that? Again he thought about Ruth. She, not Carmen, belonged on the hot seat. She had been Doc's partner, his confidant, in every scheme. That lousy, conniving bitch . . .

"Nick," McGarvey said, bounding in the door, "let's try this again."

"I want immunity for both of us," Nick repeated. "It's not negotiable. That's the only way we're going to cooperate."

"It isn't that easy, Nick. You're putting me in a hell of a position. I want your cooperation. I want both of you so we can put Engleman away. If I could cut the deal, I would, Nick."

"You can persuade them to cut it," he said. As he said it, he was sure he'd hit the truth. He was the one who could get it done, if anyone could. He would bet McGarvey was the one who'd pulled in the Doc. Nick had learned from years of following the Doc around to smell out the power, the people who had control if for no other reason than they had the guts to take it. "If you want it done, you can get it done."

They looked at each other across the table for a while. Mc-Crady returned with coffee. Nick watched the glance they exchanged, which told him Carmen was holding firm. A few more moments of silence passed, and McGarvey left the room again.

"We really haven't got a choice," McGarvey said to the lawyers. "He isn't backing down. By morning he'll have a lawyer, and the game's over. A lawyer will tell him, Don't say anything. We'll still end up making the same deal with him a month or two or three down the road. The lawyer will have to earn his fee. You know that."

Westfall passed his hand over his face. It had been hours since Gordo had paged him at the Flaming Pit restaurant, where he was attending a Cub Scout banquet with his family. The exhilaration he'd felt when he'd heard Engleman and Handy were already in custody had given way to frustration so long ago, he'd almost forgotten that initial rush.

"It's the only way to go, Buzz," Ankney prodded.

"I don't like it," Buckles said, knowing he was stuck with whatever decision Westfall made because the county was doing them a favor, not vice versa. "But if we're going to do it, I have to call Kingsland for formal approval."

Westfall met Ankney's glance and saw the amusement in his eyes at the word "approval." *Come on, Buzz,* the expression said. *You can make your own decisions.* Sure he could. But he also had to defend them to the press. How many citizens would call protesting this one? And could he blame them?

"Well?" McGarvey said. "The longer we give him, the more likely he's going to ask for counsel."

"Intellectually it's not a hard decision," Westfall admitted. "We haven't got a good case against Engleman without Handy or Carmen. We aren't going to get Handy. So we haven't got much choice. We sure aren't going to make a deal with him to get her—not that he'd make the deal anyway."

"Well?" McGarvey repeated.

"Emotionally, it's a tough decision. She should go to prison for what she's done. The voters will hate to let her go. Hell, McGarvey, *I* hate to let her go." They waited. Slowly he turned to Buckles. "We aren't going to get her for nothing. I'm in for the deal. Call Kingsland and see what he thinks."

Buckles nodded, stood up, went to the phone. In ten minutes they had Kingsland's approval. McGarvey walked back out the door.

"Tell him he did good for his sister tonight," Westfall said sardonically. "Tell him he did a real good job."

"But don't tell him he could have done better if he'd asked for a lawyer," Ankney added.

PART FIVE:
Nick and Carmen

He read through the agreement one more time before signing it.

Nicholas Ralph Miranda will not be prosecuted or charged for the murder of Peter Halm on September 5, 1976, in St. Louis County. No charges of any kind concerning the Halm murder will be brought by St. Louis County. The same holds true of Carmen Miranda Halm. In exchange, Nicholas Ralph Miranda agrees to tell St. Louis County detectives, St. Louis City detectives, and A.T.F. (Alcohol, Tobacco, and Firearms) agents everything he knows about the Halm murder, the Sophie Marie Berrera attempted bombing and subsequent murder, and any other crimes for which Dr. Glennon Engleman is under investigation.

Mr. Miranda further understands that the statements he is about to make to the detectives and agents will be used against him in prosecution against himself and his sister, Carmen, if he is not 100% truthful and 100% cooperative during any and all prosecutions against Glennon Engleman or Robert Handy.

Carmen Halm agrees to the identical proposition. This agreement obviously includes actual testimony in any and all prosecution against Glennon Engleman and Robert Handy.

The other document, from the U.S. Attorney's office, said basically the same thing, except the crime was mail fraud for collection of the insurance money. Nick had done it—bought Carmen's freedom. For the first time since he hadn't intervened to stop Eric Frey's murder, he felt good about himself. McCrady and McGarvey and another county cop, Steve Burris, were setting up a tape recorder. McCrady was going to interview him while the others listened. He took a large swallow of water and realized he was thirsty enough to drink a pitcher of it, and hungry too. It was 10:23 P.M. when they started the tape. He hadn't eaten since noon.

"This is going to be an informal interview, Nick," McCrady said. "If you have anything to say, say it. Feel free to ask questions. We want to concentrate for now on the murder of Peter Halm."

McCrady tested the tape, then read the documents he had signed into the tape. Hearing them out loud, Nick marveled again at what he had negotiated. Two little pieces of paper saved Carmen and kept him out of jail—if he could have gone there for long in the first place. Those two little pieces of paper also absolved him in the religious sense of the word. They gave him permission to speak, to confess for the first time. He was almost eager to begin. His face, bathed in sweat, glowed with sweet relief.

> MCCRADY: *All right, why don't you start and explain to us when you first got involved in this, or when you knew about it?*
> NICK MIRANDA: *Well, I was in California in '76. I went out about, as I recall, about March or April of that year to pursue a career in producing films and managing television artists. I had been out there for several months. One evening I got a call from my wife. It was the night that Peter was shot. She was very upset . . .*

"Shot?" he repeated. His first thought was a hunting accident. Did Peter hunt? Was it even the season for hunting anything? "What happened? How serious is it?"

"It's very serious," Barbara said, and then he could tell she was crying. "You'd better come home right away."

When he hung up the phone, he couldn't remember if she had actually said Peter was dead—but of course he had to be. Why else would they want him home? He looked out the window for a long time, staring at the palm trees growing along the roadway. It was hard to believe in ghosts, yet inexplicably his mind was drawn to Eric Frey. There was something very wrong about this. He almost called Barbara back, but he knew the questions he had to ask weren't questions he could ask of her. Instead he picked up the phone and began making the arrangements to return to St. Louis. He would stay through the funeral, then he would come right back. He was busy putting together a show on cheerleaders. Surely what he wouldn't even allow himself to think couldn't be true.

His whole family was more upset than they should have been, he thought. Carmen had been married to Peter for less than a year, and during that time the groom hadn't done anything to ingratiate himself with the bride's family. In fact, he'd behaved as if he had wakened one day to find himself married to a poor Mexican girl and, not knowing how it had happened, at least found solace in blaming her family for *being* Mexican. Peter was the quintessential American working-class boy: stubborn, racially prejudiced, interested in cars and spectator sports, basically good-hearted, if in a limited sense, a plodder who probably would have shared beers with the same group of buddies in the same neighborhood hangouts for the rest of his life if he hadn't been killed. There was nothing special about Peter except his dying.

Perhaps they were upset for Carmen, who still seemed in a state of shock. His sisters Nedra and Lupie were particularly jumpy. When he had gotten off the plane the night of the wake and asked them how it happened, they had hesitated before telling him. It was as if they knew but didn't know, wouldn't allow themselves to know something more awful than accidental murder had occurred. He didn't ask them if they thought there was—didn't suggest there could be—something wrong with Peter's death. "Unknown assailant," they all said, parroting the newspaper writers. *Unknown assailant*, right. It smelled to him; it just smelled of something bad. Later they said, *Glen was at the wake. Glen asked when you were coming in.* And it smelled worse.

A day after the funeral, he walked into his own living room and saw Carmen sitting on the couch. His sisters were in the kitchen with Barbara. The children were playing outside. Jesus, what's going on here? he thought, looking at Carmen. He sat down beside her, pulled her against him in a hug.

"Carmen, what is this all about?" he whispered. She just looked at him, her eyes wide, staring at him, so frightened he was scared too. She'd cried so much the tears would no longer form, but he saw her trying to make them in her eyes the way a mute tries to speak. "Is this what I think it is?"

"Yes," she whispered, lowering her eyes shamefully because they were dry.

"He killed him, didn't he?" Nick said, his arm tightening around her. The bastard had done it; he'd killed Carmen's husband. "Glen killed him, didn't he?"

"Yes. Glen and Bob Handy." Her voice caught. "We went out to Pacific to this place where Glen had taken me before. He told me to take Peter that day and he and Bob Handy would be waiting and they would kill him. They had tried to kill him before, two times before—and I didn't think it would happen. I never thought it would happen. Then I took him to this place, and he was shot. He said he'd been shot and slumped over and died. I never thought it would happen."

"Carmen," he said, holding her tighter because she was shaking. "Does anyone else know?" He was afraid she would crack emotionally if she kept going on, so he didn't want to ask her for more details. "Did you tell anyone else?"

"No," she said. She was quiet for a minute; then she told him, "He said if I did it I would have enough money to buy Mother a home. He said he would do it with me to help me. But now I don't want the insurance money, Nick. I don't want anything."

"Honey, we'll talk about this later. For now, just don't say anything to anybody else, all right?"

She nodded, and he continued to hold her. Barbara came to the door. When she looked at them, her eyes filled with tears and she turned respectfully away. He could never talk to his wife about this. She was a religious person, a very spiritual woman. This would shock her. Christ, it shocked him and he wasn't an easy person to shock. He had sat at Madre's table all those years, listening to her and Glen, listening to them expound and develop an antisocial philosophy of life. And he was still shocked when it had come to this. Madre believed some organizations were fair game, the banks and insurance companies, the government, the utilities, anything big, beyond their control. You could steal from those places and it wasn't stealing, she said, it was getting yours back. Glen had taken her beliefs as his and built upon them. Madre thought anything Glen did was justified, from fathering illegitimate children to murder. Nick knew it. He had seen Glen's sense of personal power expanding with her approval; and still he was shocked when it came down to this.

"What will happen?" Carmen whispered.

"Nothing," he said, patting her shoulder. "Nothing. I'll take care of you. You'll be fine."

A few days later her brothers and sisters agreed in a family meeting that Carmen had to be hospitalized for a while. She had told them she was feeling so "black" she didn't care what happened to her anymore. They were very much afraid she would commit suicide. While she was hospitalized, they kept the police away from her. She wasn't able to answer questions about the accident, they said, and her doctors concurred. After several weeks, when she was well enough to leave the hospital, Nick decided to take Carmen back to California with him so he could protect her and prevent further questioning.

"What is he supposed to get out of this?" he asked her. He was holding her hand, sitting at her bedside. They were alone in the hospital room the day before she was to check out. She turned her head toward the wall. "Honey, just tell me, and I'll take care of it. I'll see he gets paid what he's supposed to get. You can forget about everything then."

"Ten thousand dollars. He said he would do it for ten thousand dollars. There was supposed to be more insurance, but there wasn't . . . Peter didn't . . ." Her voice trailed off and her eyes glazed. "Ten thousand," she repeated. "That's all he wants."

"Well, I don't want you to see him again. I don't want you near the man. I'll take care of it for you. I'll take you back to L.A. with me, and I'll take care of him for you."

He called Glen that night and told him he had Carmen's power of attorney. He would collect the insurance and pay him off when it was settled. Glen said that was fine, and then told him about how difficult it had been to shoot his brother-in-law. "It took us three tries," he said. "Third time was a charm," and he laughed. Nick could picture him holding the phone, laughing, his free elbow flapping like mad. "Your brother-in-law," he said, "was a hard son of a bitch to kill."

Flying back to California with Carmen, Nick suddenly remembered a conversation they'd had two years before. She had told him Glen had a plan for helping her, a way for her to get ahead in the world. It was a bad plan, she'd said, and she had only listened in the first place because she wanted to help her mother. But she had told him it was a bad plan. Nick remembered now how he had tuned her out. There were so many things about Glen he had just not listened to. He had tuned Carmen out when he should have grabbed her by the shoulders and said, Listen, listen, I'm getting you out of there, do you hear me? But he had ignored her, left her under the power of a man who knew exactly what buttons to push to get her to react the way he wanted. That was the dangerous thing about Glen, his knowing what combination to press for each person, his choosing people who had no way of knowing for themselves.

> MCGARVEY: *Did they say why they did it? You know, was there a conversation with Carmen about their reasons for doing it?*
>
> MIRANDA: *The actual motives you mean?*
>
> MCGARVEY: *The motive for it, right.*
>
> MIRANDA: *A combination of things. She told me that he wanted to help her, help my mother . . . At the time he said Peter was beating my sister up . . . I don't know if he was or wasn't . . .*
>
> MCCRADY: *To your knowledge did Dr. Engleman have any specific controls over Carmen at that time or did he not? Was he blackmailing her or anything of that sort? To your knowledge?*
>
> MIRANDA: *I don't know . . . not to my knowledge . . . no.*

MCGARVEY: *Do you recall her ever expressing any fear about Dr. Engleman or Handy?*
MIRANDA: *Yes . . .*

He wiped his face and asked for more water. They brought the water and food, turned off the tape recorder so he could eat the food. How could he ever make them understand the way Glen controlled people when he didn't understand it himself? How to explain the fear—and more than fear, the loyalty and love even when you knew he wasn't someone you should love?

When Glen had lived on Compton, the Englemans had a black ironing lady, Lavenia, who came once a week. Part of her deal was a free lunch, which she shared with Glen and often Nick. He used to wonder why Lavenia loved "the doctor" so much when he, under the guise of educating her about her race, constantly put down blacks over lunch. *Do you know, Lavenia, that eighty percent of the thirteen-year-old girls of your race have already had sexual intercourse? Do you know, Lavenia, statistics for crime, for rape, and incest and so forth from your race? Huhmmmm,* Lavenia would say, *huhmmmmm, those bad girls, so bad, those bad mens.* She said "mens" for "men" and persisted in saying it, no matter how often Doc corrected her. Even as a kid, Nick knew Lavenia was an Uncle Tom, considering herself privileged to break bread with a man who disdained her race. But then what was the comparable phrase for Nick Miranda?

While Nick, McGarvey, and McCrady were eating sandwiches, Nick told them a story about Glen, about him bombing Bobby's Books, a porno bookstore. Glen wanted to put Bobby out of business because he was offended by pornography. You had to laugh at a man who committed murder but found pornography offensive. It was the first of many stories Nick would tell them about Glen. He felt like a clown earning his meal, but he was grateful to tell it and would keep telling stories, would keep on earning his meal with them. He had the best deal in the world and he knew it . . . would do whatever they wanted. I've got another one for you, I've got so many you won't believe . . . For years, another story went, Doc had railed against the owner of a shop that was located next to his office. When he noticed the guy's air conditioner dripping onto the sidewalk, he had thought of a way to put him out of business. He'd paid a bum twenty bucks, taken him back to the office, shot him full of Novocain and roughed his forehead with a file. Then he and Nick had carried the bum outside, planning to drop him under the air conditioner in the puddle on the sidewalk. The bum would sue the owner, claiming he had slipped in the water and hurt his head. Dragging the semiconscious man between them, they both looked up at the same time and discovered the air conditioner was not in the window. The pissant had taken it in for repairs. They dropped the bum and left him there on the sidewalk in the heat. Everyone had a good laugh over that one, the bum with his roughed up forehead. "Have you heard the one about the taco stand?" Nick asked. "We burned it down for insurance." The laughter was another form of release.

MCGARVEY: *Did he ever mention the ten thousand dollars to you?*

MIRANDA: *Yes, he did. He called me at home one day and said he wanted to see me about the money. Most of the time, I've never called the man. Never. Never. Never, but he would always get wind that I was in town, and he would call me.*

"I have to see you," Doc told him. "Meet me at the office and we'll go to lunch."

"Why do you have to have lunch with him?" Barbara asked him. "We have so little time with you. Why can't you stay here and have lunch with us?"

"I have to go," he snapped at her, and he hated himself when he talked harshly to her. He and Doc always met at the office and then went to lunch. That's what they did. And he had to go, no question about it, he had to go. Peter had been dead nearly four months and the insurance still wasn't settled. He'd been writing letters, but the insurance companies were dragging their feet. Carmen was okay, doing better, but, he thought, far from well. She was flying back to St. Louis a lot because she missed the family. They were spending money they really didn't have . . . Christ, spending it like crazy, like they were crazy. Yet really she didn't have anything. She apologized for buying groceries, clothes. All their money was spent on airfare. She couldn't stay here because of Doc, but she couldn't stay away from here either. Both of them, they were crazy, torn.

"What's going on?" Glen asked him. "What's taking so long? The I.R.S. is on my back. I need that money."

"Well, my sister has received nothing to date. She doesn't have anywhere near this kind of money. You have to wait." He hated himself, being so obsequious, needing to live so badly he would scrape and bow like this. "I've got a letter," he said. "I brought you a letter from the insurance commissioner of the State of Missouri." If it had been up to Carmen, she wouldn't have made a claim on the policies. He produced the letter, which proved he was still trying, albeit unsuccessfully, to collect the money. "I brought you a letter . . ."

"Okay," Doc said, examining the letterhead carefully. "Okay, but when you get it, let me know."

A few weeks after that, Carmen got a check for $11,000. It came to her address in Los Angeles. They flew home with the check and took it to the Commerce Bank in Kirkwood. Nedra waited with them so she could take Carmen out another door without seeing the doctor in case he showed up at the bank. The vice-president tried to talk them out of cashing the check. He turned his attention to Nick, who was clearly in charge, ignoring Carmen, whose name was on the check. *Why don't you deposit it in an account for your sister? You don't want to walk out on the street with all that money. It's dangerous having that much cash in your pocket.* He took the full amount in hundred-dollar bills. Doc was waiting in a nearby church parking lot. It would have been dangerous to walk outside *without* that money.

"I'm surprised there won't be more," Doc said. By now he had realized she wasn't going to get as much insurance as he'd expected. "She should have made sure that change-of-beneficiary form was signed and turned in. What a waste. The Halms getting the rest of that money! What a goddamn waste."

Soon there was more money—money that didn't have to be paid to Glen. Nick couldn't recall how much money. He opened an account in California under C & N Enterprises, for Carmen and Nick. The plan was that he'd invest the money and they would have something, become something with the money in spite of how it was gained. Carmen didn't want to hear the plans anyway. She just wanted the money for airfare so she could go back and forth to St. Louis. Just before one check came in, she'd written a personal check to TWA with no funds in the bank, knowing, hoping the money would be there by the time the check got to the bank. She really didn't want the money, so she really didn't care when it was gone. Maybe he really didn't want the money either; that's why he'd wasted it on bad investments and a Mercedes-Benz, which he wanted to like a lot more than he did.

No, he told the cops listening to his story, he didn't remember exactly how much money there was or where it had gone. But he still had the records somewhere in a filing cabinet. He would find them. No, he couldn't remember. Sometimes he could remember exactly what had happened fifteen or twenty years ago, and sometimes he couldn't tell you what he'd had for breakfast.

It was 12:32 A.M. on Monday, February 25, when they ended the interview. His sister, they told him, was next.

Carmen looked at the three men Nick said she now had to trust. Had to trust, not could trust. No choice in the matter, like she had no choice in the matter of trusting Doc. At least this time everyone could understand why she had no choice. The man named Burris had said he would ask the questions, but they were all free to jump in. She was free too . . . to ask them questions. What could they tell her that she would want to know?

BURRIS: *Okay, Carmen, why don't you go ahead and tell us about your relationship with Dr. Engleman? How you happened to be associated with him or exactly what the relationship is?*

CARMEN MIRANDA HALM: *I have known Dr. Engleman all my life.*

BURRIS: *Was he a friend of the family?*

HALM: *Yes, he was a friend of the family.*

BURRIS: *Were you ever in his employ?*

HALM: *Yes.*

She could not remember the first time she was aware of the Doc. He said he knew her better than she knew herself. Often he surprised her because he knew things about the way she was raised, about how it was when she was young, things she didn't know. He said her father was a drunk and her brother Bobby was no good and would end up in jail and she and her family didn't have enough food to eat, things like that . . . he knew things like that. She and Nedra and Lupie, they had cleaned his house and his office and baby-sat for Sandy Frey's baby Melissa—his baby, he said, his baby too—and later they baby-sat for David, his son with Ruth. She could not remember the first time she had noticed the Doc in her life. He had always been there.

"What did you do that for?" Mama yelled. "How are you ever going to get anywhere, get a decent job if you don't finish your diploma?"

She had dropped out of high school in the middle of the tenth grade, just like that; and her mama was furious. Nick wasn't around much then, but he would be angry too when he heard. Her brother Nick read books all the time and he knew more big words than the Doc now. He argued with Glen's wives; he thought Glen beat them. She guessed he did. And Glen. What would Glen say about Carmen quitting school? While Mama was yelling, she was thinking about what Glen would say. She valued his opinion above everyone else's.

Carmen was going with a boy at the time. It was easy, so easy, just to drop out and spend her days sleeping and cleaning and going around with Nedra in her girlfriend Squeakers's car. So easy. She got pregnant the same way, easy, because it wasn't any trouble, and it would have been trouble not to. He was like a puppy, eager, straining against her body; and she gave in to him because refusing him required too much energy. There was a certain comfortable languor in lying back, submitting, taking the parts she liked, the hugging and kissing, and consenting to the rest. It just happened, as things happened to her; and then she was sorry later. She was seventeen. Nedra and Squeakers took her to Glen's office on Compton at night so he could take care of it, the pregnancy. He could end it easy, he said.

"I'm going to put a tube in your vagina, Carmen," he told her in his gentle voice, which made her feel she wasn't so bad after all. No other man she knew had such a soft voice and those clean white hands. It had hurt, having the tube stuck in, but he had told her it didn't hurt. He wouldn't hurt her—couldn't—or so she tried to pretend. "And a piece of tube will be sticking out, taped to your leg. When you start to bleed through the tube, take it out. It will be just like having a period, Carmen, a regular period, maybe a little heavier, that's all. Nothing to worry about." His voice mesmerized her, hypnotized her into believing. "Nothing to worry about . . . nothing . . ." She had been listening to his voice forever and believing, hadn't she?

When the cramps started later, she remembered his words: *Nothing, nothing to worry about.* She started bleeding and pulled the tube out, just as he had told her to do. Carefully she covered herself with a Kotex and went to bed. Nedra came in and placed a towel under her; it was that bad. She needed a towel and still there were spots on the sheets. How would she clean the sheets without Mama seeing?

"Carmen, Carmen," Nedra was crying beside her bed. It was three in the morning, or maybe four; she was dizzy, weak, she didn't know. "Carmen, you're bleeding so bad! Carmen, look at you!"

Weakly she sat up on one elbow. Nedra had pulled back the sheet, and the bed was a mass of blood and blood clots. She leaned back again, afraid she would be sick. He said it would be okay, nothing, nothing to worry about, and so it would.

"I'd better call an ambulance, Carmen," Nedra cried. "You're bleeding too much!"

"No, Ned," she said. "It'll be okay. Give it a little longer. He said I would bleed."

He had said she would bleed, but that nothing bad would happen to her. Nothing. Nedra waited longer, perhaps an hour. She didn't know, she was too weak, passing in and out of consciousness, hearing her name and not being able to catch the place in the air from where it was coming. This time when Nedra pulled back the sheets, the draft made her shake.

"I'm calling Mama," Nedra said, crying. "If she finds out, it's better . . . it's better than if . . . if something happens to you."

Suddenly Mama was standing by the bed, her face white. Her voice shook as she asked Nedra, "What's going on? What's happening to Carmen?" She fainted. Then Mama was standing beside her weeping as she lay on a table in the hospital.

"Who did this to you?" the doctor said, peering into her face. To her mother he said, "She would have bled to death if you'd waited much longer." And again to her, "Tell me who did this to you."

"No one," she whispered, looking at Mama, who would never have to know it was Glen. "I did it to myself." It wasn't Glen's fault really, if something went wrong, it had to be her fault, not his. He had helped her. "I did it to myself."

"I want you to work for me, Carmen," he said. "I'm going to teach you to be a dental technician. Then you'll always be able to get work, no matter what. You will have a profession."

"But I haven't finished high school," she said. She was shy with him following the abortion, though she had made Nedra promise he wouldn't be told about the hospital. Nedra surely hadn't told, and neither had she. Somehow it seemed like she had let him down by going to the hospital; she didn't want him to know that part. "I don't even have a diploma. Mama says I can't do anything without one."

"She's mostly right. No one else would hire you. I want to help you, teach you."

"Thank you," she said. "Thank you." No one else would give her that chance. Once again she was grateful to him.

Shortly after she began working for Engleman as a dental technician, she went on a weekend float trip with some friends. One of the boys slipped into her sleeping bag at night. The night was warm and she hadn't zipped the bag. Suddenly he was on top of her, his hardness pressed against her groin. He was panting and licking in her ear so that she giggled. He took her laughter for encouragement. "Touch me," he said, guiding her hand to him. "Feel it, feel how hard it is." They always said this, bragging over how hard it was when each one felt the same to her. She touched him because he wanted to be touched. Then the next week, he

called her and said he had something, she'd better be checked
too.

She didn't know why she always ran to Glen all the time, but
she was ashamed, embarrassed. Who else could she tell if she had
something? He told her to sit in the chair, the dental chair; and he
would examine her. Then he took a long cotton swab and put it
up her vagina. *This doesn't hurt,* he said. *Why are you flinching? Come
on now, Carmen, you've had an abortion, this is nothing, nothing.* She
watched him smear her juices on a thin piece of glass. And he told
her he would take the glass, a slide he called it, to a place where
someone would test it and tell her if she had something. Of course
she did; and he gave her the penicillin to cure it.

> BURRIS: *And these times when Dr. Engleman helped you, you
> never had a sexual relationship with him?*
> HALM: *Never. He tried one time. And I told him . . .*
> BURRIS: *And what did you tell him?*
> HALM: *He tried it one time, and I asked him please not to. He
> had talked a few times about him and I, suggesting we could, you
> know, do that together; and I had pacified him, never coming out
> and saying, you know, I didn't want to do it. But then he tried it;
> and I asked him please not to.*

"I've done it before," he said. They were alone in the office in
the morning getting it ready for patients. This was the time she
usually talked to him, telling him about her problems. He had
been telling her for days now that he had the solution to her
problems, that the solution was very simple. She would marry
someone and he would kill him. "I've done it before. I killed
Bullock. You know that, but you were just a little girl. Do you
know that Christmas I gave your mother the money for your
presents? There wouldn't have been any presents under the tree
that year, Carmen, if Doc hadn't put them there. I've done it
before, Carmen. I killed Eric Frey. You remember him; and you
remember the apartment Sandy lived in after he died. You and
Nedra went swimming there."

She listened, not quite believing, but mesmerized by the world
he created with his voice: a world where she could swim in an

apartment pool and have presents under her Christmas tree, all thanks to him. Every day he added details to the plan. She didn't believe, but she listened the way she ate meals, lapping up the details like dessert, skipping over the parts she didn't want to hear, leaving most of them on her plate.

"It just bothers me, you know," she told him, "that I can't get ahead in life, that I am just existing."

"You are just existing like your mother has existed, Carmen. She's a hardworking woman, but she never had the chance to get ahead. People like you, Carmen, have to make those chances. They don't just happen. You never get anywhere working a pissant job and paying your taxes."

He talked to her endlessly, his voice like a stream. Most of the time when he talked to her he didn't say those words that she hated to hear. He didn't scream curses about the Jews and niggers and homosexuals, not most of the time, not with her, unless a patient or someone else had made him really mad. She was afraid to make him mad.

"I want to have more than my mother had," she told him. "I want to help my mother. It isn't fair that she works so hard and she doesn't have a house of her own. It isn't fair."

"I can help you," he said. "If you marry someone, I'll kill him. You'll have a start in life then, Carmen."

She listened but she didn't believe the part about the killing. The part about the start, though, a house for her mother and an apartment with a swimming pool . . . she liked that part and pretended to believe it. That part was a fairy tale. In fairy tales the killings were not real. Doc seemed to know when she was most bothered and depressed, and he brought it up right away, the subject of marrying a man to kill.

"How would I know who to marry?" she asked. She wasn't going with anyone at the time. It was harmless to talk about marrying someone the doctor would kill if she had no boyfriend, wasn't it? He was educated and she respected him, hoped he would pass some of his education on to her. "How would I know who?" she said. "How? I don't know any rich men."

"Carmen, you wouldn't want to marry a rich man. There are too many questions asked when rich men die. You stay away from doctors, business owners, policemen, lawyers . . . you stay away from anyone whose death would be questioned too much. You're looking for a man with a solid job at a big company, an average man. Those big companies pay benefits, honey. After you marry him, you can take out more insurance, sometimes through the mail. And then we kill him, Bob Handy and I kill him for you. We make it look like an accident and we get some of the money, and the rest is yours."

She had a headache. She closed her eyes, thinking about how her mother had looked, white and shaking, standing next to her bed when she was bleeding and how she might look standing proudly in a house of her own.

For nearly a year they had the same conversation. She would marry and lure her husband to a wooded place, somewhere in Franklin County, where Eric Frey had been killed and the sheriff asked no questions, and he and Bob Handy would arrange an accident. This place in the woods was fuzzy in her mind, a spot where all the laws fell away because the sheriff did not care and Glen was God. He and Handy would set up targets and arrange wine and beer bottles, maybe marijuana cigarettes. It would look like her husband had been killed by a group of drunken teenagers playing with guns. She had listened to the story for so long, she didn't believe it would happen, but it was romantic to pretend herself a beautiful widow whose husband had been killed in the woods, leaving her his money. Romantic. None of the men she had dated was right anyway, the doctor said, until she told him about Peter Halm.

> BURRIS: *So you began to date Peter Halm during the time that you worked for Dr. Engleman?*
>
> HALM: *No, I dated Peter when I was even younger than that. I dated Peter when I was fifteen or sixteen; and we broke up. We went back together, then we broke up and went back together and broke up, off and on.*
>
> BURRIS: *When did you begin to date him steadily for the last time prior to your marriage?*
>
> HALM: *I think a year before our marriage.*

"He's the one, Carmen," the doctor said. They were alone again in the office in the morning, getting ready for patients. Again he told her he had been homicidally intimate with Sandy Frey; and he told her about the golden girl, who was, he said, following his plan. She knew who the golden girl, Barbara, was. She'd met Barbara before her first marriage, the one that ended in divorce, and she'd seen Barbara in the office plenty of times, before and since. Barbara's first baby, a daughter conceived before her marriage, they said, was his. Glen said Barbara was smart, he let her know, very smart, maybe smarter than Carmen, and she was following his plan. "Southwestern Bell, honey, they have very good benefits. I've been looking into it. And you'll get a year's salary after his death in addition to the insurance benefits, honey. He's the one, Carmen. An average working man from an average, working-class family. No one will care enough to ask any questions when he's gone, honey. They'll look at the scene and it will look like an accident because Handy and I have made it look like an accident . . . He's the one."

"But what if he doesn't propose?" she said. "I've been dating him for a long time, and he's not proposed yet."

"Honey, you can get him to propose," the doctor said, smiling at her in the way which let her know she'd said something very naive. "You will get him to marry you the same way women throughout the ages have gotten their men to marry them: through sex, Carmen, through sex." She blushed, and as if reading her mind, he said, "I know you've been having sex with him, Carmen, but you have to do more than just lie there and submit if you're going to make him want you bad enough to marry you. Honey, you have to be seductive, seductive."

The next morning he brought her a copy of *The Riverfront Times*. He had circled an ad for a belly-dancing class. "You're going to sign up for this," he said. "Then you're going to belly dance for Peter. It will drive him wild, honey."

He instructed her in the noises she should make while Peter was making love to her. Make those noises, he said, whether you feel like it or not; and move around, honey, don't just lie there and submit. Any woman can do that for him. He described his sexual life with Ruth and Barbara and the other women he had, even Lupie, but she told him, No, no, I don't want to hear about Lupie, not her. He said he wouldn't talk about Lupie if they'd work on the plan.

He told her how to pleasure Peter. What drives a man wild, he said, is fellatio. She had never heard the word "fellatio," and putting down her head nervously, not wanting to look in his eyes, in case it was a disgusting thing, she asked him, "What does it mean?"

"Head, Carmen, giving head. You've heard that, haven't you? You do it, don't you? Don't you put your pretty little mouth around Peter's big stiff cock, honey?" Those hard words were like the rapids in the river of his voice, but she had been riding the river for so long now, she took the rapids almost without flinching. She didn't like the words, and he knew it. She thought he punished her with those words. "Well, don't you, honey? Maybe you aren't doing it right. From now on I want you to give head the way I tell you to do it, Carmen. Nothing can go wrong if you do things the way I tell you to do them."

"Yes," she said. Maybe if she did what he told her to do, Peter would propose, and then she would have done what the doctor thought was right. "Yes."

"Okay, honey, you take it in your hand, his cock, with your hand around the base." He put two fingers of his left hand together, pretending they were a penis, and made a circle with his right hand around them. "Take that big stiff cock in your hand, honey, and lower your mouth to it." She almost laughed when he put his own mouth down over the tops of his fingers, talking out the side as he demonstrated. "Lick up the shaft slowly, honey, on both sides, then take the balls in your mouth, carefully, one at a time, no teeth, and suck them, then lick up the shaft again and put your mouth down on the head." He had given up demonstrating at the place where his fingers had no balls, so he stood there with the fingers of one hand circling the fingers of another. "Suck the head, Carmen, no teeth, suck it until your jaw aches, honey, suck it."

When she did those things to Peter, she heard the doctor's voice playing. He was the soundtrack in her mind. She made herself hear him. Perhaps the listening was her penance.

BURRIS: *When did you first tell Dr. Engleman that you had intensions of marrying Peter?*

HALM: *Well, when I was working for Dr. Engleman, um, he told me that I would have to stop working for him as soon as things seemed to be serious between me and Peter, as soon as he proposed. So when he proposed, Dr. Engleman got me a job with Dr. Albair and he told me to call him, like every other day, to stay in touch with him every other day or so and let him know any developments, and I did.*

BURRIS: *You told him that you were going to get married and you stayed constantly in touch with him?*

HALM: *Yes.*

BURRIS: *At that time you told him you were contemplating marriage, did he ever mention the fact that he might kill the person that you were going to marry for money?*

HALM: *Every time I spoke to him.*

BURRIS: *Did you continue to stay in touch with Dr. Engleman after you and Peter were married?*

HALM: *Yes, yes.*

"Carmen, I think we should meet to discuss the plan. Can you come to the office Saturday afternoon?"

"Well," she hesitated, but he was insistent. *Carmen, Carmen, we have to discuss the plan.* She was married now, and she didn't believe it would happen, not really. It was hard to believe he had ever killed anyone. Maybe he said those things to make himself look important. She was married now, and, like the princess in some fairy tale she vaguely remembered, she didn't want to pay the price to the man who had arranged the marriage. "Well . . ."

"You know you are supposed to call me every two or three days, Carmen; and I haven't heard from you in five days. Five. Now I want you to be here Saturday afternoon," he said, his voice rising, scaring her. "Saturday afternoon, Carmen. Do you understand?"

"Yes," she said. "Yes, I will be there."

She was married now, and she didn't want to be with him on Saturday afternoon. The marriage was not what she once dreamed marriage might be, but it was not as bad as she knew it could be either. They argued sometimes, and when he was really angry at her, Peter pushed her. She knew he was disappointed too. Whomever it was he thought he had married, he hadn't.

Carmen didn't want to be there, but she sat on the counter in the room Glen called his lab, where he made the impressions of teeth that would be sent out to another lab where they actually made false teeth. She sat up on the counter. He had a late patient, and he told her to sit there and wait until he came back. Then he started touching her, putting his hands on her breasts, her crotch, and she said, "No, please, don't."

"Wait here," he said, "and when we have an intimate moment, we will discuss the things I am planning."

She was afraid that when he came back he would touch her again, but he didn't.

"Have you made sure he signed the insurance forms changing the beneficiary from his parents to you? Are you sure the house is in both your names and he has mortgage insurance?" he asked. She said she had, but she was lying. "Did you call the insurance companies I told you to call and sign up for more insurance?" Again, she said she had and again she was lying. They did have more insurance but only because a friend of Peter's, Wayne Leeka, who rode motorcycles with him, sold insurance and had asked them to buy some. "Okay," he said, rubbing his hands together. "Okay, Carmen, you have done well. You have done what you were supposed to do. Now the rest is easy. Nothing can go wrong. Handy and I are ready."

He was looking at her so hard that she closed her eyes for a minute. The last time she had told him she didn't want to do it. He had gotten very angry, very disappointed in her. Glen didn't get angry like other people. He turned very red, like everything inside him was boiling up. She had not seen him explode, and she was afraid to see it. If he blew up, she would be hurt in the explosion; she knew that for sure. He had told her he was disappointed, so she had said, "All right, okay, I'll do it, I'll do it, I'm sorry," until the red began to recede and slowly he returned to normal, crushed back down inside himself; and she could breathe. Now she just agreed with him and believed it wouldn't happen.

"When I kill Peter, I want to kill your brother Bobby too," he said. "Bring him along so I can kill him."

He hated Bobby; she didn't quite know why. Maybe he hated Bobby because Bobby had never believed in him the way Nick had. But she said, "Yes, yes, of course, I will," though she had no intention of doing such a thing, of bringing her own brother to him to be killed.

> BURRIS: *Were some specific plans made between the two of you toward Peter's death?*
>
> HALM: *Yes, a month or two before Peter was killed we made plans which didn't work out.*

She and Peter had a friend named Tim Carmody who lived in High Ridge, a wooded area that the doctor said was good because it was outside St. Louis County Police territory. He told her to take Peter there one day, that he and Handy would be waiting in the woods, and they would kill him. It was not hard to get Peter there because he liked going to Tim's.

"Don't nag me about drinking too much beer," he told her in the car driving down. She had already made him mad by insisting they take a car, not a motorcycle. They had argued, but he had forgiven her. He was letting her know she was forgiven by the tone of his voice, easy, not hard as he warned her about nagging him; and besides he cradled the back of her neck with one hand, squeezing gently, the way she liked him to do, especially if she had headaches. "I want to have a good time, for God's sake, so don't nag me about a few beers."

"Okay, as long as you let me drive home," she said. It occurred to her then he wasn't supposed to be coming home. That was the plan, wasn't it? She thought about the doctor and Handy, hiding in the woods around Tim's house, waiting with shotguns, but she couldn't believe it would happen. Peter was alive next to her; he was not going to die today. "Okay," she said, smiling at him, cupping the hand which caressed her neck. "Okay." It was easier most of the time to agree with men than argue.

They had been at Tim's for an hour or so when his dog attacked a man in the woods. Tim had seen the man running from his dog but did not know who he was. The next day Carmen learned he was Dr. Glennon Engleman. "The goddamn son-of-a-bitch dog bit me in the leg," he said. "I should sue the fuck who owns him."

When they made the next plan she was sure it too would fail. Maybe he just liked making plans.

"You know what you should do with your money, Carmen," Glen told her, "you should invest in a condominium in south St. Louis or maybe south County. Condominiums are the coming thing, honey. You can't lose, can't lose on a deal like that now."

She didn't even know what a condominium was; and he explained to her they were like apartments you buy instead of rent. They were driving to this place he knew where he said he would kill Peter, a covered bridge, which was close to the place she had to go anyway to claim her grandfather clock. She had won the clock when a telephone solicitor asked her a question and she knew the answer. Glen was surprised she'd won. Then when she told him the details he'd laughed. "Oh, honey, it's just one of those rackets. They give you some pissant prize, your clock will be about six inches tall, honey, to get you out there to look at property they're selling at inflated prices. That's all, honey, but it's good. It will give you a good excuse for taking Peter out here."

When they got to the bridge, he insisted they get out of the car and walk over it. She thought the bridge was pretty. The roof was red, and the stream beneath it was almost clean, dancing over the rocks as if it thought it were somewhere exciting, not eastern Missouri. She had never seen a covered bridge before.

"Why does it have a roof?" she asked; and he told her about covered bridges, that there weren't many left in the country and they had roofs because cattle were driven across them and cattle got scared if they could see anywhere but straight ahead. He knew so many things. "I like the roof," she told him; and he took her elbow, leading her, like a father this time. She felt safe.

When she led Peter to the bridge, she told him about the cattle; and he said that was bullshit. "Where did you get that idea? he said. Where do you get the stuff you think, anyway? You didn't even finish high school and you have all this bullshit in your head.

It's like your stupid little clock, Carmen. We drove all the way out here to collect a clock you could put in a dollhouse. Some asshole wants to sell you something and you can't tell the difference; you think you won a prize. Maybe you should have kept that baby, Carmen, maybe that's what you need after all." They stood on the bridge for a while, watching the water flow under them. He wasn't exactly angry with her, just bored, disappointed maybe. They weren't the only people who had come to claim their clocks, and some of the people were dressed in nice clothes, driving pretty cars. Were they dumb too? In the distance they heard the sounds of children and dogs. Nothing happened. She had never really thought it would. "It's true," she told him, "about the cattle. I read it in a book."

"Those goddamn kids," the doctor told her the next day. "Those kids and their dogs. We had to get out of there. They saw our faces. We couldn't kill him, the lucky fuck has more lives than a cat."

> BURRIS: *The third attempt actually resulted in Peter's death . . . Is that correct?*
> HALM: *Yes.*
> BURRIS: *When did the discussion about the third attempt take place?*
> HALM: *Probably two weeks prior to his death. I met Dr. Engleman in his office, and we drove to the spot.*
> BURRIS: *He drove you there?*
> HALM: *Yes.*

The weather was hot, and her car wasn't air-conditioned. The drive from her house in Kirkwood to the Ground Round on Lindbergh where he had told her to leave her car took fifteen minutes or so, long enough for her shirt to be sticking to her back. It was Thursday, so the doctor had no appointments. He was waiting for her, impatient to begin the drive. This time, he said, nothing would go wrong. He and Handy would be waiting there, and nothing would go wrong.

"I'm so thirsty," she said, looking wistfully at the restaurant. They were taking his car, which was air-conditioned, but she was still feeling hot and wanted to cool off before they started a long drive. "Could we stop for a soda?" She wanted him to take her inside the restaurant. Peter seldom took her out to eat, and when he did it was White Castle or McDonald's.

"We can't be seen together, Carmen," he told her; and she felt suddenly impatient with his scheming, his planning for something that would never happen. "I'll stop somewhere and get a soda for you, but you'll have to wait in the car."

Soon he stopped the car at a 7-Eleven and brought her a large frozen Coke. Greedily, she sucked on the straw, half-listening while he told her they were driving to caves near Pacific, Missouri, just past Six Flags amusement park, where he would kill Peter. *Where he would kill Peter* . . . How much longer would they make these plans? Since he had become consumed with this plan, she hadn't been able to tell him her troubles anymore, and she missed the telling. She couldn't tell him her marriage to Peter wasn't happy and she was flirting with other men, teasing him, hoping he would leave her. No, she couldn't tell the doctor her private things anymore.

He parked the car and led her down a path toward a group of small caves. "Everything will be marked," he told her. "All you have to do is lead him down here. Take him along this path and stop in front of the cave where we've set up the target. I will do the rest. Nothing can go wrong this time, honey. Nothing can go wrong." He told her about the gun, which Handy had obtained from a fence, someone who sold things that had been stolen from other people. He explained everything to her so she would know what he meant.

"Handy knows everything, honey. Handy will be here, but don't talk about this to Handy. Do you understand, Carmen?" His arm was on her back, fatherly, propelling her back up the path. There were people on the path behind them. He kept his head down, and so did she. "It's dangerous to talk. We are homicidally intimate now, and you mustn't talk about this to anyone else, not even Handy, not even to me, unless I tell you it's okay to talk. Do you understand?"

He was going to kill Peter on Sunday, but on Sunday their driveway was being laid, so it had to wait another week.

HALM: *When Nick came back from California, just by the way he heard about it, that Peter was killed with a gun, he said that he thought it was Dr. Engleman. Then he asked me, uh, he just said why, asked me why I did it.*

MCGARVEY: *What was your response?*

HALM: *I don't know. I felt trapped.*

BURRIS: *Trapped by what? Trapped by Dr. Engleman? Trapped by a marriage to somebody you didn't love?*

HALM: *All of those things.*

MCCRADY: *Were you afraid of Dr. Engleman?*

HALM: *Sometimes I was and sometimes I wasn't. Sometimes he was so cruel and kind. Like I said, when he got mad, it was like I was really afraid he was going to beat me or hit me but it was like it was a secretive, it was like he was angry and I knew it, but I didn't know what he was going to do about being angry.*

Carmen woke on Sunday, September 5, with the feeling that she would never get out of her own life. She was trapped in it and she didn't like it. It was like being sewn into a dress you hate, only a dress would eventually rot away. They had fought again the night before, so Peter was in a bad mood. He rolled toward her, reached his arm across her, and she recoiled. His breath reeked of last night's beer. From across the bed, she nudged him, reminded him he had to get up because they had plans, they had something to do. He told her to fuck off and let him sleep. They were an hour late by the time they got to the caves. This made her very nervous, because this time, when the plan failed, the doctor would blame it on her.

She was in such a hurry to get out of the car, which she parked in the spot exactly where the doctor had parked his, that she grabbed her purse, then had to run back, and throw it in the car because it would have been in her way. "What the fuck is it you want me to see?" he was saying, which made her think of when she had told him she was pregnant. "What the fuck do you have to tell me?" he had said. "What's the big news anyway?" He probably would have let her have the baby, he would have gotten over his little upset and been all right about it, but she went to Planned Parenthood and got rid of the baby anyway. Afterward he told her gently it was probably the right thing to do because they were fixing the house and it was so expensive to fix up a house. But he would have let her keep it if she had cried and said she wanted it badly enough.

"What the fuck is it you want me to see?" he repeated; and she began to take him on the path the doctor had taken her.

She was looking for the doctor everywhere, but she really didn't expect him to be there, didn't believe it would happen until it did. The shot rang out; Peter fell dead at her feet. From that moment, she started sinking. Finally one day she looked out her eyes and saw nothing but black. She told them, her family, how black she felt, and they put her in the hospital. Nick wanted her in the hospital anyway, so the police couldn't get her. He said she was safer there. She didn't care. I just can't wake up another day like this, she told him.

> BURRIS: *Carmen, we want to talk to you about the financial end . . . as far as the result of Peter's death, what monies did you receive and what did you pay out? And what were those arrangements? Can you talk about that?*
>
> HALM: *I don't know the exact amount of the money that came in because Nick, my brother, took care of all that. And I didn't care, I really didn't care. I didn't want the money and at the time my brother was financially in trouble himself. He was backlogged. When he sold my house, uh, I gave him all the money, or he borrowed all the money, and you know, uh, he paid what he owed on his house and . . . Oh, God, I wasn't able really to sign anything or do anything. At the time because Peter's mother was uh, hard up for some money, I gave it to her, because I didn't want any of it. And my mother and sisters who didn't really know anything, they said, "Boy, that's crazy you know. Why give them money." And I couldn't tell them why, but I didn't want the money but, uh, I don't remember that much about it and I really didn't have that much to do with it.*
>
> BURRIS: *What about the payoff, the ten thousand dollars to Dr. Engleman? Did you handle that?*
>
> HALM: *No, Nick paid him.*
>
> MCGARVEY: *Did Nick ever pay you back the money he bor-*

rowed? Did you buy anything in particular with the insurance money? A new car? A condominium?

HALM: *No, I had money all the time for a little while and I would just use it to buy new clothes sometimes. I went grocery shopping. I never did buy any big objects. And most of the money, you know, I didn't want it. Nick borrowed most of the money. Since then, he gives me money on occasions when I don't have money. But I told Nick that I don't want him to pay me back.*

At 3:31 A.M., they told her the interview concerning the death of Peter Halm was finished. She couldn't think about anything then except the time she walked from American to TWA because she had no money, but TWA would take her check and she wanted a ticket home. She had no money in her checking account at the time, but she knew a big check was coming, and the money would probably be there when the check got to the bank. The lady from TWA had smiled so nicely and taken her check, and she thought about the lady now, for no reason.

"We would like to ask you a few more questions." McGarvey said. "Doc has said there are more murders. Is he bullshitting us or do you really think there are?"

McGarvey looked for Buckles when he came out of the interrogation room, but someone told him Buckles had left around two-thirty. Jeez, he didn't blame him. Rubbing his smarting eyes, he briefly considered going home himself, but he wanted to play back some of the testimony again. He waited until Carmen had been escorted back to Nick and the two of them were out of the building. Then he sat back down at the table with McCrady.

"Christ," McCrady said. "I wondered if she was going to get through this for a while." He shook his head. "It's hard to understand, isn't it? I still don't . . ."

McGarvey had listened to the hyperbole of the lawyers, who were already making comparisons to Hitler and Manson, and invoking Jekyl and Hyde, but he wasn't putting out his own theories on what motivated the Doc or Carmen. He and McCrady played back Carmen's voice, fragile and gentle, talking in whispers about plans she never thought would be executed. It was almost as if the Doc had held her in thrall. Even given his advantages in years and education, how did he get her, and not just her, but other women too, under this thumb?

McCrady pushed a button and once again they heard Carmen Miranda Halm say, "I went to work one day, I went to work every day, I would come in with problems, and I'd ask Dr. Engleman because I respected him and I'd look up to him and I admired him, I thought he was educated and I hoped that he could pass some of that on to me, and I guess there were times that he could tell that I was bothered or depressed or, you know, about not getting ahead, you know, about just existing in life, which I think bothered me at times. He suggested that I marry someone and that he would, uh, kill them."

It was almost six A.M. when they left the building together. The *Globe-Democrat* was already on the streets. The headline read, DENTIST IS CHARGED AS KILLER FOR PROFIT. Engleman was photographed in cuffs. The side article was titled, FRIENDS CALL ENGLEMAN 'NICE MAN.' McGarvey read the first few lines of the piece and laughed.

> To the police who have focused on him on and off for 22 years, climaxing in his arrest Sunday on a charge of capital murder, he is an enigma.
> To friends and neighbors, he is a nice, pleasant man, always helpful, often retiring and protective of his privacy.

He folded the paper and tossed it in the front seat of his car. Jeez, he needed a shower and a shave. For the first time in the past twenty-four hours, he thought of Sophie, whose death had led to this point. They would make the bastard on that one too.

PART SIX:

In Pursuit of the Golden Girl

Before she became an obsession, she was just this glittery movement in the distance. We could see her ahead of us, see her just well enough to stay in pursuit. —Don Weber, former Madison County, Illinois, State's Attorney

Friday, March 14, 1980

McGarvey was reading the *Globe-Democrat*. "Dr. Glennon E. Engleman—whose recorded conversations with his former wife, known as Informant X, capped an investigation into his alleged criminal activity—was indicted for capital murder Thursday by a St. Louis County grand jury." He chuckled at the dramatic term, Informant X.

The murder-for-profit headlines the *Globe* had been running were simplistic. They didn't do justice to a complicated story. And how much profit had there really been in Glennon Engleman's murder business? Seven murders had netted him approximately $50,000 in hard cash in addition to the dropping of Sophie's $15,000 lawsuit. If he'd taken his dentistry more seriously, he could have made this and more additional income in a year's time. That he was not a particularly good dentist, however, was becoming obvious too. Following his arrest, former patients who had spent thousands to correct his inferior work—including

Bob Handy's sister Millie—began to come forward. The reason
Sophie Berrera had charged Engleman more than she charged
other dentists was also disclosed. The impressions for bridgework
and false teeth that he'd sent her were so sloppily executed, her
technicians had to spend more time working on them than they
had to on impressions from other dentists.

While McGarvey avidly followed the newspaper coverage on
the Doc, he thought the real story, much of which was already
unfolding in courtrooms, was more interesting. They'd brought
Ruth in for the grand juries, federal and local, and she had done
well on the stand, extremely well. He couldn't be more pleased
with Ruth. Doc and Handy, being held without bond, had been
indicted on federal charges for sixteen counts of mail fraud and
conspiracy in connection with the Peter Halm murder. Doc had
been indicted on two capital murder charges, for the deaths of
Peter Halm and Sophie Berrera. The mail fraud and conspiracy
cases were being tried together. Originally the plan had been to
try Engleman for the two murders together, but they couldn't do
so, however, because Handy was part of the Halm mail fraud
indictment but not charged with Berrera. The Berrera indictment
marked the first time anyone in the office could remember an
indictment in a car bombing, the most difficult crime to solve.
There was a general feeling of cautious optimism.

That, he thought, rearranging the piles of old police reports on
his desk, was the good news. There was also bad news. The
Halm murder had occurred when the death penalty was not in
effect, so Doc couldn't get death on that one. It was doubtful
anyone would ever make Doc on the Bullock or Frey murders
after all these years. George Peach, the city prosecutor, had read
the Bullock file again and, barring the development of new evidence, didn't see any better chance of making the case than
Thomas Eagleton had twenty-two years ago. And Eric Frey had
been cremated without an autopsy. It was hard to go to court
without a body. That left one good shot at the death penalty—for
Sophie's murder—which many familiar with the case thought
Doc should get.

He lit another cigarette and moved the Bullock and Frey material to the side. The Gusewelle murders still intrigued him. He

found the story no less fantastic now than he had when Ruth first told it, when she couldn't remember their names right. Griswell, she had said. Unfortunately, the story seemed even more fantastic to the Illinois authorities, who didn't have the advantage of familiarity with the Doc's history. It was, after all, a twisted saga that had to grow on you.

When he'd taken Nick over there for the first time February 28, the Illinois authorities had listened politely, clearly humoring him, and he couldn't blame them. They had Andre Jones's confession on paper, and it looked good to them. He certainly wasn't able to explain how Jones could know all the details he did about Ron Gusewelle's murder if he hadn't played a part in it. But, Andre Jones notwithstanding, the odds that Engleman had murdered the son looked good to McGarvey now because the crime fit his pattern of insurance fraud and murder—female associate weds blue-collar stiff, she takes out insurance, Doc takes out gun—a pattern broken only by Sophie's murder. Had someone else murdered the parents—or had the Doc and his golden girl really planned this one as a two-part scheme? He picked up the folder and began to read again.

Murders Four and Five: Arthur and Vernita Gusewelle, Thursday, November 3, 1977

"I've been shot, I need an ambulance . . . Hurry . . . hurry . . . my wife's been shot."

"Where are you, sir? I need an address."

"I've been shot . . . my wife . . . hurry, hurry . . ."

"Where are you, sir? Please, sir, I need an address!"

"Two miles south . . . Carpenter Road . . ."

The front of the house was dark, so the ambulance attendants walked around back and entered through the rear door. They walked into a utility room to the kitchen where they saw a white female, later identified as Vernita Gusewelle, fifty-five, lying facedown with her head near the base of the sink. One man turned the body over and checked for vital signs. The blood had already stopped pouring from the three bullet wounds in her head. The powder burns indicated the murderer had placed the gun next to the skull before firing. She was dressed in purple slacks, a multicolored shirt, and slip-on soft black shoes. The watch on her wrist, filled with blood, had stopped at 6:50. The rings on the fingers of each hand were crusted with blood. Finding no signs of life, the attendant covered her body with a sheet. The other attendant found the man, her husband, Arthur Gusewelle, seventy-one, in the adjoining family room. His hair matted in blood, the blood still oozing from a wound in the back of his head, he was sitting in a recliner mumbling, "I've been robbed . . . I can't see . . . I've been shot and robbed . . . My wife has been hurt . . . She needs an ambulance . . . I can't see . . . I need an ambulance." The two attendants picked up the couch cushions that had been tossed on the floor, blocking their path to Gusewelle, who was dressed in bib overalls and a blue work shirt, and put him on a stretcher that they carried out through the sliding glass doors after moving aside the television set thrown in front of the doors. "Two," Gusewelle mumbled. "Two."

A light rain was falling outside the rural Edwardsville, Illinois, farmhouse, and the temperature was a balmy sixty-two degrees, when the first police officer, Joseph Urban, arrived on the scene at 7:35 P.M., less than ten minutes after he'd been told that a man, apparently weak and elderly, had called the fire department for help. The Hamel ambulance service had pulled into the drive minutes ahead of him. When he got out of the car, the driver told Urban they already had the wounded man in the ambulance and were proceeding to the hospital. The woman inside was dead.

"Did he say anything?" Urban asked.

" 'Two,' he kept saying the word 'two' . . . there were probably two men." The doors slammed shut. And Arthur Gusewelle would never say another word, though he would repeat that same word, "two," at Anderson Hospital before he died at 9:27 P.M.

Urban went inside. Packages of frozen foods, commercially prepared peas, french fries, home-prepared vegetables, and pastries were thrown about the floor of the utility room. In the kitchen, blood was splattered on the refrigerator and the wall near the phone, on the floor and the wall of the family room. He walked from room to room. The house had been ransacked, but a woman's handbag, lying in the middle of the hallway, contained seventy dollars in cash. There were no signs of forced entry.

Shortly after eight o'clock, sheriff's deputies notified Richard and Ronald, the two sons of Arthur and Vernita Gusewelle, that their parents had been shot. Richard lived with his wife Donna and their two children in a house directly behind their parent's residence, and Ronald lived with his wife Barbara and her three children from a previous marriage two houses to the north. The sons and their wives drove to Anderson Hospital.

They were told the elder Gusewelle, blind from the moment he was shot, was clinging to life and would be transported shortly to Firmin Desloge Hospital in St. Louis. The sons asked if he was able to say anything. Did Donna Marshall, the emergency room supervisor, know what happened? "He said there were two," Marshall responded. "He was shot by two." One of the wives, the pretty blond one, became quite agitated then. "Is that all he said," she kept repeating, "is that all he said? . . . Will he be able to tell us anything more?"

He died before they could transfer him. When the relatives were given the news, the blond woman sobbed loudly. She kept saying, "I just sent my daughter over there at four-thirty this afternoon to borrow some Tide and they were fine, they were fine, they were fine then, they were fine." Marshall thought it odd she would be so upset, but then, she told another nurse, "You can't ever tell how people will handle a shock, can you?"

The investigation briefly included the FBI because the murders were similar to those committed by an organized burglary team operating throughout the bistate area. Certainly no one could discover a connection between the Gusewelles, a hardworking farm couple, and the mob, but the method of killing, execution style, by shooting at close range into the head also smacked of the Mafia. The Gusewelles were decent people who worked hard all their lives, believed in saving and not aiming too high. "He's getting above himself," was the reproving remark they made about people who spent all they earned and then some. Who *would* murder people like that? The bullets had been fired from the same .22 caliber gun—which was about all the law enforcement agencies knew after months of investigation. The

Gusewelle estate, valued at over half a million dollars, was tied up in probate for a year and then was divided between the two sons.

McGarvey closed the folder. It was tempting to see the hand of the Doc in this one. The .22 caliber bullets, the faked home invasion to create a diversion, the use of a companion, the suddenly hysterical blond daughter-in-law all pointed in his direction. On the other hand, nothing concrete had connected him to this crime: no fingerprints, witnesses, *obvious* motive. It was a lot cleaner than his last murder, Sophie's. Maybe it was too clean to be Doc's. Maybe he had claimed it as his own while bragging to Nick and Ruth because he wished it were his. Doc, who held the Mafia in high regard, would have liked to be a Mafia hit man. He flattered himself that he *could* have been. Maybe the Gusewelle murders represented a fantasy of his.

The only way to get him on this one was to turn someone, and Barbara was a better possibility than Handy. Grinning, McGarvey picked up a transcript of Nick's last interview. Nick was in their pocket now; he wasn't particularly comfortable with the position, but he understood it. Nick might open the door to Barbara. She had confided in him in the past and might again. Word of his deal hadn't leaked, so it was worth a shot. Nick might be able to play on the fear Doc's arrest must have engendered in her and convince her the game was over for all of them. He didn't expect much, but it was worth a shot. Meanwhile, the newspapers were sniffing around too. Word of the agency's interest in the Gusewelle murders had leaked out. They might also play into his hands.

Sunday, March 16, 1980

> *Dr. Glennon E. Engleman, the south St. Louis dentist indicted Friday on capital murder charges in the bombing death of Sophie Marie Berrera, is a suspect in the unsolved killings of an elderly couple in Madison County in 1977 and their 33-year-old son 17 months later . . . One source close to the Madison County case said Engleman bragged about it as 'his biggest project.' "—*
> St. Louis Post-Dispatch, Sunday, March 16, 1980

"Okay, Nick, we just want to see what we can accomplish here with a phone call," McGarvey said. They were sitting at a table in the back of Stagger Inn, an Edwardsville bar, with some of the local cops. "If you can get her to talk to you at all, great . . . don't push it by asking her tough questions right away. We'd like to get her to agree to a meeting with you. We just want to see where you stand with her, if there's a possibility she'll trust you enough to say something incriminating."

The phone call had been McGarvey's idea, Nick supposed. Still, he didn't think it would lead anywhere. Nor did he think McGarvey expected it to. He sighed. Christ, why would she meet with him now? She'd have to be crazy.

He repeated what he had said when the call was proposed. "I think Barb is too savvy to say anything to me on the phone. And I doubt if she'll see me . . ."

"Well, you can try, Nick, all you can do is try . . ."

If they thought Barb could be manipulated the way he and Ruth and Carmen had been, they were probably wrong. The circumstances were different. She was in the catbird seat now—or surely thought she was. He didn't think she had ever feared Doc the way they did. By finding Ron Gusewelle, who represented his big score, she'd put herself in so solid with Doc she seemed unshakable. And there was the sex too. Doc and Handy were in jail, and she had to know they weren't getting out to hurt her—or weren't about to confess to three more murders while they were awaiting trial either. Some moron had confessed to murdering Ron, so she was clear on that charge. Why would she talk to him, or anyone, now? All she had to do was count the cash. She wasn't like Carmen either; she wouldn't have any qualms about the money, no conscience to tear her apart. If they thought she was going to be like the rest of them, eager to spill her guts as soon as they took her in their arms, they were wrong. She was different. The golden girl, Doc called her. Well, he was right about this one. Her *luck* was golden.

After telling the Madison County authorities all he could remember about the Gusewelle murders, as he had been informed about them by Doc and Handy, he was supposed to pick up the phone and call Barbara. The idea made him nervous. "Try to get her to talk. Don't worry about it," McGarvey said, "we're just sounding her out through you. If she sounds tentative, or better yet, positive, we'll develop the lead further." He didn't think he could get her to talk and he hoped the failure to do so wouldn't cause him any problems.

MCGARVEY: *When did you become aware of Engleman, Handy, and Barbara Gusewelle's involvement in these murders?*
MIRANDA: *Approximately a couple years ago. I met Barb when she was living in an apartment which was the upstairs portion of Glen's mother's house, in '60 or '61. He had an affair with her. She married a dentist in St. Louis, someone Glen knew. After she married and had three kids, I lost touch with what she was doing. Then she got divorced, and Glen said he was supporting her, giving her four hundred dollars a month and sometimes more and free dental care because her ex wasn't giving her enough child support. He bragged about having sexual relations with her too. But he said helping her financially would pay off because she was going to be his golden girl. Then he told me she had married Ron Gusewelle and discovered his parents had money. He told me he and Handy had a two-part plan: They would kill her parents and then they would kill her husband. He expected to get, ultimately, fifty thousand dollars for this.*

Murder 6: Ron Gusewelle, Saturday, March 31, 1979

Ronald Allen Gusewelle, age thirty-three, spent the last morning of his life working on a secondhand Chevy he'd bought for his stepdaughter, Jamie Boyle. As he worked on the silver '72 Camaro, sweat mixing with grease, bathing his face, hands, and arms in the familiar slick, his wife Barbara was in the kitchen fixing a sack lunch for him to take to work on the evening shift at Amoco Oil Refinery in nearby Wood River, Illinois. His life—except for the unsolved murder of his parents seventeen months ago—was as ordinary as his brown-haired, bespectacled countenance promised it would be.

People who knew him would have expected Ronald Gusewelle to remove his greasy shoes and step lightly on stocking feet over the carpet his wife kept vacuumed because he was well-known as a "good boy." In that quietly prosperous rural area northeast of Edwardsville, men are divided into two categories: those the locals watched grow up, who are either good or bad, and those who came from somewhere else, outsiders. Most of the outsiders are connected to Southern Illinois University at Edwardsville and are liked, admired, but never considered part of the community. An unassuming man often described as "kind of to himself," Gusewelle was as much a part of the community as the road signs warning of curves, signs the locals knew as well as the lines of their palms. He did what he was expected to do: worked without complaining, brought his paycheck home, tinkered with engines, drank an occasional beer.

His wife, however, beautiful blond Barbara Varney Boyle Gusewelle, looked a little out of place in rural Edwardsville living next to women like Richard's wife, Donna, whose ample round face framed in brown hair frizzed in a cheap beauty-shop perm was *the* look of an area where women spent far less than they could afford to spend on beauty. A stranger seeing Barbara, with softly styled golden curls and long polished nails, a curvaceous body still attractive though she'd added weight in the marriage, would probably wonder why she was carefully folding brown paper sacks containing lunches. Even for working in the kitchen she dressed in matching or coordinated clothes. A pair of the high-heeled ankle-strapped shoes she loved were waiting by the door. In Edwardsville, women like that marry lawyers with a penchant for flashy blondes.

Ron had met her at a Denny's restaurant, renewed the acquaintance later in a laundromat, and married her May 28, 1976, six weeks after she first batted her blue eyes at him over Styrofoam cups of machine coffee and their separate piles of dirty clothes. He told people how important clean clothes were to her, especially towels, big and fluffy towels.

If he had unhappy thoughts during the last hours he spent at home on March 31, they were probably thoughts of his parents. His friends would say he and Barbara quarreled frequently following his parents' murders. Her friends would say she worried about him after those murders because he often stood outside staring in the distance toward the family home. And they insisted she was happy in her modest ranch house on Carpenter Road, where she enjoyed decorating and cooking for Ron and her three children from her previous marriage. They could look back at Barbara Boyle, who tended her babies and bowled with her girlfriends, and see the continuation of a line—interrupted by divorce—in her life with Gusewelle. The two went grocery shopping together at National Food Store and planted trees in the yard.

"Well, she called him 'Ronnie' after all," her mother would tell a reporter for the *Edwardsville Intelligencer*, as if that made it clear she could not possibly have meant him any harm. And she probably called him "Ronnie" the last time she told him good-bye.

He told Barbara he would drive the Camaro to work because he "needed to check it out," to be sure it was safe for Jamie to drive. Besides, Jamie said it didn't get good mileage, so he was keeping careful track of the mileage to determine what the problem was. When he left home, a little before two in the afternoon, dressed in Levi's and layered shirts, plaid and corduroy, he patted his wife on the ass by way of good-bye. He had promised her a car, a candy-red Corvette, if she would lose some of the weight she'd gained since marriage, and the pat on the ass was his way of reminding her about the deal. He didn't like to nag her, but he surely must have been disappointed to think she might run to fat exactly as the other rural wives had done.

Leaving Carpenter Road for Route 140 in Bethalto, he headed west toward Route 111 and the sprawl of tidy, low brick buildings, flanked in the distance by huge white receptacles, which was the refinery. Richard Baum, the shift foreman that day, said Gusewelle arrived around two-thirty so he could begin work before three, abiding by the early relief policy. He took his place at the bank of gauges, windows, and controls. The work was boring and dull, but Ron Gusewelle didn't mind it.

No one remembers anything significant happening inside the refinery building until Gusewelle received a phone call from outside around nine-thirty. He spoke briefly with his back to the room. Kenneth Davis, the operator who worked beside him, heard him say, "Thanks for the information," before he hung up.

He didn't appear to be upset by the call, but he told Davis, "I'll have to skip the beer tonight. We'll do it another time, okay?"

At ten-thirty, Gusewelle was relieved from his shift. He drove to the shower house close to the main gate, took a shower, and walked back to the Camaro. It was 10:55. Davis, whose car was parked next to his, was a few minutes behind him. He clearly saw the right-turn signal light flashing on the Camaro, then saw Gusewelle make a right-hand turn back toward Route 111. A left turn would have led him over the railroad tracks to Route 3. Going south on 3, he would have headed through Granite City toward East St. Louis. He could have gone all the way through southern Illinois on this route if he had turned left, but Davis would later swear in court that he didn't.

When he pulled into his driveway, the crunch of the tires on gravel alerted two men waiting inside the garage. Ron Gusewelle got out of his car, raised the garage door, and was shot in the chest, then struck with a hammer as he fell. When the body was shoved into the backseat of the Camaro, one of the legs was also broken. The Camaro was driven to and abandoned on the parking lot of Coleman's Plaza, a former Holiday Inn, on Seventh and Broadway, the downtown hooker district of East St. Louis, Illinois, perhaps the darkest city in the nation after the sun goes down. In this city, where most of the streetlights aren't functioning, unemployment is seventy-five percent and neon signs flashing LIQUOR over grated windows dominate the retail scene, you can throw a body down in front of twenty people in daylight and no one will see you do it.

During the five days in which Ron Gusewelle's body lay in the silver Camaro on the parking lot of Coleman's Plaza awaiting discovery, Barbara's neighbors brought consolation and dinners on Chinet plates covered first with plastic wrap, then aluminum foil. The members of Eden Church in Bethalto conducted a prayer service for the family. Barbara attended with red and swollen eyes.

On Wednesday evening, April 4, Samuel Jamison, the maintenance manager at Coleman's Plaza, decided to look inside the silver Camaro that had been parked there for days. He saw the body slumped over and covered with towels and a garbage bag, and called the police. By the time an officer responded, a crowd had gathered. The officer used a wire coat hanger to unlock the door. The stench of rotting flesh came out the way a blast of August heat hits one in the face upon leaving an air-conditioned building, and the crowd moved back.

Clad in blue jeans, a red, yellow, and green plaid shirt, and a light tan corduroy overshirt, the body, swollen to the point of straining its clothing, was curled in an embryo position, with the left leg broken. There was a bullet wound in the chest. The head was largely caved in, and an X-shaped wound on the left side was visible. A pack of Winstons, a Bic lighter, $3.19 in two ones and change, and a packet of Trojan brand prophylactics were removed from the pockets. The unofficial police theory was that Gusewelle had gone to East St. Louis in search of some "black pussy" and gotten himself killed. One crime-lab technician commented that the towels used to wrap the head didn't look like they'd come from a hooker's den. They were large, fluffy, and apparently treated with fabric softener. So what? another tech said. Can't hookers use fabric softener too?

The news of a third murder in the family terrorized the rural community. Mrs. Chester Buchta, Barbara's neighbor, told the *Edwardsville Intelligencer,* "Well, I'm just stunned. I took dinner to Barbara just last night, fried chicken, mashed potatoes, and canned corn, and she couldn't eat a bit of it; and she said she thought maybe Ronnie had taken a ride. She kept thinking he'd be coming back, poor thing. And we'd had that beautiful prayer service at Eden Church for the family. Who could believe this would happen again? The first time we thought it was a freak, a mistake. I don't even know what's normal anymore."

Two or three days after the body was found, Barbara consented to a search of the house and, in fact, almost insisted the police search Ron's dresser drawer. When they found a packet of Trojans, she tearfully told them she didn't know why he needed rubbers, since she'd had a tubal ligation years ago. They also found trash bags, the same brand of trash bags that had covered Ron's body. But everybody used trash bags. Then in October, Andre Jones, a convicted killer sentenced to death, confessed to murdering the Gusewelles.

MCGARVEY: *Did Dr. Engleman tell you that he and Handy
had in fact committed the murders?*

MIRANDA: *Yes. I remember a conversation in May of '78 in
which he told me that several phases of their plan with the golden
girl had happened: that she had married the wealthy man and they
had killed his parents. Then after the murder of Ron Gusewelle he
told me it was done. I remember a specific conversation after
Andre Jones confessed. Glen said, "We lucked out on that deal; the
heat's been diverted from Barb." He was especially proud of this
whole plan. He liked to say he planned his crimes from the witness
stand back; and in this scheme, he thought he'd planned very well.*

Nick took a swallow of his Coke and looked around the Edwardsville bar. He liked the old oak back bar, the exposed brick
walls, but the clientele looked like country boys. He felt he'd
helped the cops all he could with the Gusewelle murders. He'd
had no involvement in the crimes. His knowledge was limited to a
series of conversations, each of which had been duly reported and
recorded. What more could he do? McGarvey had been taking
him over to Edwardsville several times a week for the past three
weeks. He'd been sent to knock on Barbara's door like a school
kid selling candy, and she never answered, but he always scooted
back down the drive halfway expecting someone to shoot his ass.
So far the newspapers didn't know or hadn't reported his cooperation with the police, and McGarvey thought he would be able to
get Barbara to confide in him by telling her things were falling
apart and he was scared. Fat chance. Barbara wasn't very smart,
but the odds were she had some guy looking after her interests
now, as she always did. He was nervous about this operation
because he knew he wasn't going to be able to pull it off.

"Nick, let's try it now." McGarvey rose, signaling him to follow. They walked back to the pay phone temporarily rigged with
a recording device for his call.

He liked working with McGarvey and McCrady, but this
straight arrow from Madison County watching him now was another matter! These guys clearly didn't buy the story about Doc.
It was okay with him if they didn't; McGarvey was doing them a
favor, and if they preferred not to take a better look at their

confessed criminal so they could take advantage of the favor, okay. He picked up the phone, punched in Barbara's number, and hoped she would finally answer and tell him to go to hell so he could be off the hook. A woman answered; he thought it was Barbara, but he wasn't sure. She sounded loaded. It could have been her daughter.

"Barbara please."

"Who is this?"

"This is a friend of hers calling . . . and I gotta talk to her."

"Hello," a man's voice said.

"Yeah . . . I'm calling for Barbara Varney, please."

"This is her attorney. Who's calling please?"

"I'm sorry . . . Who is this?"

"Her attorney . . . who's calling please?"

"Well, this is just a friend of hers."

"What is your name, sir?"

"I'd rather tell her if you don't mind . . ."

"I'd appreciate it, sir, if you didn't call her anymore. Thank you."

Nick looked at McGarvey, who said, "We were looking for a reaction, Nick, that's all, so we got it."

They went back to the table and played the little tape for the others, who laughed when they heard it. Apparently he'd just caught her attorney at his client's house enhancing—in their minds at least—the persistent rumors of an affair between the two. Well, he'd made the day for these guys, hadn't he? He wondered if it had occurred to McGarvey yet they couldn't touch Barbara now, no way. She had just told them the one thing they hadn't known: She wasn't going to be intimidated into talking because she was in the protective care of some guy.

"Well, that pretty much does that for now," McGarvey said as they were driving back to St. Louis. "It doesn't look like anything will happen there very soon."

"She never will talk," he said, relieved it was over and he apparently wasn't being blamed for the failure. "Barb may not be the smartest thing in the world, but she's good at stonewalling."

PART SEVEN:
The Trials

. . . whereas in the beginning, the difficulty had been to throw off the body of Jekyll, it had of late gradually but decidedly transferred itself to the other side. All things therefore seemed to point to this; that I was slowly losing hold of my original and better self, and becoming slowly incorporated with my second and worse.—from *Dr. Jekyll and Mr. Hyde* by Robert Louis Stevenson

St. Paul, Minnesota, Monday, August 4, 1980

Frederick "Rick" Buckles had never put in more hours preparing to try a case, and he was noted for exhaustive preparatory work. He was regarded as one of the government's best at anticipating possible defense strategies. Considering the publicity the Engleman case had generated, losing in court would have been an embarrassment to the agency. Yet Buckles appeared confident and self-assured making his opening statement for the prosecution, a statement that symbolically, at least, opened the whole series of trials.

The federal and local prosecutors had agreed the mail fraud and conspiracy trials of Engleman and Handy in the murder of Peter Halm should precede the murder trial for several reasons. The Justice Department preferred having first trial rights before granting immunity to Ruth and the Mirandas, and the federal immunity was necessary to guarantee the witnesses they absolutely wouldn't be prosecuted later by local authorities—and to qualify Ruth for the Witness Protection Program. Also, case law in the area of double jeopardy was gray enough to make Kingsland's superiors in Washington concerned about the possibility of Doc getting out of the federal charges on double jeopardy if the state's case went first. And finally, the first case had to be solid. If the defense created any loopholes or discredited any witness, those problems would affect the future trials. The federal government had the manpower and money to put behind such a trial preparation, but St. Louis county or city certainly did not.

Thus the work of preparing the first case, which would be the basis for the other cases, fell to Buckles. Gordon Ankney, who was set to try the Halm murder in St. Louis County for Westfall, would be watching much of this trial. In spite of the pressure on Buckles, he seemed more concerned about how Carmen Halm would hold up than he was about his own performance. In the five months they'd been working with her, Buckles and Ankney had come to regard her as another of the Doc's victims. "She's a pitiful thing," Buckles had recently confided, his original hard line regarding Carmen forgotten. He thought the possibility of her breaking down during the trial was a good one.

"The prosecution will show how Dr. Glennon Engleman masterminded a plot which included marrying off Carmen Miranda, a woman he had known since she was a child, to Peter Halm, who would be killed for his life-insurance benefits. He coached Carmen Miranda on what type of man to marry and whom not to marry," Buckles said, keeping his voice at an even pitch as he spoke to the jury, letting the words carry their own heavy weight. "He received ten thousand dollars from Carmen and her brother Nicholas Miranda, and he used most of that money to settle a six-thousand-nine-hundred-dollar tax dispute with the federal government."

Buckles had the jury's attention from the start. How often does a murderer commit the crime to pay his taxes? The trial had been moved to Minnesota because of the pretrial publicity in St. Louis, so these people were new to the story, and the shock and disbelief was already registering on their faces. Observing their reaction,

Doc leaned toward his attorney, Dick Dempsey, and whispered a comment. His cool, superior demeanor hadn't been changed by five months of sitting in the St. Louis County jail. Often he seemed to be enjoying himself. When he had listened to the tapes, for example, he had yanked off his earphones and gleefully cried, "Well, that's the end of your case, gentleman!" at a point in a conversation with Ruth where he had denied killing people. He still maintained his innocence and wouldn't allow Dempsey to use the insanity plea. He steadfastly refused to see a psychiatrist—which delighted the prosecutors and hamstrung Dempsey.

"We have traced the murder weapon from a burglary in Steelville, Missouri, to an intermediary who sold it for three hundred dollars to Bob Handy, who turned it over to Engleman," Buckles said. The "intermediary," Kenneth Cope, was McCrady's find, which McGarvey considered one of the best pieces of police work he'd ever seen.

After Buckles had outlined the prosecution's case, he returned to Carmen. She would be the most important witness for the prosecution. They had tried to prepare her for the attempt the defense would surely make to discredit her as a murderess herself, but he knew nothing could really prepare her for the emotional battering she was about to endure.

"She had known Engleman all her life, cleaning his office and baby-sitting for him when he went to the Grand Canyon," Buckles said. "She quit school after the ninth grade and began working for Engleman, a man she trusted and respected, as a dental assistant. This man she trusted told her she would be poor all her life if she didn't let him help her. And how would he help her? He told her, 'You can marry somebody and I'll kill him.' He instructed her to stay away from professional people and law-enforcement people and look for someone who worked for a big company."

Frequently the members of the jury would look past Buckles at the apparently mild-mannered dentist in the old blue suit. He could see their eyebrows knitting in consternation as they attempted to relate Buckles's words to that man. Glennon Engleman looked like a *dentist*. He looked exactly like the kindly neighborhood dentist his lawyer would paint him to be.

Tuesday, August 5, 1980

Under federal rules, witnesses are not allowed in the courtroom during the trial outside of their own testimony. The only exception is the case agent, who sits with the U.S. Attorney and assists him, when needed, in prosecuting. Carmen, in spite of the importance of her role, read the other testimony in the paper like every other interested observer. After the first day she read that the father of the little family at the caves had said he gave her the Mickey Mouse pillowcase and told her to put it on Peter's wound, but when the ambulance came she was standing there, the pillowcase in her hand. She didn't remember that. And the ambulance driver had said he'd tried to clean the sand from Peter's mouth to help him breathe before he knew he was dead. She didn't remember that either.

Her testimony began after lunch on the second day of the trial.

Do you see Glennon Engleman in the courtroom today?

She hadn't wanted to look at him, but she had to do so now.

Yes, I do.
Would you point to where he's sitting and describe to me the clothing he has on?
He's sitting right there and he has on a blue suit with stripes.

She focused on the suit, avoiding his eyes at first, then quickly looking up to meet them. He was watching her with frank, kindly interest, the way he had often looked at her when she came to him with her problems. He had looked like that when he told her she would be poor all her life if they didn't do something to change it.

Yes, he was her employer. She had begun cleaning his house when she was nine, and she'd worked in the concession stand at the drag strip when she was ten. And, yes, she was about fifteen or sixteen when she met Peter Joseph Halm, Jr. She knew where Mr. Buckles was taking her, down the path again to the place where Peter was killed. He had taken her as far as "Yes, he told me to marry someone and he would kill them," before court was adjourned for the day.

On Wednesday she picked up her story in the same flat voice. This time when she began to speak she looked directly at the doctor, and he returned her gaze intensely. She was wearing a short-sleeved two-piece dress in beige, and a large watchband encircled her tiny wrist. An artist was sketching her; she was aware of his hand moving quickly over a pad of paper and wanted to turn away from him and hide, the way people did when they were photographed being arrested, but she didn't.

> BUCKLES: *After Dr. Engleman made that suggestion to you, did you ever ask him any questions about that plan or how it would work?*
>
> HALM: *Yes, I did. I asked him how it would be done. And he said it would just be several insurance policies taken out on Peter.*
>
> BUCKLES: *What else did he tell you about this plan?*
>
> HALM: *Well, he told me it could be done because he had done it before. He told me that he had killed Eric Frey, and he and Sandy had taken insurance out on Eric.*

Buckles had explained to her the importance of bringing up Eric Frey. It was to set a precedent for what Doc had done to her in the jurors' minds and make them understand he had done it before Peter and would do it again, whereas she hadn't and wouldn't. It was so they wouldn't mind as much about her deal. When she said she had known Eric Frey and later she had baby-sat for the doctor and Sandy, she looked at Glen again. He still looked at her in the kindly way, but his expression was touched with sadness now. She searched his face, looking for anger, but it wasn't there, not yet. She was afraid, though she knew he couldn't hurt her, couldn't touch her in the courtroom. So why was she afraid?

> BUCKLES: *Do you recall the day you were married?*
>
> HALM: *October the thirty-first, 1975.*
>
> BUCKLES: *Keep your voice up please. We could not hear your answer.*
>
> HALM: *October the thirty-first, 1975, yes.*

The judge reminded her there was no loudspeaker system in the court, and she would have to speak up so the jurors particularly could hear. She tried again. "October the thirty-first, yes." And his eyes were still on her, looking at her, saying, Carmen, honey, why do you want to do this to me? Her answers came slower now. She was aware of Mr. Buckles standing in front of her, willing her to speak. He was pulling her down the path. Yes, she knew where Peter worked and that he had just bought a house. She put her head down on her arms for a few minutes, then yes, she knew about the company benefits, the insurance he had.

> BUCKLES: *After you told Dr. Engleman all those things about Peter, what did he say? What did Dr. Engleman say?*
> HALM: *He said that Peter sounded good.*
> BUCKLES: *Peter sounded good for what?*
> HALM: *To kill.*

Her last answer took so long someone in the back of the courtroom fell asleep, and the judge banged his gavel hard. Everyone jumped; everyone jumped but Carmen and the doctor. He held her eyes while the judge lectured the sleeper. And finally she answered the question: *To kill.* To kill. She heard the judge asking Mr. Buckles why it took her so long to answer, was she sedated or stimulated, was someone signaling her? His patience was wearing thin. After Mr. Dempsey finished cross-examining her, she looked at the doctor. There were tears running down his cheeks.

Friday, August 8, 1980

> BUCKLES: *Mr. Miranda, how would you describe your financial condition in the summer and fall of 1976?*
> MIRANDA: *Not too good.*
> BUCKLES: *Wouldn't desperate be a better word?*
> MIRANDA: *It would be a good word.*

Watching Nick on the stand, McGarvey was reminded of how far they'd come since the night in February they'd negotiated the deal. They had worked with Nick for five months to get him ready for this testimony. They'd told him they had to have every dirty little detail on all the shit he'd ever pulled, all the people he'd screwed throughout his life—because the defense would have a whole line of people waiting to tell exactly how Nick Miranda had screwed them. No recovering alcoholic in the confessional stages had ever so thoroughly spilled the reeking contents of his gut. They felt they knew every dirty secret Nick had when he came to St. Paul to testify. And they liked him anyway.

Then he'd showed up with an order to produce his income-tax returns from the defense. With the shit-eating grin McGarvey had seen numerous times before, he said, "I ain't got any. What should I do?" They told him, "Some things, Nick, you just have to eat"; and Nick was up there on the stand, eating it and sweating buckets. Dempsey knew he hadn't paid his taxes and also knew how much jurors hated people who made a lot of money and didn't pay any taxes. The only thing Nick feared as much as going to jail was the I.R.S. "They're relentless," he said. Jeez, McGarvey thought, it wasn't easy to admit you'd taken nearly $75,000 in ill-gotten insurance money and blown it in less than a year, largely on a Mercedes-Benz and an unsuccessful theatrical business—but to admit you'd done it *and* hadn't paid taxes . . .

Dempsey might have succeeded in making him look like an opportunist, a petty con man, and a tax dodger, but he couldn't shake his testimony about Peter Halm's murder. Nick Miranda told the jury that Engleman's only expressed regret had been anger at himself for shooting Halm in St. Louis County instead of Franklin County—where Eric Frey's murder had not even been investigated. With emotion in his voice, he described the murder of Eric Frey, which had convinced him of the Doc's violent capabilities, then his role in the financial arrangements following Halm's murder. As he detailed the Doc's phone calls, badgering him to collect the money, McGarvey watched the jury. They seemed to believe him by the end of the story, where he described the $10,000 payoff in hundred-dollar bills, which took place in a church parking lot in Kirkwood. Maybe they figured no one would eat as much shit as Nick had if he wasn't caught between the feds on one hand and a murderer on the other.

Nick had sweat so much during his testimony that his tan suit was soaking wet. When he stood to leave the witness box, his pants and his coat were stuck in the crack of his ass. He looked straight ahead as he walked out the door. McGarvey thought it was a goddamn good thing he'd looked straight ahead and not at him or McCrady or they would have howled.

Ruth, who followed Nick, carefully avoided Doc's gaze. She called his attorney "Mr. Dempsey" in a severe tone of voice that discouraged even him from going too far. McGarvey thought Dempsey was afraid of her. His full silver beard wagged almost respectfully when he questioned her. McGarvey's original estimation of Ruth's intelligence was constantly being upgraded. She was smart and she was tough. But Jack Carter, who followed Ruth, McGarvey thought, was the nail in the coffin. No one could mistake the genuine sorrow in his voice as he recounted the Frey murder, important to the prosecution because it clearly set the precedent for murdering Halm, convincing the jury the Doc meant to kill.

He had watched Doc carefully while Ruth testified, and he was disappointed to see so little reaction on the man's face. Doc was still treating this as a game he expected to win. When the defense did win a concession, as they had in Judge Hungate's refusal to let jurors have the typed transcripts of the tapes, he'd jeered, "Too bad, boys," and laughed in a cawing fashion, flapping his arms up and down like some berserk bird. He seemed to be enjoying himself.

Tuesday, August 12, 1980

Doc was confident he made a good appearance in his blue pinstripe suit. Surely the jurors saw him sitting there, relaxed and confident, and wondered if the garbled tapes they'd listened to on Saturday had really said what they thought after all. People wanted things to be like they appeared to be. Upon taking the oath, he smiled at Melody and Kim sitting in the courtroom, then looked directly into Dick Dempsey's eyes, the way an honest man would face a firing squad he meant to disarm. He would explain himself in such a way as to nail Ruth, that goddamn greedy bitch, to the wall—and embarrass her lousy federal pimp

APPOINTMENT FOR MURDER / 201

McGarvey in the process. The feds had played fair enough until it came to bugging the bedroom, invading a man's sanctum sanctorum . . . They had gone too far with that one, too far then. Yes, he was confident. He would beat them. They thought they were smart, but he would beat them.

> DEMPSEY: *Would you tell the jury how long you have known the Miranda family?*
>
> ENGLEMAN: *Like my sister said, from infancy. Mrs. Miranda is a Mexican national; so was Nick's father. Nick is a Mexican national. My mother was a Texan. She grew up in the Rio Grande Valley of Texas. She was very familiar with Mexicans. She spoke Spanish and so Mrs. Miranda—they adopted her; we adopted them. And shortly after the last child—she had nine children—the last child was born, Mr. Miranda died.*
>
> DEMPSEY: *Doctor, how long have you known Carmen?*
>
> ENGLEMAN: *Carmen was placed in my arms when she was an infant . . .*

He told them the Miranda children had all passed through his home as house domestics. He thought he handled the explanation well, speaking more fully than the law required, educating them about certain points because this was his way. The Mirandas were a bunch of high-school dropouts, but he'd helped them in every way he could. Why, he would pile a lot of them in his car and take them out to the lake for picnics. He trained two of Carmen's sisters before her as dental assistants, and she had worked out very well too. She caught on readily, and blood didn't nauseate her. Yes, he noted the effect of the revelation on the jury. Blood didn't bother her at all.

"She regretted she quit high school and she welcomed the opportunity to improve herself as a dental assistant and get away from slinging hash, as she termed it. Carmen definitely reached a point in life where she wanted to better herself. That, basically, is it."

As to Nick, "He would be the last human being ever that I would ever tell anything to if I was in the commission of a crime."

Yes, he owned an extensive collection of guns and was an expert shot, but he hadn't shot Peter Halm. His sister, he told them, had a nineteen-room mansion with a swimming pool, seven bathrooms. Her daughter was getting married and so he was busy repairing leaky faucets in those seven bathrooms the day Peter was killed. And after he had dispatched that little story nicely, educating them about the fact there were only three covered bridges in Missouri and explaining the geology of the limestone caves, he proceeded to demolish Ruth. The crux of the problem, he said, was money and the custody of their son. They were divorced, but they still slept together, shacked up, common-law, whatever you want to call it. He still had the key to the condo. They were divorced in name only; they still operated as a family. She had stolen his valuable coin collection, and now she wanted to steal his son too. He had made up this wild crazy story about killing people after Sophie Berrera's death to scare her . . . to intimidate her into returning the coins and surrendering David.

DEMPSEY: *Did she ever make any suggestion to you as to how you might get your money back?*

ENGLEMAN: *Flat-out blackmail. Ruth, since our divorce and the circumstances leading up to it, Ruth had an abnormal, absolute neurotic possession of our son. And David is a very beautiful and intelligent boy. And Ruth had many, many psychological hang-ups about what the conduct of a father and son should be. You don't wrestle with a boy when he gets to be a certain age because that tends to make him a homosexual. Well, I'm sorry. You do wrestle with a boy. That keeps him from being a homosexual, and so forth. So we had a go at that.*

David, he had a bladder operation, and Ruth, she went to the hospital like any mother would go. She crawled in bed with David—in the hospital bed—the night before the operation. There was a trundle bed provided to her. She never used that; she crawled in the actual bed. The surgery was performed the next day. Ruthie proceeded to spend that night on her elbow with David and all these tubes and a ruckus with the nurses in the hospital.

David would come in and he would want something from the icebox, hot and sweat[y]. "Give me kisses." And David would have to come up with a hot, sweaty kiss in order to get something out of the icebox.

Ruth was a good mother, but she was flawed in that respect.

DEMPSEY: *What sort of proposition, if any, did she make to you, Doctor, with reference to David and the money?*

ENGLEMAN: *She wanted to go to Memphis. If I would give permanent custody of David to her, I could have the money—all of it—back.*

DEMPSEY: *Now, I ask you, Doctor, whether sometime in the winter of '79, first part of '80, there was another development in the relationship between you and your former wife?*

ENGLEMAN: *Well, after the money showed up missing, our relationship deteriorated. There is no question about that. We argued; I wanted the money back. There was no way I could get the money back other than give up David; and I wouldn't give up David. Ruth started. It degenerated. That was all there was to it. Ruthie proceeded to tell me that I had had affairs with some of my patients and we never really had any reason to stay together, and so forth. I denied these things. They were untrue.*

DEMPSEY: *Did she ever discuss you having an affair with Carmen Miranda?*

ENGLEMAN: *Yes, she definitely did.*

DEMPSEY: *Did she ever make any accusations to you, Doctor, about being involved somehow in the death of Peter Halm?*

ENGLEMAN: *Ruth was always suspicious of the circumstances under which Carmen's husband died. And when she found out that Carmen had inherited some money, she often wondered about Nick having a hand in it. She even went so far as to ask me if I had anything to do with that hanky-panky.*

DEMPSEY: *What was your reaction to that?*

ENGLEMAN: *No, I simply told her, "No, come on, babe."*

DEMPSEY: *Did you ever, thereafter, however, change that statement to her?*

ENGLEMAN: *Yes. I played a smarty. I just plain tried to scare old Ruthie into thinking that I'd had something to do with Peter's homicide.*

He looked straight at the jury when he said this. And he was sure they believed him. Under cross-examination by Buckles he admitted the coin collection, which he valued at $200,000, hadn't been appraised. You have something appraised, you invite theft, he said. Ladies and gentleman of the jury, his expression seemed to say, you know about crime in America, I know you do.

Thursday, August 14, 1980

The jury had been out for nearly twelve hours, and now they were filing back in. Twelve hours was longer than McGarvey thought it should have taken, and the delay had caused Buckles some concern. While they were deliberating, the jurors had asked to hear the Valentine's Day tape again. Hungate had refused, surprising all of them. But Hungate, outspoken against wiretapping, had not been happy with those tapes all along.

They'd been lucky to get testimony about the Frey murder admitted. According to federal law, evidence of previous crimes could be introduced only under limited circumstances. The previous crime had to be exact or very similar in nature—no problem for them—but committed during roughly the same time period as the one for which the defendant was being tried. The Frey murder was thirteen years prior to the Halm murder, but Buckles got it admitted by arguing that the special nature of the crime and the time lag in collecting insurance monies justified an exception. He had set new case law in the process.

McGarvey looked at the faces of the jurors searching for clues as they took their seats. Buckles's closing argument the day before had been a convincing and powerful summation of the facts. The Doc, in keeping with his tendency to chatter, had told the prosecutor during a break that he finally understood the meaning of the phrase "make a federal case out of it."

"You've worked so hard on this," he taunted, "I almost hate to see you boys lose."

Dempsey and Marty Hadican, Handy's attorney, had, of course, attacked Carmen and Nick. Hadican had termed Carmen "a queen of darkness, princess of evil," and Nick, "a fast-buck artist, Mr. Negotiator. He epitomizes self-interest, greed, love of one's self to the hilt." Dempsey insisted Carmen had killed her own husband because Peter beat her and she was in love with another man. Both lawyers attacked Ruth, Hadican by insinuating she'd been sexually rejected by Handy, and Dempsey by insisting she was motivated by the desire to have sole custody of her son and keep Engleman's coin collection. He stuck to his client's defense as articulated when Engleman took the stand—that he had made up the murder stories to scare Ruth into returning the coins and giving him more visitation rights with David.

McGarvey looked again at the jurors and was pretty sure they hadn't bought the bullshit defense. As the guilty verdicts—guilty on each count of conspiracy—were read, he watched the Doc, who stood affecting nonchalance with his left hand in his jacket pocket. When it was over, Doc leaned forward with both hands on the table and stared at the jury blankly. He hadn't expected to lose.

Behind him his sister Melody was crying and his niece Kim appeared in shock. McGarvey thought Kim was probably the only person in the courtroom who had believed in Doc's innocence. He turned away from the sight of her crumbling face and in a low voice congratulated Buckles on the outcome.

The jurors were already talking to reporters, giving the media their impressions of the principals: The doctor was "money-hungry, felt superior to the Mirandas, and had used them"; Nick was "a leech"; and Carmen was "destroyed." The deliberations had taken so long because one young man hadn't believed a dentist could do something like this. He had finally surrendered to the convictions of the other eleven. Ruth was admired for coming forward. Ironically, Peter Halm's mother, also named Ruth, was saying the same thing in a phone interview to the *Globe-Democrat*.

"I feel it was his wife that started the ball rolling," Ruth Halm said. "I think it was Engleman's wife that finally came forth."

Jefferson City, Missouri, Wednesday, September 10, 1980

It was the third day of the Halm murder trial, and McGarvey thought everything was proceeding nicely. Ankney was allowed to use the transcripts of the tapes, and he had quoted liberally from them in an opening statement that seemed to have considerable impact on the jurors. His style was more emotional than Buckles's but it fit the crime. Dempsey was stuck again with the defense Doc had created: His murder confession to her was a cock-and-bull story invented to scare Ruth. Carmen had seemed to be handling the trauma better than she had in St. Paul until Dempsey's cross-examination techniques made her cry. Then Nick had taken the stand.

He was finished with his testimony and leaving the witness box when Engleman mouthed something to him.

"What did you say?" Nick demanded. "He just told me, 'I'm going to kill you,'" Nick said to Ankney.

"You heard me, fatso," Doc said to scattered titters in the courtroom.

During recess, Dempsey was busily denying that Doc had threatened Nick's life. "Nobody else heard it," he insisted. "This alleged threat is as truthful as everything else Nick Miranda says."

The exchange seemed to buoy Doc's mood even more. His adrenaline was flowing. After the testimony, he held an impromptu press conference with the assembled reporters. Appearing very relaxed, he answered their questions, maintaining his innocence steadfastly.

"You always hope for acquittal," he said. "I now appreciate the rights granted under the Constitution after going through two trials. In Mother Russia I wouldn't have these rights."

When one of the reporters asked about his health, he said he'd lost several pounds from eating jail food but he had kept his mental vigor.

Ankney looked at McGarvey and grinned. Doc was whetting the media appetite for tomorrow when he would take the stand. In spite of one conviction, he appeared to be as cocky and condescending as he'd ever been.

"You think you can shake him up tomorrow?" he asked Ankney on the way out of the courtroom. The prosecutor shrugged.

Engleman was dismissing the press with his closing remark: "I want to tell you I consider Dick Dempsey, my legal eagle, the F. Lee Bailey of St. Louis. With his help, I fully expect to be acquitted. I am an innocent man."

Thursday, September 11, 1980

The day had begun with his questioning of Ruth Engleman. Ankney suspected this woman was more evil than anyone knew— she hadn't come forward until her own neck was under the blade, had she?—but she was a credible witness anyway. Now the Doc was on the stand, rattling on in his own defense. Ankney half-listened to his first comments. Yesterday's exchange between Carmen and Dempsey still rang in his ears.

> DEMPSEY: *You knowingly and willingly participated in a plan to murder an innocent man?*
>
> HALM: *Yes.*
>
> DEMPSEY: *Is it your testimony that when this man told you of this atrocious, outrageous plan for you to marry someone he would kill, you didn't run screaming out of his office?*
>
> HALM: *Yes.*
>
> DEMPSEY: *Tell the jury your reaction when he told you he was going to butcher some innocent boy for money.*
>
> HALM: *I can't recall.*

Shortly after that, she had broken down. He felt bad for Carmen—and Nick, he liked Nick. Okay, the guy had been a con man all his life, but who'd taught him how to con, anyway? Basically, he thought Nick was a lovable guy trapped in a criminal alliance he'd entered into as a kid. Now the Doc was on the stand refuting Nick and Carmen's testimony.

"Nick Miranda tells lies faster than a person can think," Doc said. "He's one of the biggest liars God ever set guts into. When he dies, they'll have to screw him into the ground. Why, he can lie faster than the average person can think, even a lawyer."

His last remark drew the expected chuckles from the spectators. *How to draw him out . . . How . . .* Ankney wrote on his legal pad. He and Buckles had talked about the subject and reached no conclusions. Hamstrung by the limitations regarding the transcripts that Hungate had put on him, Buckles hadn't been able to cross-examine from the tapes. He was disappointed in himself for not drawing Doc out, though Ankney thought he had handled the Doc well by letting him ramble, giving him time to expose his megalomania to the jurors.

"Basically," Buckles, who thought less of Doc's intelligence than many of his adversaries, had told him, "the guy's a psychotic. He's a cut above the ordinary criminal, but he's not that smart. However, he is smart enough to spot a strategy and match it. If you have a strategy, he'll read it. He won't let you take him down that road. If anyone gets to him, it will be through a random visceral shot."

Ankney doodled on the notepad while Dempsey finished his questioning of his client. A hard shot to the gut. He thought Buckles was right. A hard, unexpected, perhaps random shot to the gut.

"Mr. Engleman . . ." he began.

"*Dr.* Engleman," the defendant corrected him. A flash of irritation showed in his eyes. "It's *Dr.* Engleman."

"Excuse me," he said, his voice conveying an exaggerated note of politeness, deliberately projecting the condecension Doc projected when he talked about the "poor" Mirandas. "*Dr.* Engleman."

He began the questioning. The doctor set off, attempting to run the same obstacle course he'd run in St. Paul, but he was hobbled at the start by irritation. After he had repeatedly answered Ankney's questions with long and unnecessary explanations, Judge Byron Kinder admonished him to "answer the questions and spare the court the educational discourses." Again the anger flashed in Engleman's eyes.

When Dempsey intervened by saying, "If you don't answer the question we'll be here all night," he retorted, "I'll be here fifty years!"

Ankney asked him to explain the implied confession of homicide in the tapes. He responded by repeating his contention that he had merely been attempting to threaten Ruth. That "homicide" was not Peter Halm, he said.

ANKNEY: *What homicide are you talking about, if not Peter Halm?*

ENGLEMAN: *Any homicide, I would be capable of any homicide to scare this woman!*

His voice remained raised as he continued venting his wrath against Ruth, thief of his coin collection, more importantly, thief of his son. Ankney deliberately let him ramble, staring at the floor, finally consulting his notes while Engleman raved. He was giving Kinder impetus to intervene and poke the doctor again—but the poke wasn't needed. Ankney heard pain in his voice when he said the word "son." He deliberately stepped on the word, as if it were a raw nerve running directly into the gut.

ANKNEY: *Dr. Engleman, are you saying you concocted a complex murder story to see more of your son?*

ENGLEMAN: *One day he is going to be an adult and he is going to say, "Mom, what happened to my dad?" Just beautiful . . . just beautiful the way that bitch has taken him out of my life. Half of David is me. Half of David is me! Mr. Ankney . . ."*

His face flushed deep and angry red, and he tightened his grip on the arms of his chair as if a sudden infusion of energy had just come into his body through that very chair. His voice grew deeper, descending to the level of animal growls. The two women jurors closest to him pushed back into their chairs.

I would tell my wife any damn thing, Mr. Ankney!

His face grew even redder, tinged in purple, and blood seemed to fill his eyes. His chin went down until his neck seemed to disappear and his head sat between his shoulders. Finally his eyes went back into his head.

. . . in order to get my son back. Scare that female . . . Yes! I would scare her, tell her any kind of lie. Is that too unreasonable to believe? My son is gone. Gone! He's just not there anymore.

Ankney had watched the dentist in fascination and, yes, in fear. The man could have killed him, he thought, could have jumped right out of the chair and killed him. He felt like he'd seen before him the transformation of Dr. Jekyll to Mr. Hyde. The courtroom was completely silent.

"Where is David?" Engleman resumed, his voice coming down somewhat. "I've got a little picture here of him . . . Is that all . . ."

The judge was yelling above him, calling for a recess, asking Engleman to leave the stand and come into his chambers. Dempsey tried to take his client by the arm, but Engleman shook him off.

"Damn it, Dick! They're trying to put me in prison for fifty years. This isn't a traffic ticket . . . David . . . I'll tell anything to get him back."

He had shown the jury the face of a murderer and given Gordon Ankney a hook upon which to hang his closing arguments.

Gordon Ankney spoke in low, well-modulated tones. He agreed Carmen was guilty of murder too—attempting to smooth that particular rough spot for the jurors immediately. But, he explained, she and her brother, whose involvement was peripheral and after the fact, were given immunity because their cooperation, which couldn't be achieved any other way, was necessary to build a case strong enough to convict Engleman.

Pointing to Engleman, he said, "This is Mr. Hyde. But the story you heard isn't fiction, it's true. This is not the way he looked when he was scoping in on Peter Halm's back."

> *Carmen Miranda Halm, that agent of death, that poisonous fruit, that embodiment of evil . . . she's a banshee . . .*

Dempsey's closing arguments were being shouted to the jury. Ankney didn't know if the jurors realized as well as he did what tack the defense attorney was pursuing—talk loudly and attack the prosecution witnesses—but he suspected Dr. Engleman had made up their minds for them already. Privately the defense attorney had admitted he would be doing all he'd promised Melody he could do if he'd kept Doc off death row at the end of the trials. He watched Dempsey emotionally flogging himself into a state that would pass for conviction and felt sorry for the guy. He liked Dempsey. The man was a little too close to the criminal in this case to fully respect, but he liked him.

> *Nick provided a comic element . . .*

Ankney was more interested in watching the Doc than Dempsey now. Apparently Engleman had pulled himself back together. He once again wore the countenance of a respectable dentist as he sat in the same blue pinstripe suit he'd worn to two trials, listening to his defense lawyer describe him as a man whose heart was broken over the loss of his son. That, Ankney thought, might be the only truth Dempsey had spoken all day.

> *Clutching her son in one hand and the money in the other . . .*
> *Ruth's a liar, cold-blooded, a contriving, deliberate liar . . .*

He was finally winding down, even if his voice was still up.

After the jury's verdict of guilty, with the accompanying sentence of life without parole for fifty years, was delivered, Dr. Engleman, who appeared relaxed and philosophical, said, "I'm fifty-three years old. In fifty years, there won't be anything but dust. Well, I don't relish this guilty verdict, but we will appeal." He patted Dempsey on the back. "I have all the confidence in the world in this man."

Across the room, Melody was telling Gordon Ankney, "My brother is really two men. You brought that out on the stand, but you don't really know the full story. No one does."

St. Louis, Saturday, December 6, 1980

> *Dr. Glennon E. Engleman began to live out his sister's prophecy that "at the end of my life I would be away from my family and friends," when he entered the Missouri Penitentiary Friday to start serving a life sentence for murder.*—St. Louis Globe-Democrat,
> December 6, 1980

Although he'd been held in jails since his arrest in February, Engleman was only now moving into his permanent home. Following the Halm murder trial in which he had so spectacularly lost his cool on the stand, he'd been sentenced to thirty years for the first federal mail fraud conviction, tried on federal bombing charges in the Berrera murder, found guilty, and sentenced to another thirty years—and been through a mistrial for the Berrera murder in Hermann, Missouri. That trial, number four, was scheduled to start again in January. Picking himself up from the misstep in Jeff City, Doc had continued to taunt and tease them, profess his innocence, and attempt to ingratiate himself to the jury and spectators. He had added *Dr. Jekyll and Mr. Hyde* to his recommended reading list for reporters. Handy had gone down for mail fraud and conspiracy to commit mail fraud—gone down without opening his mouth against his friend. For the first time, however, Doc could get the death penalty in the Berrera murder. Would he take the stand again—or would Dempsey convince him not to risk it this time? Like everyone else, McGarvey thought he'd convict himself if he opened his mouth.

The black-and-white picture of the Doc in prison clothes made him look like a killer. Maybe he'd spent enough time in jails so the veneer of the dentist was roughed off. Ankney would probably say Mr. Hyde was more visible now. McGarvey studied the picture for clues, but there were none in the sullen face looking back at him.

It was ironic Doc looked more the part of the killer now that they had subdued him and he couldn't kill again. He was trapped inside whatever was the truth of his own identity, and he wouldn't be getting out of it to kill anyone else. Removed from his south St. Louis milieu, he was a man forced to live inside himself. In fact, the saga of Doc Engleman following the Halm murder trial had disintegrated into a comedy act. McGarvey and all the other participants had just been collecting Doc stories, the way little boys used to collect baseball cards when he was a kid.

From Jeff City, the show had moved to the Gasconade County Courthouse in Hermann, a hundred-year-old red brick building with a Civil War cannon on the lawn. The start of the trial, however, was delayed because somebody had forgotten to tell St.

Louis County jail officials to bring the defendant down for the proceedings. McGarvey and Tom Dittmeir, the city prosecutor, had barely been able to conceal their amusement when they heard Engleman, bound by leg irons and chains, clanking up the stairs—"He sounds like Marley's ghost," Dempsey had whispered—two hours late for his own trial while the judge fumed.

The next day Dempsey and the circuit judge were having dinner at a tavern when the sheriff, who had been ordered to stay with the sequestered jury, stopped in for a drink. He'd walked past Dempsey and the judge to join a woman deputy who was having a drink with a female juror. Dempsey's mouth fell open. He closed it and wrote the motion for a mistrial on a paper napkin, handed it to the judge, and ordered another drink.

Doc, of course, loved that one. He had brought to Hermann a copy of his horoscope, cast by Melody, which he said proved his fate was incarceration and betrayal at the hands of women. The mistrial insured him enough media attention to properly exploit his message. "It was predestined at my birth," he said. He also pointed out to the press his birthday was February 6, the same as Ronald Reagan's, whom he supported, which made McGarvey uncomfortable since he supported Reagan, too.

Increasingly Doc talked about astrology and astral projection to anyone who would listen. Reportedly he had told the warden what books he should read in the occult areas, and the warden had politely ignored him. But a real contender for the all-time best Doc quote came when he was asked to comment on the mistrial for TV cameras: He said he was borrowing a quote from Mrs. Berrera herself in saying, "Whatever will be, will be."

The anecdotes kept building and the legend of Doc grew like a snowball rolling downhill. He was already comparing himself to Jesse James and the Dalton boys. McGarvey tapped the newspaper picture, an unflattering shot in which the dentist looked like any other vicious killer, but too dim for the big leagues he put himself in. The party was almost over. Doc would surely get the death penalty in Hermann next month.

He shoved the paper aside. The Doc was finished. He was involved in another investigation, and this one was done. The Gusewelles nagged at him, and he had to ignore their nagging.

This was a job like any other. You divorce yourself from the emotions and you do your job. The thought of the golden girl enjoying the money bothered him, but he couldn't stop her, could he?

He'd filed a clipping that he'd seen in the papers shortly after Nick's dead-end phone call: GUSEWELLE MURDER CASE SOLVED, AUTHORITIES SAY. That was their response to the story he'd planted implicating Doc. Well, it was comfortable for the authorities to say so. He couldn't blame them, could he?

PART EIGHT:
Turning Handy

Svengali had but two friends. There was Gecko . . . who lived . . . close by . . . who indeed owed his master his great talent not yet revealed to the world.—from *Trilby* by George du Maurier.

Edwardsville, Illinois, Monday, August 31, 1981

Driving over the Poplar Street Bridge into Illinois, McGarvey began going over the Gusewelle case again in his mind. The original investigation had implicated Engleman and Handy in yet another murder and mail fraud scheme, but none of the principals, including Barb, had come in on a deal. Madison County authorities were content to stick with the Andre Jones's confession. If Doc had gotten the death sentence in Hermann, maybe he would have considered the book closed too.

The jurors had found him guilty with a sentence of life imprisonment. He guessed the Doc had been saved by two things: not taking the stand in his own defense and the fact that he hadn't put the bomb on the car. He'd hired someone else to do that part. To the jury's mind, this fraction-of-an-inch space he'd put between himself and the physical splattering of Sophie perhaps made him a little less guilty. In his experience, a jury had to be convinced beyond a glimmer of doubt the defendant was as guilty as a person can be before giving a death sentence. The Doc had surprised everyone by taking Dempsey's advice and staying off the stand. Actually, the Doc had surprised everyone by letting his fear of death show for the first time. He might have gone through his paces for the press, telling them about Melody's prediction of his fate and all the other bullshit, but it hadn't sounded like he was convincing himself this time.

McGarvey remembered catching Doc's eye as he stood on the courthouse steps in Hermann discoursing on the prison population. It included, he said, some frightening people, "sociopaths" and "psychopaths," men who were "violent." But some of those men were "beautiful, intelligent souls." He'd looked Doc square in the eye on that one.

He'd heard about Doc's circle of followers within the prison community. The irony was not in Doc finding his role as a teacher of men again, but in the racial composition of his new followers, who were largely black. Glennon Engleman, avowed racist, was now spiritual guru to a racially mixed group anxious to believe they could astral-project themselves back into their wives' bedrooms at night.

If things had changed for Doc, they'd changed for Handy too. In May of 1981 the original conviction of mail fraud and conspiracy had been overturned in a court of appeals. Then he'd been convicted again in August by another jury in a retrial. Now he was putting out feelers through his attorney. Handy was "interested in exploring the possibility of cooperating with the government in the investigation of the three killings in the metro-east area" in exchange for "making his cooperation known to the trial judge for consideration in a possible reduction of his seventeen-year prison sentence." In other words, he wanted to make a deal, but it would have to be very good because Handy was too street-smart to risk becoming a snitch for anything less.

With only a modicum of hope such a deal was possible, McGarvey pulled into the parking lot of the St. Clair County jail. Before getting out of the car, he opened one of the bottles of Pepto-Bismol he kept on the dash—there were usually two next to a carton of cigarettes—and took a swig.

"I want to know how I can shorten my jail term," Handy said. He looked thinner than he had in court, the lines in his face settling more deeply into his flesh. "I want to get into some kind of program or something in prison to do that."

"I can't promise you anything, Handy," McGarvey said, lighting a cigarette to keep his hands busy. He'd promised he wouldn't take notes. In fact, he was posing as Handy's new lawyer, their previously agreed tactic for deflecting the trouble Handy would get from inmates if he was seen as a snitch. "I have to know the extent of your involvement—and you have to be truthful. We can't do anything for you unless you're completely honest and truthful."

"You know I didn't get anything out of this, any money or anything," he said, swinging easily into conversation. "I may have had knowledge of the Halm killing prior to its happening and I may have inadvertently aided Glen in the completion of his scheme—but I didn't get nothing out of it. No money. And I didn't help Ruth launder no money."

"No," McGarvey replied, raising his eyebrows.

"And prior to those meetings with Glen and Nick at Carnegie's and the Other Mother and Grone's Cafeteria, I hadn't seen Nick since 1974 when he made a pass at my daughter." He was enjoying himself now. Talking to the cops was one way to get out of the cell for a few hours, and he'd found a way to do it safely. "Most of those meetings they talked about the plan for murdering Michael Spinks, you know. I wasn't involved in that at all. Yeah, I was working for Glen redecorating the office, you know, when Halm got killed. I see now why he wasn't in any hurry to finish. He was working with Carmen. You know I should have contacted Carmen and attempted to talk her out of the plan since I had knowledge of it, but he would have killed me if I did. That's why I decided not to do anything about it." He was clearly on a roll. "I tried to talk him out of killing Sophie Berrera, you know."

"Listen, Handy, I want to believe you, but when you tell me things which are in contradiction with the facts, I have trouble believing you."

"Glen told Ruth a lot of things about me and the murder scenes that aren't necessarily true," he said defensively.

"Well, why don't we start at the beginning. Tell me when you first met Engleman and take me through your involvements with him."

He began with their meeting at Lake Tishamingo in the early '60s and rambled leisurely down the path of their friendship. It was a decidedly rosier path than anyone else had described. McGarvey didn't believe him, and he wasn't sure Handy expected him to. This was just one phase in his dance. He wouldn't dance any closer until he had some idea of what he'd get out of the partnership. And McGarvey couldn't promise him anything on the basis of what he was dishing out.

"I don't feel I owe Glen anything anymore," he said. "He used me, as have so many people in my life. My sister Millie was right about that, I guess. You know, Melody is behind a lot of what Glen does. She's aware of everything Glen is involved in . . . I think he did a lot of those things to pay for her lifestyle. You know he put a lot of money into that house of hers. Personally," Handy finished, "I don't like Melody at all."

McGarvey suppressed a laugh. None of Doc's close associates liked each other. He'd driven across the river just to hear what one member of this soap-opera crime family thought about another, but he hadn't expected much from this first meeting anyway. When a man has spent his life lying to the police and hiding criminal activity, he doesn't start telling the truth easily.

"Anyway," Handy said. "I have no contact with Glen anymore except through an old friend. I was in Terre Haute with him, and now he's in Jeff City with Glen. I hear through him about Glen."

He said he wanted to talk again. McGarvey told him he'd have to have the complete and total truth because once he was caught lying his credibility would be shot down and they'd be unable to use his information or testimony. These guys all came down on Ruth so hard, but her credibility had held through four trials. They all insinuated she'd had more involvement than she admitted to—but if she had they would have found it, and, he was convinced, Dempsey would have nailed her with it. Handy's credibility was nowhere near Ruth's.

"I want to believe you, but I'm having doubts, Handy, I'm having doubts," he said, pausing at the door to deliver his final statement. "A prosecutable case may not exist against you now, but if further investigation turns up the evidence, your bargaining position decreases accordingly."

"I'll take my chances," he said. "You know I wouldn't want my family, my sister and my kids, to know I was involved in something as bad as murder."

The Recanted Confession of Andre Vernell Jones, Tuesday, May 22, 1984

On May 15, Major Robert Hertz of the Madison County Sheriff's Department, accompanied by Special Agent Dennis Kuba of the Illinois Department of Law Enforcement, Division of Criminal Investigation, and Madison County State's Attorney Donald Weber went to Menard Penitentiary in Chester, Illinois, to interview Andre Jones on death row. He refused to talk to them until he could consult with his attorney. The three men drove back upstate to Belleville, Illinois, to see his attorney, who was out of the office. A meeting was finally arranged and approval granted for the interview. This time they had Jones transported to Edwardsville.

At 10:00 A.M., Jones's attorney briefed him. At 10:05, Hertz, Kuba, and Weber were allowed to speak to Jones. All in their early thirties, they were an otherwise disparate group: Hertz, a severely controlled man with short, thinning dark hair, determined to stand unblemished in a county noted for corruption and scandals; Kuba, a low-key, intelligent detective with the sort of looks and flair associated with TV heroes; and Weber, the chinless and slightly chubby politically embattled aggressive state's attorney as obsessed with justice as Hertz was with procedure. Jones must have felt singled out for special attention when they asked him if he still contended he was the person responsible for the murder of Ronald Gusewelle.

He stated he and his girlfriend Lori Elam, since dead of a drug overdose, were directly responsible for the killing. Pretending to solicit him for purposes of prostitution, she lured Gusewelle into a room at Coleman's Plaza where Jones meant to rob him. Gusewelle, "a heavyset white guy," fought back. Then, according to Jones, he picked up a lamp and struck the white guy three times in the head until his victim was dead. He and Lori stuffed the body into the Camaro.

Hertz and Kuba told him his original statement had gone into far more detail. In fact, Weber had thought from the beginning the wealth of detail in his original statement was suspicious, but Hertz had said it was too complete not to accept it. Jones said time had passed and he'd forgotten those details. He had confessed to a total of six murders, including the brutal slaying and beheading of an elderly white man. According to his written confession of that crime, he'd had a fight with his grandmother and stormed out the door looking for trouble when a deep voice from inside told him to walk up to a house, knock on the door, and kill the old couple inside. Apparently the same voice told him to cut off the man's head with a knife, place it in a paper sack, and carry it to the apartment in the projects where his mother was staying. When his brother asked what was in the sack, he said he'd tell him later because he was tired and needed some sleep. If Ronald Gusewelle had been killed in East St. Louis, Andre Vernell Jones was clearly the sort of man who would have killed him.

"Will you go to the scene with us and show us how it happened?" Weber asked him. He said he would.

Surprisingly, Jones had had an apartment at Coleman's Plaza, opposite the building from where Gusewelle had been dumped. When he attempted to show them where the Camaro had been parked, he picked the wrong side. They were noncommittal. "I did it," he swore, "it's just been a while."

The next day, however, in the courtroom chapel area of the jail, he admitted to the same group of people he was *not* responsible for the killing of Ronald Gusewelle, as he had maintained he was for four years. They told him if he gave them the true story they would arrange for him to hug his grandmother. It bothered him, he said, that he could only see her through glass partitions; he wanted to hug her bad. They videotaped his recantation.

> HERTZ: *Okay . . . then Tuesday of this week, which would have been the twenty-second of May, at approximately nine-thirty, ten in the morning, we did, in fact, all get together in another room of this building and we talked about this Gusewelle case, is that correct?*
> JONES: *That's right . . .*
> HERTZ: *And, at that time, we indicated to you the possibility of us having some reservations about your truthfulness in that state-*

ment, and, at that time, which was Tuesday, what did you indicate to us as to your involvement in killing Mr. Gusewelle?

JONES: *Well, at that time, I had again said that I had committed the crime but in reality, I didn't commit the crime and my reason for saying that I committed the crime was because I was pressured, in a matter of speaking, to sign a statement saying that I committed the crime, but the reason I signed the statement was to protect my family.*

HERTZ: *Okay . . . that interview Tuesday, you did not indicate that last part of what you just said to us . . .*

JONES: *Oh, no, I . . .*

HERTZ: *Am I correct in saying that Tuesday when we talked to you, you had still maintained that you had killed Mr. Gusewelle . . .*

JONES: *Oh, yes, I did . . .*

HERTZ: *Okay . . . then at approximately three-thirty this afternoon we again asked you if you remembered any additional details about that . . . the killing of Mr. Gusewelle and it was then, at that time, that you indicated to us what?*

JONES: *That I did not kill Ronald Gusewelle . . .*

HERTZ: *Okay. Then, at this time I would ask you to relate to us exactly what did take place. Did you, in fact, kill Ronald Gusewelle?*

JONES: *No, I did not.*

HERTZ: *Then, why in late 1979 and more specifically, January 31, 1980, did you make a statement to authorities that you did in fact kill this man?*

JONES: *Uh . . . well, I . . . the reason why I said that was because I was given a statement, I was given police reports and I was given autopsy reports and I was shown these reports and I was told to go over these reports, to memorize these reports and which I did. And, at this time, uh . . . it was indirectly stated to me that if I didn't sign this statement sayin' that I did this, that . . . uh . . . it wouldn't be in the best interest of my family if I . . . uh . . . didn't sign the statement. And this is why I signed the statement.*

HERTZ: *Okay, who initially spoke with you concerning the Gusewelle case?*

JONES: *Detective Robert Miller.*

HERTZ: *Okay, and what intially did he bring up to you to get the ball rolling on the Gusewelle case?*

JONES: *Well, he had came to me in reference to a case . . . some people that got killed in this place called Mexico City Cafe, and he had received some information from other guys that I was the one that was . . . I was the one that did the actual killing at the time. I told him I wasn't . . . And he mentioned do I know a Ronald Gusewelle. I don't know anything about Gusewelle. And, at this particular time I told him I didn't know anything about the case and he told me it happened in East St. Louis around Coleman's Plaza . . . do I know where Coleman's Plaza is at . . . I told him yes I did and he told me that he had been talking with my people, with my grandmother and you know, and specific, with my mother and with a girlfriend of mine and that if I didn't sign a statement and read the reports and study the reports, that something would happen to my family. He said this in an indirect way . . . he didn't say it directly, but this is what he said and this was my reason for admitting to the Ronald Gusewelle killing . . ."*

He further admitted, while he *was* guilty of the three murders for which he'd been given the death sentence, he'd confessed to two other murders he didn't commit. He went along with Mr. Miller because he was depressed and didn't care what happened—and to keep his family safe. After talking with his grandmother, he said, and praying that nothing happened to his family, he felt it was time to get the truth out. While he talked, Weber was trying to remember if it was two or three promotions which Robert Miller had received as the result of solving these and several other murders in rapid succession. He thought it was two.

HERTZ: *Did Miller indicate what his interest was in wanting you to confess to something that you maintained that you weren't responsible for?*

JONES: *Yes . . . as he put it, to uh . . . to clear his case up . . . I was under the impression that he was investigating the case and that it was . . . uh . . . that he was one of the arresting officers on the case or whatever . . . but I found out later that he actually, I guess, didn't really have nothing to do with the case, he was just using me to make himself look good . . .*

Hertz showed Jones the statement he'd signed. Jones said Detective Miller had written it, though he himself "invented up" the part about luring Gusewelle into the room via a prostitute because that's how things were done in that part of town. When Hertz asked him where he got the details, he said he'd been given the police and autopsy reports of the crime. Detective Miller had had his secretary make a copy of the entire file for Jones to study in his cell.

> HERTZ: *Did Miller give any special privileges for you while you were . . . or perform any special privileges for you while you were incarcerated at the St. Clair County jail?*
>
> JONES: *Yes . . . uh . . . well . . . um . . . money . . . uh, money was given to me and money was placed on my books . . . uh, at which time, I didn't receive any money from my family and I could use this money to go to the commissary, what have you, and . . . uh . . . I was given Valiums . . . at this time because I was going through a depression . . . I was given Valiums by Mr. Miller . . . I don't know where he got these Valiums from . . . uh . . . or I don't even care . . . but . . . uh, that is basically about it.*

Weber looked at Hertz, straight-arrow, by-the-book Hertz, standing emotionless in front of the video camera giving his spiel closing the interview. He had to admire his ability to hide his feelings. The man must be mad as hell, he thought. Mad as hell. One thing you had to give Hertz, however, was his stoic acceptance of the consequences if something went wrong. He wouldn't try to put it off on somebody else. Maybe if he'd looked at the confession a little closer instead of being seduced by the overwhelming details, instead of letting the number of ways that the confession matched the facts make him faster than any black hooker ever could have made Ron Gusewelle—maybe he wouldn't be standing here now swallowing his own smoke.

Edwardsville, Illinois, Saturday, June 9, 1984

"Okay, Nick, we're just about set up here to make this phone call . . ." McGarvey said.

Nick had told them everything he knew about the Gusewelle

murders, which wasn't much, one more time. They'd wired him and run him, sweating profusely, up to Barb's door several times. Either she wasn't home or she just wouldn't come to the door and talk to him. Christ, he was glad she wouldn't. What the hell would he do if she pulled a gun on him or something? But he couldn't tell them that. And now it was, "One more phone call, Nick, one more try."

McGarvey had said they needed to flip her or Handy, and Nick couldn't see either one of them flipping, at least not through him. This was going to be, he hoped, the last game plan involving him. Working with Hertz was like submitting to a toothache. McGarvey had a dry sense of humor that Nick liked, and he accepted you as a person as long as you were straight with him. Hertz, on the other hand, always seemed on the verge of turning him over to God or a pest-control service. Nervously, he dialed the number in Barb's Glen Carbon home, the $100,000 house she'd bought after selling Ron's place.

> MIRANDA: *Hi, Barb?*
> BARBARA: *Yes . . .*
> MIRANDA: *Barb, this is Nick Miranda calling . . . How have you been?*
> BARBARA: *I don't even know you . . . so please don't bother me.*
> MIRANDA: *Listen, I have a message for you . . .*

She hung up. "Try it again, will you Nick?" Hertz asked. He punched the numbers. A man's voice answered. Apparently it was not her attorney this time because their eyes didn't light up. The man told him not to call her anymore. Shrugging good-naturedly, Nick Miranda hung up the phone.

Alton, Illinois, Thursday, June 28, 1984

Once they had dispensed with Andre Jones, they moved to flip one of the three principals, Engleman, Handy, or Barbara. As Kuba and Detective Donald Spaul drove with Weber to pick up McGarvey in St. Louis for the interview with Handy, they filled him in on the previous day's contact with Barbara. Kuba and Spaul had intercepted Barbara, who had begun using the surname

"Boyle" again at the Alton, Illinois, Police Department when she arrived to post bail for her son, who'd just been arrested for burglary. (He eventually was acquitted of the charges.) They told her they were updating the files on the murders and let her know Andre Jones had never been criminally charged. She said talking about the murders upset her. When Kuba told her they were interested in discussing the number and type of life insurance policies on the life of Ronald Gusewelle, she became very nervous.

"I don't want to go through this again. I've cried my eyes out every night for three years," she said, her upper right arm visibly trembling.

As she was walking out the door, Kuba had said, "We're going to interview Glennon Engleman. Do you want us to tell Glennon anything?" Her eyes had opened wider as she hurried out the door, calling, "Good-bye, boys," over her shoulder.

Weber had her wedding picture tacked up in his office, next to a picture of General Custer captioned NEVER UNDERESTIMATE YOUR ENEMY, and a photo of Karla Brown, the victim whose murder had obsessed him for the five years it took to capture and prosecute her killer. He wasn't obsessed with getting Barbara, but he wanted to get her. Her picture—the fat sausage curls under the lacy big hat, the fatter smile—focused him. He'd never bought the Andre Jones confession, and driving to work each day past the Gusewelle homes, he'd felt an eery sadness. Something wasn't right about it, and he wanted to put things right. Since McGarvey had come to him in March with the insurance records ATF had collected and the information gleaned from interviews with Ruth and Nick Miranda, he'd been convinced Barbara married Ron to kill him. He wanted to see her go to jail for it. Without Handy, he'd have a hard time putting her there.

McGarvey had convinced him he was the one to turn Handy. A lot of people had played roles in the saga of Glennon Engleman's crimes. Maybe this was meant to be his. The idea pleased him.

"Handy's a con, a fearless con," McGarvey reminded him as they drove. "He's been in and out of the system so many times, he knows exactly how it works—and how to work it for whatever he can. You can't con him. He knows when to keep his mouth shut and when to talk. And he's not afraid to take a rap."

According to McGarvey's reading of him, Handy wouldn't talk until he had "The Man" in front of him, the man who could make the deal. Handy wasn't going to deal with you if he had to wait while you called for authorization. He wanted to deal with the guy who had the power to make decisions. In the Gusewelle murders, he, Weber, was the guy.

"Don't tell him anything you can't back up," McGarvey said. "He won't be snowed. You're in a good position with him going in. His lawyer told him he should believe what you say."

At first glance, Handy was exactly what Weber expected him to be: rough, wary, a man with all his defenses securely in place. He smiled and shook hands affably. This guy was clearly enjoying the attention he was getting now, the chance to get out of his cell for a few hours and talk and to eat the hamburgers they'd brought him from the outside. Weber thought it was ironic how things changed once a man went inside. A visit from the cops could be the highlight of his day now.

"I'm going to ruin your day," he said to Handy. "I've put two guys on death row already this year, and I'm going to put two more there for the Gusewelle murders. One of them is going to be Engleman." He watched the smile run off Handy's face like makeup off a fat woman in August. "The other will be you or Barb. I have to make a deal with one of you." He laid out the evidence he had against Handy and Engleman: the insurance documentation, the testimony of Ruth and Miranda, and some of the small corroborating details, including a phone call made on Ruth's phone to the Wood River refinery. "Talk to me today or I talk to Barb."

Handy glanced quickly at McGarvey before saying to Weber, "You ruined my day all right." After a slight hesitation, he said, "Okay, I'm ready to talk."

"I don't want any bullshit. Don't tell me, 'Yeah, Engleman did it and Barb was in on it.' I want details, everything you've got."

"I've been in prison a while. I know what you need."

For two and a half hours, he talked.

Wood River, Illinois, Spring 1971

Glen liked to drive when they went places, so he was driving that day. He liked to drive, and he always liked to pay, whether they went to dinner or movies or both. Glen was a generous man with his friends. He owned one suit and probably his whole wardrobe wasn't worth two hundred dollars, shoes, socks, and all. He drove a moderate-priced car, but he liked to be the one who opened his wallet. He paid. That was okay with Handy, the paying and the driving. He liked riding, especially on a nice day like this when he could roll down the window and feel the wind on his face.

"That's one thing you miss in prison," he told Glen, "the wind in your face."

Glen chuckled. Handy hadn't mentioned prison very often since he'd gotten out in September of 1968. He'd taken the rap on a counterfeiting scheme, which had been Glen's idea, but then he felt he'd deserved to take the rap. His mistake was what led to the discovery of the money floating in the drainage ditch anyway. So he hadn't talked much about the stint in prison since the party Glen threw for him the night he got out. He remembered how mad his sister Millie had been. After driving to the prison in Terre Haute, Indiana, to bring him home, she had planned to stay in the house with him and the kids that night, but he'd asked her to leave. He was grateful to her for keeping up the house payments and looking after the kids, who had been left in his custody following the divorce, while he was in jail, but she wasn't any fun at parties. And besides, she and Glen didn't get along.

"You'll like Barbara," Glen said, "she's a good girl, a very hardworking girl and pretty. Her husband was running around on her with some woman, face like a dog, reminds me of the bitch Melody's husband's been sniffing up. Barb's husband, a dentist making good money, you can bet, in the practice he's got . . . and handing her a few dollars a month and so forth. She can't live on what he gives her. It's been hard on her, leaving St. Louis County to come back over here and live like that with three little kids."

Handy nodded in agreement, but he wasn't particularly interested in Barbara or her plight. All he knew about Barb was she'd lived in the apartment inside Glen's mother's house and married a dentist who'd worked at Union Electric when Glen did. It was all he cared to know. He liked doing things with Glen. They were action guys. Their first project together had been working on Glen's brother Vernon's place at Lake Tishamingo in 1963 before he married June, before the kids were born and she left them with him. He still liked doing things with Glen. Sometimes he thought he had more in common with Vern, who went belly up in every business venture he'd ever tried and even managed to lose money developing houses at Lake Tishamingo, when every other developer was making a killing out there. But it was Glen he liked being with.

They pulled into the parking area on the side of a small apartment complex, the kind he called ticky-tacky, made of Perma-Stone brick facing and creosoted wood. Each little apartment door was exactly alike and most had a pot of something green or flowering outside the door, but Glen walked unhesitatingly up to the right door. As soon as he knocked, she opened the door. She was wearing jeans and high, open-back heels, a lavender blouse with a plunging ruffled neck and puffy sleeves, the kind of blouse women wear to the bars when they're looking to get picked up. When she shook his hand, her long fingernails, painted a pinky lavender, grazed his palm.

He and Glen put the youth beds together for her twin five-year-old boys, David and James, while she made coffee and piled cookies on a plate. The job didn't take twenty minutes. Glen could have done it alone, easy. Handy had the uncomfortable feeling he'd been taken along just so he could meet Barbara, and he wasn't sure why. She acted like she was at a tea party, fluffing open her napkin, holding her store-bought cookie in two fingers before she took a bite. Yeah, he thought she was pretty in that ripe kind of way, like Marilyn Monroe, only a little riper, so ripe she was almost on the verge of going bad. He thought if you touched her skin, juice would flow out of her like an overripe peach. Anyway, she was not as sexy as Marilyn Monroe and not exactly his type. She'd rubbed up against Glen a few times, so he didn't understand why he was getting the pitch to date her. Maybe Glen was looking for a way to get out from under her—or maybe Ruth had caught him and he just wanted to divert the heat.

"What did you think of her?" Glen asked when they were driving home.

"Pretty," he said. Glen waited, obviously expecting more, so he said, "Awful long way to drive to court a girl."

Handy didn't hear much more about Barbara until the following year, in the early summer, when Glen asked him if he'd take her to a barbecue at Lake Tishamingo. By then, Handy had figured out she and Glen were having a sexual affair. Glen was, as a matter of fact, pretty hot for her, which only confused him more when he thought about the day they'd put together the beds. He wasn't anxious to drive to Wood River to pick her up, but Glen wanted her out at the lake for some reason, so he said he'd do it. He called her and she said she'd be happy to meet him at his house.

She was wearing a snug white jumpsuit, short sleeves, with the snaps undone enough so the tops of her breasts showed, and those high, high heels. Her toenails were painted pink to match her fingernails, and her blond hair was freshly done. He was momentarily sorry he'd promised his sister Millie and the kids they could go along, but they were all ready, their coolers full of hot dogs for the grill and potato salad packed in the car, so he couldn't back out now. She took his hand again, and he was sure she did that thing with her nails grazing his palm on purpose. It did send shivers up his spine.

She and Millie hardly spoke for the forty minutes it took them to drive. He could see that Millie, as fiercely plain as she was and insisted on being, her tight little curls spelling it all out for anybody just how tight she held herself, didn't like Barbara. After June left him, all he heard from Millie was, "That's what you can expect when you mix up with women like her. All they care about is fixing up their faces and going out. When you stop taking them out, then humpty-dumpty, they're gone." Every action Millie described was preceeded by the phrase "humpty-dumpty." Nobody ever did anything without Millie humpty-dumpty-ing them first. Goddamn, that got on his nerves. He peeked at Barb the first time she said it and saw the giggle forming in her mouth, like bubbles of gas, swallowed back down. He winked.

The usual group, twenty-five or thirty people, mostly relatives, were already there when they pulled into the gravel drive. He watched the looks on some of their faces when Barb stepped out of the car and knew it had been a mistake to bring her there. Ruth, who looked pretty dumpy in her red plaid Bermuda shorts and white shirt, glared at her, then him. Nobody fooled Ruth about anything, including Glen. He knew she'd figured out the situation as soon as Barb's high-heeled foot hit the gravel. Who wouldn't figure it out, the way Glen stood there salivating over her ankle? Melody and Glen's mother came over to make her welcome, which only irritated Ruth more. Things weren't that good between Ruth and Melody, especially since Melody had proclaimed herself a witch with psychic powers—her way of getting one-up on everybody, Handy thought. Glen had tried to get him into the psychic stuff. He had his doubts, and the whole idea made him nervous. But then, there *was* something eery about Melody.

The whole situation made him so uncomfortable he more or less ignored Barbara and talked to other people. Finally, Millie took pity on her and walked round and round the lake with her until people began leaving the barbecue. The two women sat in Handy's car with the doors open talking until he finally acknowledged they were ready to go and got in the car to drive them home. After Barb had gotten into her own car at his place and left for Wood River, Millie admonished him. *She was so unhappy you ignored her. Couldn't you see that? Why did you invite her if you didn't want nothing to do with her?* He told her to stop nagging.

After that day, he saw Barb one more time in the summer of 1972—and only because Glennon Engleman kept pushing him to call her. "Take her out," he said. "She's lonely. She likes you. Take her out." So he complied one time. He drove over to Wood River and stayed maybe an hour, an hour and a half. She poured Riunite wine for them, but he wasn't a wine drinker. His back was hurting him so he went home. He was sure the sex was available if he'd wanted, and he didn't exactly know why he didn't.

"It's too far to go to court a girl," he told Glen the next time Barb's name came up, and that was the end of the suggestions about dating her. Periodically, Glen mentioned seeing Barb or Handy bumped into her when she was leaving the office. They said hello to each other, but never had any real conversations.

Now that he was no longer trying to fix them up, Glen was open about their sexual relationship. He liked to tell Handy the details. She preferred doing it in the dental chair, he said, to the cot, which he somehow managed to keep hidden from Ruth; and on more than one occasion, Ruth had sneaked into the office and been standing outside listening while they fucked.

In the spring of 1976, Handy noticed Barb had begun covering her golden curls with a scarf when she visited Glen. Handy was spending a lot of time working on the Gravois office. He worked on the wiring and plumbing and helped Glen build the little triangular magazine table into the wall in the waiting room. They were particularly proud of the table, painted with the same aqua paint as the walls to blend right in. In fact, on the day they'd finished the table, Barb, wearing her scarf, had come to visit. He asked why she wore the scarf, and that's when he was told about the plan.

"The golden girl is getting married next week," Glen said with satisfaction. "She's handling it a lot better than Carmen did, none of that whining, 'Oh, Glen, I don't want to do this anymore,' once the plans are made. Carmen's real moody, delicate, and so forth, but Barb, with her increased maturity, knows what she's doing."

In the beginning it was the standard plan: Barb would marry this man with a solid job for a big company, some guy she'd met at a Denny's restaurant, and take out more insurance on him. Then they would kill him. Glen said he needed the money for taxes, and he just assumed Handy would be part of the plan. It occurred to him briefly that maybe he'd been meant to play a different role in the plan in the beginning, that maybe Glen had wanted him to date Barb so he'd fall in love with her and marry her and he'd be the one whose life was suddenly heavily insured. That occurred to him, but he dismissed it as something he couldn't afford to think about—just like it occurred to him to tell Glen he didn't want to be part of the plan, but figured he couldn't afford to say that either.

After she got married, Barb, wearing her scarf, came into the office one day when he and Glen were getting ready to go out to lunch.

"His parents are pretty wealthy people," she told them. Her

eyes were glittering brighter than her hair. "What do you think about that?"

"Well, well, well . . ." Glen said, and Handy's first thought was they would be in for some long planning sessions in the days ahead. Glen never did anything without talking about it so long he figured you had it drummed pretty good in your head. Glen kept talking, but he was looking at Barb in a way Handy definitely recognized as a sexual signal, so he excused himself and went to the hardware store to pick up some materials they needed for the work they were doing on the roof.

SPAUL: *So the plan was that, after Barbara had married Ron Gusewelle, was to kill the parents. And then the two sons would inherit the money. Then Engleman told you that the plan also included at some later date the killing of Ron Gusewelle?*

MCGARVEY: *And that was for money. Did Engleman say whose idea it was to kill the parents? Was that Engleman's idea or was it someone else's?*

HANDY: *Well, it's hard to say if it was Engleman's idea or Barbara's idea, but I don't see how Glen would have gotten that information without Barbara.*

Murders Four and Five: Thursday, November 3, 1977

Glennon Engleman dressed carefully in his only suit, a blue pinstripe, a white shirt, and the maroon patterned tie Ruth had bought for him several Christmases ago. For a year and a half he and Barb and Handy had been planning the murders of Arthur and Vernita Gusewelle, Barb's in-laws. Using Barb's directions to guide him, he had made a trial run past the house in a borrowed car. Now he patted the knot of his tie into place and smiled at his reflection in the mirror. Yes, he looked exactly like a representative from the Farm Bureau. They would most certainly invite him inside and lie right down when he told them to do so because they were country people who wouldn't suspect a white man in a suit of any wrongdoing. He put the .22-caliber blue steel long-barreled pistol and two pairs of rubber gloves in his pocket and the new length of clothesline, held together by a paper wrapper, inside his suit coat, clutching the cloth to his body to hide it until he got inside the car. He was particularly fond of this gun; he'd taken it on float trips with Handy and used it often for target shooting on the practice range he'd built into one wall of Melody's basement.

Handy was watching television when he rapped once on the door, opened it, and walked inside. As soon as he saw Engleman, Handy shut off the TV, stood, and pulled on his short tan jacket. "Attaché case is right there," he said, pointing to a black fiberglass case on the sofa. Engleman opened it, put the rope inside.

They took Handy's car, a '72 Chrysler, and as they drove on Highway 55 downtown and over the bridge, Engleman talked: "Ron beats Barb," he said, "and runs around on her. He's a no-good worthless shit. She deserves better, and he's going to get exactly what he deserves when the will is probated and everything's in the golden girl's hands."

Engleman was in that agitated state, a jumpy kind of excitement that preceeded criminal acts, especially murder, and so was Handy. Whenever they were carrying out criminal plans, they were more highly charged than usual. Doc's philosophy was that government and large institutions like banks and insurance companies cheated people all the time, and anything you could do to cheat them was justifiable, was only getting a little something back that belonged to you all along. He cheated as much as he could on his taxes by underreporting his income, but even so he had to pay something. The Gusewelles were going to die because Glennon Engleman had to pay his taxes. If anyone's to blame for their deaths, he said to Handy, it's the fucking federal system. His partner agreed. When they turned off the interstate onto Route 140, a two-lane blacktop road, Engleman pulled into the parking lot of a filling station and made a call from the pay phone booth.

"I called Barb. She sent the kids to the house to borrow soap powder to make sure the parents were home, and they are. When this is all cleared up, I'll do right by you," he promised. "It's going to take a while to probate this thing, get it all settled, and then kill Ron. We knew it was a long-range plan when we developed it, but it's worth it. We'll be rich men, me and you, Handy, when this is done."

They drove behind the house and parked the car. It was dark, and the porch light was on. Engleman got out first and walked to the door. He knocked and Arthur Gusewelle answered. Engleman identified himself as a Farm Bureau representative and was invited inside by a man who had lived in rural Edwardsville all his life and never had reason to be suspicious of strangers as long as they were white. As soon as Arthur Gusewelle closed the door behind him, the dentist pulled out his gun and ordered the couple to lie facedown on the kitchen floor. He showed them the rope and said, "If you lie down quietly so I can tie your hands, I won't have to hurt you." They told him he could have anything in the house if he didn't hurt them, and they lay down for him. He put the silencer on the gun and held it to the woman's head first.

According to plan, Handy waited outside. After he had been waiting three minutes, Vernita Gusewelle had been shot three times in the head, the blood was running down her face, obliterating her features, and Engleman was firing the gun into Arthur Gusewelle's head. He then began methodically tearing up the house to make it look like a home invasion. On his way out the door, Engleman stopped at the freezer, pulled it open and threw packages of frozen food on the floor. A lot of people hide money and valuables in the freezer, he thought.

"It went so smooth," he bragged to Handy as they were driving back toward St. Louis. "I showed them the rope. They just laid right down for me when I told them to, laid down so nice on the floor, putting their heads down for the gun. It was that easy."

Both men were a little tense until they pulled back onto the highway headed for St. Louis. They would have been more tense if they'd realized Arthur Gusewelle had not died and had, in fact, regained consciousness and pulled himself blindly up the wall, inch by bloody inch, to reach the phone and call for help. Engleman said he was glad he didn't have to use the rope, a new coil of rope, because, after all, he had other uses for it. And he said again, that when the third phase of the plan had been successfully completed as the second phase now was, he would reward Handy one day. About this time, Gusewelle was sitting in his chair, drifting in and out of consciousness, waiting for help.

"After my taxes are paid, I'll do right by you," Engleman promised, and Handy felt warmed by the promise.

The next day television broadcasts and news articles reported the double murder. A grinning Engleman brought a small clipping from the Illinois section of the *Globe* to Handy's house that night. "Those pissant Illinois cops will never figure out what happened," he said.

> SPAUL: *Did you continue to have conversations with Engleman about this plan during that time interval between the time of the death of his parents and the death of Ron?*
>
> HANDY: *He would sometimes tell me that, you know, he would have to wait for probate and soon as all that cleared up, well, then he was gonna go shoot Ron Gusewelle.*
>
> SPAUL: *Did he ever discuss any plans that he intended to use or any of the approaches that he was gonna use to kill Ron Gusewelle?*
>
> HANDY: *He mentioned one time what he thought he would do was wait on the side of the road and when Ron got off work he was gonna flag him down with a flashlight and act like he had car problems and have Ron stop and then he was gonna shoot him right there on the road. That was one plan.*
>
> SPAUL: *Were there any others that you were aware of, perhaps involving Barb?*
>
> HANDY: *There was one time he suggested that they was gonna go over there and, ah, he was gonna tie Barbara up and leave her in bed tied and then shoot Ron Gusewelle and act like this was a burglary or something and Ron resisted him and he got Ron and then he just tied up the wife. That was one of the plans.*

Murder Six: Saturday, March 31, 1979

It was after eight-thirty in the evening when Engleman pulled up his '73 green Ford Maverick in front of Handy's house. He glanced around the neighborhood when he got out of the car: lights were on, drapes closed, people inside. It was a month, six weeks too early for sitting on the porch. A man with a purpose, he climbed Handy's front steps, rang the bell, and waited. He was expected, and Handy was ready to go, so Engleman didn't walk right in this time.

Waiting for Handy, he bounced up and down on the balls of his feet. He was agitated, and it felt good. Barbara had never been liked and accepted by the people in that little hick town, Edwardsville, and soon she would be a wealthy widow, well rid of them. Ron's new will naming her his sole heir had been signed after the first of the year, and she'd been buying insurance policies since they got married. She must have close to $200,000 of insurance coming now, more than he had suggested, not counting the benefits Amoco Oil would pay, plus her share of the parents' estate, which would be another $200,000. Handy had no idea how much money was involved, but Handy, his true friend, was willing to go along, knowing he would be taken care of in the end.

He punched the bell again. Handy was usually two steps behind, the reverent follower. Patting the pocket of his blue windbreaker, Engleman hitched his pants. When Handy opened the door, he pulled a .38 pearl-handled blue steel revolver from that pocket, palmed it for Handy to see, like a date displaying the corsage. "Ready?" He grinned.

Handy grinned back. He had the kind of midwestern face that could lend itself to mug shots or paintings of the American Gothic, depending on the moral fiber of the person possessing it: broad forehead, flat features, the nose growing more bulbous with years. The two men had been hanging around together so long they were beginning to look a little bit like each other, attributable surely to the way the one followed the other. They left Handy's house together in Engleman's little Maverick. There were two sets of gloves and a box of plastic trash bags in the car.

"How's Barb?" Handy asked. She wasn't supposed to call Engleman from Illinois because he didn't want any record of their calls on either phone bill. So when she needed to talk to him, she drove to the Northland shopping center in St. Louis and called the office. If she couldn't get him, she called Handy, and the calls had been stepped up since the first of the year. The meetings had increased too. "She isn't losing her nerve, is she?"

"The golden girl?" he laughed. "Not her. Barbara's a rock, a rock, don't worry about her."

They took the same route they'd taken in 1977, Highway 55 across the river, but this time they pulled off at a shopping center in Fairmont City, Illinois, where Barbara was supposed to pick them up. In the parking lot, Engleman told him, "When she gets here I'm going to sit in the front seat and you in the back; and we're both going to crouch down so nobody sees us." While they waited, he tapped the steering wheel occasionally and told jokes.

"I've got one for you," Handy said. "Did you read about the nigger in East St. Louis who shot another nigger while he was fucking a bitch, then pulled the body off her and started fucking her himself? It was in one of those nigger newspapers. Alfio brought it home from somewhere."

Engleman laughed, flapping his elbows up and down in that crazy gesture, which Handy had seen most often at the poker parties the doctor frequently hosted. After Handy told his "story," Engleman went over the instructions again. The two men had few conversations together. Mostly, the doctor instructed, and the follower listened. Engleman, a well-read man, tended to speak for the most part to his associates, with the exception of Nick, as though he were quoting alternately from *The National Enquirer* and *The World Book Encyclopedia*. As he talked, he removed two plastic trash bags from the box and stuffed them in his left pocket, handed his partner one pair of gloves, and stuffed the other in his right pocket. When Barbara Gusewelle pulled into the parking lot, they quickly got into her blue Oldsmobile and crouched down so it would appear there was only one driver in the car, as planned.

The golden girl wasn't very talkative, but she didn't appear to be particularly nervous either. What she had to say formed a narrative, spaced out in sentences interjected between the doctor's instructional periods. She said the kids were with their father, a St. Louis dentist, for the night. And she was worried about Ron's brother Rich and his wife Donna, what they might do since they didn't like her anyway. But she thought they probably weren't smart enough to figure anything out and do anything anyway. Besides, there had been some tension between the brothers going back to before their parents were killed, when Ron had borrowed the elder Gusewelle's truck and damaged it slightly without offering to pay for repairs. And why should he offer, she asked, when *they* had so much money? Rich had behaved in the smug, judgmental way one sibling treats another on behalf of the parents whom he feels have been wronged. Rich was good at taking on the attitude of an abused brother and had made it known he felt Ron asked for a little more and therefore got a little more than exactly half his share anyway. The murders had brought them closer for a while, and then the old resentments had returned, leaving them exactly as they had been toward each other, but without their parents to provide the magnetic pull holding them together.

Engleman told her there was nothing to worry about, no way they could connect her to a body discovered in East St. Louis. He kept repeating his instructions. Wait a while after they'd removed the body, then call the refinery to ask if he had worked late. You're being a concerned wife and you just want to know if he's still working, and of course, they tell you he's not working; then wait another hour or two and call the hospitals, and finally in the morning call the police.

She said, "Ronnie's punctual. He'll be home right away."

They stayed crouched down on the floor as the car drove for miles down 140 toward Edwardsville, through farmland, both ramshackle farms where the aging equipment is stored in sheds plastered with faded signs advertising products no longer manufactured, and big productive operations like Rapp Farms on Quercus Grove Road near the Gusewelle's six-hundred-acre farm. When she reached the three-hundred-foot-long winding drive to her house, they moved from their confining positions and stretched, sheltered from the view of distant neighbors by stands of pine trees more than twelve feet tall. The gravel drive turned in front of the house—a one-and-a-half-story brick with mustard-stained wood, a contained rather than sprawling ranch—and then doubled around to the asphalt stretch leading to the garage doors, which opened at the side. Barbara pulled into the right-hand side of the garage as the automatic door went up.

"I heard my back crack when I got out of the car," Handy complained. He'd had problems with his back before. "Nice deck," he said, admiring the redwood deck looking over the small lake in the back, kidney-shaped like a movie star's swimming pool. "Did he build it? The deck?"

"He built the deck and had the lake dug and filled in," Barbara said. Then abruptly she ended her house tour at the door. "He's punctual. Get ready. I'm going inside and change clothes."

She went through the garage into the house via the kitchen. The lights came on inside. Engleman and Handy went into the garage, pulled down the door, and waited.

Handy was getting nervous waiting in the dark garage. His back felt stiff from riding thirty minutes on the floor of the car. Engleman was cool, walking around and flexing his hands, like a piano player warming up. Occasionally his knuckles cracked, and Handy started.

"Don't worry," he said. "You've done this before. There's nothing to it. When he comes in, I'll shoot him. Then we'll put him in the car and drive away."

The crunch of tires on gravel announced their quarry approaching on the narrow winding lane. Then the headlights of a car coming in the drive unmistakably, if briefly, shone through the curtain. Engleman got in position in front of the left-hand garage door. They heard Gusewelle get out of the car. They knew he had to get out because the left-hand door was operated manually, not automatically, and the right-hand side was always saved for Barbara's car so she wouldn't have to get out alone in the dark to open the door. His footsteps sounded. The garage door was raised.

"You're never going to fuck her again," Engleman said as he leveled the gun and fired straight at the heart. Gusewelle turned and looked past his murderer toward the kitchen door with a quizzical look on his face, as if suddenly he knew Barbara was waiting there, had been waiting all along for this night. Engleman picked up a small sledgehammer and savagely hit him on the head as he was falling. He fell forward onto the floor on the left-hand side of the garage, the blood spilling from his chest and head.

"Barb!" Engleman yelled. "Bring some towels!"

She came out of the house wearing a shapeless housecoat and barefoot, carrying an armload of neatly folded, fabric softener–scented blue and gold towels. Her husband's blood was already spilling out of his body onto the floor. She didn't flinch.

She and Engleman worked together, laying towels down beneath the body, wrapping the bloody head in two of them. He removed Gusewelle's watch and wallet from his body, tucked a packet of Trojan brand prophylactics into his shirt pocket. Then he grabbed the body around the waist and began dragging it along the asphalt to the passenger side of the Camaro.

"Handy, come over here and help me get him in the car!" he yelled. To Barb he said, "Clean it up."

Handy ran to the driver's side, stepped inside the car. He held Gusewelle by the shoulders and arms and pulled him in, while Engleman lifted his legs up from the outside and pushed. The man was six feet two inches, around 220 pounds, not easy to shove inside the small backseat of a Camaro. Something snapped. "My back," Handy said, then realized with relief it was Gusewelle's leg instead. Once they had him inside the car, Engleman put the watch, hammer, and billfold in a small white kitchen trash bag. He covered the body with a large brown leaf-and-lawn bag.

"Remember, wait a few hours before you begin making calls," he said, repeating the instructions in soft staccato fashion, emphasizing them by tapping her arm. "And space out the calls. You're supposed to become increasingly worried as the night goes by and you don't hear from him. Remember, don't contact me unless it's an emergency. Then use the pay phone in Missouri. You'd better hose down that garage."

Barb got down on her hands and knees and laid down the last of the towels to soak up the blood. She nodded and didn't look up as they got in the Camaro and started down the drive.

SPAUL: *Was there blood as a result of Ron's injuries when he hit the floor?*

HANDY: *Yeah, there was blood inside the garage on the floor. And Barb came out with some towels and started wiping the blood. While we were getting the body in the car, she was cleaning up the blood and stuff, the mess that was left in the garage.*

"I put prophylactics in his pocket," Engleman said as they pulled out of the driveway. He drove the Camaro and Handy rode in the passenger side, sitting up this time, not crouched on the floor.

Handy laughed and then asked, "Why?"

"So it would look like a sex killing, or something, like a robbery and sex killing and so forth. Make it look like he got rolled by some nigger hooker and killed by her pimp." He laughed. "It's pretty obvious, isn't it? Rubbers in the pocket. Body found in East St. Louis. What else would they think? It goes on all the time down there. The place is a sewer, a sink hole; leave niggers to govern themselves and that's what you get, and those dumbass white bankers and lawyers come down there to get black pussy, thinking they're getting something special, thinking their white hides are impervious."

"Yeah," Handy said, laughing harder this time. He was nervous and excited. While he didn't do drugs, he thought the feeling he got from being with Engleman at times like this was the same thing people got from doing drugs. "Yeah."

They were both exhilarated. Engleman's breath was coming fast, as if he had been running or getting into sex, getting into it good, in the middle stages of hard excitement. In the back of the car under the trash bag, the body emitted the odor of fresh kill. Blood. They were silent for a few minutes, and the silence between them felt good, better than it had when Barb was driving them to her house. Then Engleman explained that he had hit Gusewelle in the head to get back at him for fucking Barb. He had really put himself into that blow, and it had felt so good, like drilling a woman almost.

They pulled into the Venture parking lot in Fairmont City next to Engleman's car. There were only three other cars on the lot, including a battered orange Chevette, which looked like it wouldn't start. Handy got out, and Engleman handed him the keys. "Follow me," he said. "You don't want to get lost down there."

Handy followed him in the Maverick straight down old Route 40 and into East St. Louis, past burned and gutted houses, malfunctioning street lights, and the neon signs flashing LIQUOR. They turned into the parking lot of Coleman's Plaza on Seventh and Broadway and parked in front of a wall of doors, now faded shades of turquoise and orange, doors to cheap apartments rented mostly to prostitutes. The lot, in those early minutes of April, was nearly empty. A light fog clung in wistful patches around the edges. They left the Camaro containing the body of Ron Gusewelle gleaming in the mist.

"Do you know this building represents only the second Holiday Inn in the entire chain to fail," Engleman said, climbing into the front seat as Handy slid into the passenger side. "This is what happens . . . exposed only for a short time to the caustic social acids which are East St. Louis . . . this is what happens."

"Place makes me nervous," Handy said when the aluminum surface of the Gateway Arch was twinkling reassuringly at the right-hand side of the car. "You could get killed down here."

After dropping off Handy, Engleman went to Ruth's condo. It was about two A.M. Ruth was awake, waiting for him, with the news that Melody had called looking for him because someone had broken into his office. He was furious. Ruth was furious too. She thought he'd been with another woman and she wasn't about to swallow some cock-and-bull, mostly cock, story about murdering some man in Edwardsville. If he'd told her he was with Barb, well, she'd believe that part. He slammed the door behind him and drove to the office where he checked the damage. Nothing had been stolen. They were, he was sure, looking for drugs. Lousy juvenile delinquent creeps.

> MCGARVEY: *Did you listen to any of the news reports or see any of the articles during the time Ron Gusewelle's body sat undiscovered in the car in East St. Louis?*
>
> HANDY: *What Glen would do, he would cut the newspaper clippings out and come over and let me read 'em and we would talk and we would dispose of the clipping. And, uh, he would call me up and let me know, you know, to listen to television, and if I didn't listen to that particular newscast he'd tell me what they talked about.*
>
> SPAUL: *Do you know where he spent the night after he left you?*
>
> HANDY: *No. If he was . . . he was probably . . . I don't know unless he went to his sister Melody's house. He would live with his sister for a while, and then he would go back to his wife for a while, uh, then he would. Ruth would get mad at him and have him leave, and then he'd go to his sister.*

PART NINE:
Barbara

Cold shivers went down Trilby's back as she listened [to Svengali]. She had a singularly impressionable nature as was shown by her quick and ready susceptibility to Svengali's hypnotic influence. —from *Trilby* by George du Maurier

Edwardsville, Tuesday, July 31, 1984

"Jeez, we picked a nice day to do this," McGarvey said to Kuba.

It was a hot day, and he wiped the sweat from his forehead with the back of his hand. He and Kuba and three others, a crime-scene technician and two forensic scientists, were examining the interior of Gerald Peters's garage searching for evidence of bloodstains that would have been five years old. Peters owned the house in which Barbara had lived, the garage in which Ron had been killed, and he had willingly signed a consent to the search. His two children, teenagers, a boy and a girl, peeked discreetly and occasionally into the garage as the technical people worked. McGarvey felt that he and Kuba weren't contributing much more than they were.

"You think they'll find it?" Kuba asked. "Five years is a long time."

"Peters says he hasn't painted or poured concrete or done anything to alter the interior of the garage since he bought the house. There's a good chance they'll find the bloodstains."

They waited like expectant fathers while the other three covered the walls and floor in the area where Handy said the murder had taken place with a chemical that would glow if the bloodstains Barbara had scrubbed away were still present under the surface. The blow to Ron's head might well have caused blood to splash against the walls. The forensic scientists, a man and a woman, worked swiftly, expertly. He admired the way they did their job, isolated it from the rest of the case, and just pursued it like nothing else mattered. The crime tech, on the other hand, a large man, whose stomach and ego were both outsize, had apparently heard what was going down and wanted to talk. His claim to fame was that he had also been the tech on call when Gusewelle's body was found in the Camaro. He kept telling them he'd known Engleman was the "shooter" because of the towels, good towels that you wouldn't see in a hooker's den. McGarvey kept turning away from him when he talked as though he were rotten cheese. The self-styled Engleman experts were coming out of the wood-work on the Illinois side, and they made him tired.

"Some irony if those stains turn up, huh?" Kuba asked. "After she went to so much trouble to clean them up—and then had that little scare with the cat blood in the driveway."

McGarvey laughed. He'd read the interview with Donna Guse-welle concerning the cat's blood. She'd gone to console Barbara one day during the the interval between the murder and the finding of the body in East St. Louis. As she climbed out of her car parked in Barbara's driveway, she heard a noise, an almost human whining beneath the hood, which made her shiver. She opened the hood. A cat, the Boyle children's pet, leapt out. Apparently injured by the fan blade of her car, the cat was bleeding from a wound in the ear. When Barbara saw the blood on the driveway, she panicked.

"They'll think it's human blood," she cried. "We have to clean it up."

The sisters-in-law had taken buckets of water and brushes to the cat's blood in the driveway. Picturing them bent down scrub-bing the concrete made him laugh. After all her trouble, they had found her husband's blood after all. On the floor and splashed against the walls, low, close to the floor, in the places where Handy said the stains would be, the phosphorescent glow was spreading, telling the story like a voice from the grave. She had clearly painted over the walls where her husband's blood had splashed but in her haste, she'd left the edges untrimmed. The edges glowed, showing up her paint job for what it was, a sloppy cover-up.

He and Kuba looked at each other and nodded in satisfaction. The other three began the tedious process of collecting the stains, which would be analyzed in the laboratory. They would have important evidence to support Handy's story. For his cooperation, Handy had been allowed to plead guilty to three counts of conspiracy to murder, receiving a fourteen-year sentence per count, each sentence to be served concurrently with the others and with the eighteen-year sentence he was already serving on the Halm mail fraud and conspiracy charges. He'd also been allowed to remain in federal custody, where he felt somewhat safer.

As he waited in Gerald Peters's garage for the technicians to finish their work, McGarvey wondered if he was standing in the place where Handy had stood when he watched Glennon Engleman shoot Ron Gusewelle through the heart, then bash in the side of his head with a mallet. And he wondered when it had finally occurred to Handy that for his part in the conspiracy he had received nothing. Barbara had given the Doc $4,000 before his arrest, and then she must have thought she was really going to come out of this good, with her conspirators in jail, a confession from another man the police had bought—and all the money to herself.

When they were finished, he took one last look at the place on the floor where Gusewelle had fallen. Missy, Peters's pretty little daughter, looked too. She wrinkled her nose in distaste. McGarvey laughed. Possibly the teenage Barbara Varney would have had the same reaction to the thought of a man's violent death arranged by his wife and co-conspirators; and possibly she wouldn't have. He wondered . . . but only briefly. More than wondering who she was, he wondered where she was. A subpoena had been issued for her to appear before a grand jury, but it hadn't been served yet because she was out of town. Her hundred-thousand-dollar five-bedroom home in Glen Carbon was up for sale and she was gone. He wanted to know where.

Alton, Illinois, Thursday, August 9, 1984

The grand jury hearing was proceeding smoothly. Weber had called Hertz, who related the details of the crime scenes and showed the photographs of the bodies. There was always one picture in a batch that particularly got to Weber, and in this gruesome collection it was the shot of Mrs. Gusewelle's sheet-covered body lying next to another large bloodstain on the kitchen floor. That other stain was Mr. Gusewelle's blood. He had lain beside her to be shot and then several minutes later managed to pull himself up to the phone. It was the most poignant shot to Weber, even more gut-wrenching than Ron's face as it had looked when he'd been removed him from the car.

"If you look closely on the photograph showing Mrs. Gusewelle laying on the kitchen floor, you can see she was wearing a watch," Hertz said. "I can't remember which hand the watch was on. That watch was stopped at 6:52. It was sent to the laboratory in Washington, D.C., and in the inside mechanism of the watch they found blood which apparently dried in the watch mechanism and stopped the watch. According to their report, when they removed the speck of blood, the watch started to run again."

He listened to Hertz continue to set forth the state's evidence in the clipped voice, a no-nonsense monotone that surely helped convince the jurors he knew what he was talking about. When he had established the apparent motive for the murders, burglary had no basis since nothing was taken, he had made the jurors focus on the beneficiaries of those crimes, Ron and Richard Gusewelle. Then he moved on to the murder of Ron Gusewelle.

"During the course of our investigation we were able to determine that Mr. Gusewelle on March 31 drove that car to work for the sole reason that his daughter was complaining about the mileage, that the car was not running right and was getting very poor mileage Hertz said. "When we found the car, inside the car we found a slip of paper with the mileage reading on it. We had surmised that Mr. Gusewelle, when he took that car to work on the evening of March 31, jotted down the mileage reading and was probably going to drive the car for some time to actually calculate the mileage the car was getting, the gas mileage.

"The mileage reading on the piece of paper and the mileage reading at the time the car was found gave us a distinct figure of mileage. I personally traveled the route from Mr. Gusewelle's house to Amoco Oil, back to his house, and then to Coleman's Plaza in East St. Louis. The mileage difference between the piece of paper and the actual odometer reading on the car when it was found matched exactly with the mileage that I had determined on my own car—which indicated to me that possibly what had happened was that Mr. Gusewelle left his house to go to work on March 31, went to work, came home from work, and possibly met his demise there at the house, and then his body was transported in the car from that house to Coleman's Plaza."

Hertz kept rolling. He showed more photographs. Then he recounted the story of Andre Jones's recantation and produced insurance records. One policy after another signed with Ronald Gusewelle's name in script that handwriting experts had said was consistent with that of the samples they'd studied of Barbara Gusewelle's hand. As Hertz spoke, Weber kept seeing the photographs, flashing like slides in his mind. Ron's left hand with the wedding band on his finger. The side of his skull after the skin had been removed during autopsy and the gaping hole was made visible. The wedding photo: Ron and Barbara leaving the ceremony, looking out the back window of a car; Barbara's blond hair done in fat sausage curls under the picture hat, her bouquet tossed casually in the back of the car; Ron smiling like he thought he had latched on to someone special.

Weber wanted Edith Lovato, Barbara's mother, on the stand so he could ask her about her daughter's whereabouts while she was under oath. She answered his initial questions by pleading the Fifth. Following a consultation with Chief Criminal Judge Phillip J. Rarick and him, she was granted immunity from prosecution on any activities described in her testimony. As she took the stand again, he tried to see the physical resemblance to her beautiful daughter, which was difficult. She was thin, thinner than Barbara, and well on her way to being wizened in her old age. Her hands trembled perceptibly. She was very nervous, but whether for herself or her daughter he couldn't tell. He didn't think she would lie to him, but he realized she would avoid telling him as much as possible. If he didn't directly ask, she wouldn't directly answer.

He began by asking in what year her daughter was born, and the answers he got to each succeeding question were no more illuminating than the answer to this one, which he already knew: 1942. As Edith Lovato talked, in brief broad strokes grudgingly painting the picture of a girl who had finished high school, moved to the big city, and married young, he wondered if Barbara was as indistinct to her mother as she had been to all of those teachers, classmates, and neighbors who, when questioned, could barely remember her. After her parents divorced when she was eleven, she lived with her mother and grandparents, sang in a choral group at Alton High School, became a clerk-typist for the John Fabick Tractor Company in St. Louis. He could see the jurors politely listening to the recitation of facts that wouldn't add up to two lines on any class-reunion worksheet and question, as he once did, is this ordinary pretty woman capable of murder?

"When did she get married to Dr. Boyle?" he asked.

"When she was twenty."

"That would have been 1962?"

"Yes."

"So between 1960 and 1962 at least we have it pinned down that she was living in that apartment on Compton?"

"Right."

"During this period of time, did she ever talk to you about Dr. Engleman?"

"I don't remember it."

Her answers to the important questions were equally brief. No, she didn't know what brand of towels had been in Barbara's home. They were "nice" ones. Some she had purchased herself, at Stix or Famous, she couldn't remember. The question did not appear to upset her any more than being asked about Barbara's china, and she volunteered that Vernita took her shopping all the time and bought her things, things like curtains and things like towels.

And, no, she didn't know exactly where her daughter was. She had gone on a vacation with her daughter and one son. To Tennessee and probably to Florida.

"Does Barbara have a boyfriend around here from St. Louis?" he asked.

"She was going with a fellow from St. Louis."

"What's his name?"

"Paul."

"Paul what?"

"Paul Mills."

Weber asked her where Paul Mills lived. She told him in St. Louis. He almost didn't blame her. She was, after all, the woman's mother. And she had, inadvertently, given them the lead they needed simply by disclosing the boyfriend's name.

Next, he called Kuba and related the information obtained from Ruth Engleman. And then came Handy, looking exactly like the kind of person Barbara must have meant when she complained to a girlfriend after her divorce that she didn't meet nice people anymore. The grand jury handed down an indictment of Barbara Gusewelle in the murders of her husband and his parents. The indictment was suppressed to give the state some advantage in locating and arresting her.

Later that night, Kuba and Spaul, through talking to the family of Samuel Paul Mills, discovered Barbara and Mills were staying at the Sandy Shoes Motel in Lauderdale-by-the-Sea, Florida. At 12:55 A.M., they notified local police about the outstanding warrants for her and requested she be taken into custody.

Lauderdale-by-the-Sea, Friday, August 10, 1984

The car had circled the motel once before its occupants spotted their quarry coming from the opposite direction. Barbara Jean Boyle, twenty-one, blond and pretty like her mother, pulled into the lot driving her mother's car packed with suitcases. The officers stopped her and asked where her mother was. When she said she didn't know, they detained her. Several minutes later they found her sixteen-year-old brother Brian David walking along the beach. He was led to the car where his sister waited and held there with her.

Barbara was walking along the beach too, some distance further from the hotel than her son had been. Too restless to stay in the room with Paul after the phone call, she was barefoot, carrying her ankle-strapped shoes in one hand and dressed stylishly in a cream-colored linen two-piece dress. As soon as her daughter came back with the car, they were taking the children and getting out of there. In fact, Paul said, as soon as he had the kids together, he would head down the beach in the car and pick her up. If Jamie had been in the room with them when the call came in, they could have been gone by now. What was keeping Jamie? She was tempted to run now, on foot, run somewhere and hide until Paul collected the kids and the car and found her, but how would he know where to look?

"Relax," Paul had said, pulling her close to him for an embrace before she left the room. She thought he probably wanted to make love, quickly, before the kids came back, but she couldn't possibly, not then. "She'll be here in a little while, and we'll be on our way."

"What if it's too late?" she said. "What did the police say when they called?"

"Honey, they just asked if I knew where you were because you were wanted in Illinois. I said I didn't."

"Wanted," she repeated. "Wanted how? For questioning? How?"

She had asked the questions several times, and she went over them again in her mind now. He had said he didn't have the answers, just like he said he believed her when she told him it was all a lie, a mistake, she didn't know anything, hadn't done anything, hadn't murdered anyone. She thought about the look on his face when the phone had rung and it had been the police. He was surprised, a little scared. Was he scared for her—or for him? The breeze coming in from the ocean felt suddenly cooler than it had in the weeks they'd stayed at the Sandy Shoes. She shivered. Her full-brimmed white hat fell backward off her head, and she caught it in one hand. Tears formed in her eyes. She didn't want to lose this . . . freedom . . . she didn't want to lose it now. She had earned it, paid for it, by living in little apartments with walls so thin she could hear the springs squeak when her children turned over in their beds.

The tears ran down her cheeks, and she swiped at them angrily. She'd earned it, freedom, the money, she'd earned it for years of living on whatever amount men thought she needed. Almost as soon as her first husband was earning enough money to make her life comfortable, he'd grown tired of her. Her mother said she shouldn't leave him anyway, and bitterly she thought her mother had known more about the real world than she had. "He'll have to support me," she'd raged. "I'll take him to the cleaners." Her mother had said, "Oh, honey, you just don't know"; and she hadn't. What she'd received was $350 a month in child support, $300 in alimony, not enough, not anything at all. She couldn't have made it at all without Glen.

"You believe me, don't you?" she had asked Paul again and again. He'd murmured in her hair, her golden hair, which he admired but did not love as much as Glen had, reassuring her he did believe her. Their passports had arrived yesterday; and now, looking back, she wished she had gotten on a plane to Switzerland then instead of waiting. Why had she waited?

When she was almost back to the motel, she put her hat on her head and slipped her shoes on her feet, bending to fasten the straps. Her ankles were trim and pretty again. After Ronnie's death she'd lost the weight he'd nagged her about. While he was alive, she'd kept that weight to show him he didn't own her, couldn't have everything of her he wanted. A man who took his lunch to work in a pail . . . Did he think that was what she wanted for her whole life? She saw the police car before she went inside the room but she opened the door anyway. What else could she do? She took one step inside. An officer moved toward her, claiming he had a warrant for her arrest. Her face registered shock. She took a few steps backward, and he grabbed her. It was over as quickly as that. If she had left as soon as her passport arrived in the mail, she would be free.

Whimpering softly, she turned to look at Paul standing helplessly behind the cop.

"Don't worry," he said. "We'll call your lawyer. They don't have anything on you, honey. Don't worry."

Monday, August 13, 1984

It was her forty-second birthday, and she was handcuffed to a
chair in a Florida courtroom. Her hair hung down in tangled curls.
She'd washed it, but she hadn't had a blow dryer or hot rollers to
shape it, so she was stuck with it the way permed hair looked
when the strands dried naturally, kinking and frizzing. She'd
been held without bond since her arrest, and this hearing was to
determine whether or not Florida would honor the three-million-
dollar bond set by the state of Illinois. Her left wrist, the one
encircled by the metal cuff, hurt. Jamie and Brian were sitting
behind her. She longed to pull free from the cuff and reach behind her to hug them.

"My client is a political prisoner," her lawyer, Stuart Stein,
argued. He specialized in extradition cases, which in Florida,
with its abundance of drug traffickers, was a lucrative business.
"She is the victim of overzealous prosecution by Don W. Weber,
Madison County's state's attorney—who happens to be up for
reelection this fall."

She twisted her wrist, gently, so the metal wouldn't clang,
announcing her frustration at the bonds. On the table in front of
her were the birthday cards Paul had brought her. With her right
hand she opened the top one, which pictured a blonde who
looked like a fairy-tale princess holding a bouquet of red roses and
said "To My Darling Daughter On Her Birthday." Her throat
began to close again; she swallowed hard. She believed what her
lawyer was saying, that she was a victim, a victim of political
persecution. They had never liked her, those people in that little
hick town, never.

"Mr. Weber says Mrs. Boyle is worth millions. She's not even
worth a half a million dollars, including money from her late
husband," Stein said.

She was confused about what was going on, so she opened
another birthday card, this one from her friend Phyllis, who'd
been with her at Denny's the night she'd met Ron. It showed a
buxom blonde drinking a glass of champagne. Paul had said they
would drink champagne to celebrate as soon as her bond was set,
but she wasn't sure that would happen, that she would ever be

free of handcuffs again. They were fighting extradition to Illinois and trying to get bail set here. Her lawyer had explained that federal authorities were trying to convene a grand jury of their own to indict her on mail fraud charges. If the feds got an indictment, he said, she would be extradited quickly because they bypassed all the red tape governing extradition proceedings between the states. Tracing the outline of the blonde on the card from Phyllis, she sighed. It was all so confusing.

She glanced across the room. Representatives from Madison County, the state of Illinois, and ATF were sitting together. She knew ATF was responsible for catching Glen, and knowing they were involved in her case didn't make her feel good. But surely they couldn't do anything to her, even if that stupid black man had taken back his confession. Who would testify against her? Bob Handy or Glen? Not likely. She couldn't imagine Glen ever confessing to anything. Even when he was convicted, he swore he was innocent, and probably he believed he was, that he was above however people defined guilty. As he'd told her so many times, he didn't believe in right and wrong, guilty and innocent, the way other people talked about it. They didn't have his knowledge, so how could they judge him?

With her right hand she kept opening the envelopes, pulling out the cards, reading the messages from the people who loved her. Under the envelopes was a pile of photographs Jamie had just had developed. Pictures of their vacation. She wasn't quite ready to look at them yet. She was afraid she might cry.

The judge was telling her lawyer in what he probably thought were reasonable tones she could "short-circuit" all her legal problems by agreeing to return to Illinois and face them.

"Why should she go back?" Stein countered. "Why should she interrupt her vacation?"

She looked down at her pile of cards. If all these people loved her, could she be so bad? With her free hand she moved them aside. The first photo in the stack was a shot of her and the kids with the ocean behind them. She was squinting into the sun. Paul had taken the picture. And they were all laughing. She deserved that happiness, didn't she? After all she'd been through, raising the kids alone, walking door-to-door selling Avon products, not knowing how she would make it. She deserved to laugh, didn't she? Someone who had been so sad and cried so much deserved to laugh.

And surely Glen wouldn't talk. He had always told her the important truth was what was agreed upon between the two of them. And she shouldn't talk to anyone else, shouldn't answer their questions. He wouldn't talk, would he? Had she made a mistake in turning Melody away when she'd come to the house asking for money for Glen's legal fees? But surely Glen would understand why, would understand her giving money to Melody would link them to each other irrevocably. He would think she had done the right thing, which to Glen was always whatever advanced his plan.

"I refuse to let my client be a pawn in the election of Mr. Weber," her lawyer ranted. "It is perceived in Illinois as a political game."

He said she was being treated differently than other murder suspects, who regularly have bond set for them. She listened to him talk and sorted through the pictures with her right hand and felt sorry for herself. What had Glen told her years ago when she was first dating Jim—"Sit there and look pretty. Don't talk too much. And, when the time is right, honey, part your legs, honey"? He had told her then all she had to do was look pretty and part her legs and trust him. Once he had told her a story about Charles Manson. "He can charm birds out of trees, honey; and if you were a bird, you would have nothing to fear from him, nothing." She didn't remember the story but it had something to do with birds and being able to trust. Glen's stories confused her, but they usually had something to do with beauty and trust and intimacy. And what good were they doing her now?

"There's nothing illegal about wanting to come to sunny Florida," Stein said. "Mrs. Boyle has already cooperated with the police. Why should she cut short her vacation now? Why should she?"

Jamie leaned forward and patted her back.

Belleville, Illinois, Thursday, August 30, 1984

After the federal mail-fraud indictment had been handed down, she was held in Miami, then transferred to the St. Clair County jail in Belleville. Two officers led her in shackles to the jail. She was wearing jeans, sneakers, and a purple silk shirt. The curls in her hair were a little looser, and the breeze caught them, fanned them out from her head as she walked slowly across the parking lot.

"Why don't they take me to Edwardsville?" she asked, and the men shrugged. They didn't care. It was nothing to them. She tried to remember what Glen had told her about astral-projecting, and she wished she could do that now, project her body out of those chains.

Inside she was processed—which meant they took her own clothes and put her in an orange jumpsuit or worse, gray separates. They told her she would be arraigned on the federal charges in East St. Louis on Tuesday. She asked if she would get to wear her own clothes then, and they said she would.

She sat on her bunk in the cell and practiced controlling her breathing. Already she had learned that being labeled a murderess was good in jail. The other women left you pretty much alone. Following her instructions, her daughter had taken $250,000 and hired F. Lee Bailey to defend her. She had signed over her Glen Carbon house to Stein, his pay for prolonging her Florida vacation. It bothered her to see her money going so fast. Surely, however, Bailey would get her bail reduced and get her out of there. Those fools in Edwardsville couldn't beat F. Lee Bailey; she was sure of that.

Jefferson City, Tuesday, September 4, 1984

"That's enough pictures," Engleman shouted at the photographer, but the young man, dressed in jeans and a camelhair sportcoat, kept snapping him, handcuffed and chained, and wearing his gray prison uniform. No doubt the folks back home took satisfaction in seeing him that way—Mr. Hyde in bondage. "I said that's enough. You've had your fun. Now take your camera and get out of here, You pissant! Get out!"

The guards flanking him told him to "pipe down," which angered him even more. If his hands weren't shackled together and fastened in the center to the chain around his waist, he'd wipe up the floor with all three of them. Yes, he could do it even now, at his age, with his diabetes advancing the way it was and so forth. The young photographer laughed—laughed at him!—and took another shot. Engleman broke free of the guards and started running toward him.

"You pimp!" he yelled. "All of you newspaper people, you're all goddamn pimps!"

He lunged and used his entire body like a fist, smashing the punk into the wall, slicing into his left arm with the manacles. "You pimp," he shouted into his face. Then he sunk his teeth into the left hand cradling the camera. It took both guards to pull him off. They shoved him roughly down the hall. Engleman looked back over his shoulder and laughed at the little pimp licking his hand as they led him into a courtroom. He'd seen enough of courtrooms to last him several lifetimes.

The judge barely looked at him as he picked up an order allowing Glennon E. Engleman to be taken to Edwardsville, Illinois, to appear before the grand jury. When he had finished signing his name to the order, he said, "Dr. Engleman, you know the grand jury intends to ask you about the killings of Arthur and Vernita Gusewelle and their son, Ronald."

"It's a waste of the taxpayers' money to take me over there," he said, "because I plan on taking the Fifth. I have no intentions of saying anything which will incriminate me."

With a bored expression, the judge waved him away. The guards led him to a room where he was given an orange jumpsuit to wear for the trip to Illinois. They thought they were very clever, of course, to dress the prisoners in orange. How far could an escaped convict get wearing bright orange? He laughed at their stupidity. How many times had he told them he didn't mind being in jail at all because he had the power to transport himself away, anywhere he wanted, whenever he chose. Why, just yesterday he'd been in Palm Springs playing golf.

Two deputies and a state's attorney accompanied him on the trip to Illinois. They probably thought they were going to trap him into saying something about the Gusewelle murders, but he was too smart for them. A letter from Handy had been smuggled to him through a mutual associate on the outside, so he knew what was coming down. "Glen, I'm sorry," Handy had said, "I hate going against you, but they're making me do it. I haven't got any other choice. I know I'll never be welcome in Melody's house, or Kim's or Sherrill's, again; and that hurts me. I'm sorry, Glen." He smiled. Poor Handy had the courage of a lion but he didn't have the brains to go with it. Left on his own, he didn't have the brains.

Barb didn't have the brains either. She thought she did, but she was wrong. They told him she'd been arrested, and he hated to hear that, hated to think about the golden girl in prison. It was her greed that did it to her. If she hadn't taken out so much insurance on Ron, she'd still be free. Thinking about her, he shook his head. She could have been his best pupil, the Trilby to his Svengali. He still remembered how she looked when he'd first met her, and his prick stiffened momentarily at the memory.

He didn't pick up women in bars. You got what you deserved when you started consorting with barflies. She'd walked into his dental office on Park one spring day in 1960. "I think I lost a filling," she told him, "and someone at work suggested I try you because you wouldn't charge me an arm and a leg." He had told her how pretty her arms and legs were.

She sat back in the chair, allowing her tight skirt to ride up her thighs. As she opened her mouth wide, she looked trustingly into his eyes. Her own eyes were big and blue. Her skin, he thought, was flawless. Few people had skin so good it could stand the close scrutiny it got when he leaned over their faces. She had no enlarged pores, no blemishes, just creamy, silky skin to go with her silky blond hair. He invited her to lunch.

"I'm sharing an apartment with my cousin," she said, "and it's getting me down. She doesn't like to do anything or go anywhere at night, and she tries to make me feel bad because I do." She took a bite out of her hamburger, and he marveled again at how pretty she was. He wanted to be intimate with her. Even chewing her food didn't detract from her beauty. "My job is boring. I work at a tractor company, typing and filing. I don't meet the kind of men there I want to meet."

"You should be married to a professional man," he said, "so you can enjoy the finer things in life and so forth. Working is not for a woman like you."

"Yes." she said, nodding. "I don't want to marry some farm-boy. That's why I left Wood River. I didn't want to be stuck out there, married to someone who takes his lunch to work in a pail."

He told her he was going to help her, but really in his own mind he hadn't decided how. She perked up immediately and asked if she could have another Pepsi. He signaled the waitress and got her the Pepsi. He said she would be hearing from him soon, and she asked, "Do you mean that? Can I really believe it or are you just saying you'll call me the way men do sometimes, you know?"

"Is this the way you came when you went to Illinois?" one deputy asked, and he smiled.

"I don't remember when's the last time I did come to Illinois," he said. "It was probably with Nick Miranda, that crooked lying son of a bitch, when we were looking at the drag race strip. Do they still have drag racing over here?"

"They have the death penalty in Illinois," the second deputy said. "They had it then too, in '77 and '79."

"They have a lot of cow pasture in Illinois too, don't they?" Engleman said, looking out the window. "It's an interesting situation here in Illinois, the farmland and then you have East St. Louis, which was, in my youth, a booming city. Then the niggers took it over and you see what happens when you allow a group to govern themselves who really aren't mentally and otherwise equipped to do that, don't you?" He paused. "Did you know the Holiday Inn in East St. Louis which failed was only one of two in the entire chain that ever failed?"

He looked out the window, deliberately not looking at their faces to see what effect his last comment had had. They were playing with him; and he could play too. He didn't mind being in prison, he told them that. He had established a place for himself behind the walls in Jeff City. The spiritual inmates turned to him. He had taught many of them how to astral-project with a candle in the darkness of their cells, and he understood their voodoo, maybe understood it better than they did. They respected him. They understood what a lot of these pimps and pissants did not: not every man can kill. It takes a special kind of courage to snuff out a human life, and he was proud he had it. He didn't mind being in prison. By submitting to imprisonment, he was living out his mother's, and Melody's, prophecy. His life had been determined from his birth, and it had not been determined that he would die at the hands of pimps like these.

He thought again of Barbara, his golden girl. She was meant to be the best one, cooler and tougher than Carmen or Sandy, more beautiful than his little Ruthie, and different from Ruth, who was, had been, his partner. Ruth, the bitch who had stolen his son and his money, had been his partner, no matter what she told her federal pimp. But Barbara was meant to be his Trilby. Only she had become too greedy, behaving in the end like a stupid bitch.

He'd moved her and one of her girlfriends into the small apartment on the second floor of his mother's house on Compton. The apartment had a separate entrance. Eda wasn't happy about the girls moving in, but he had told his mother about Barbara and she approved. She saw in Barbara's aura someone special, and she assured him a study of Barbara's past lives would show she had been a courtesan of wealthy and powerful men. His mother was studying past lives before any of these people, Shirley MacLaine and all of them, the celebrities, ever knew anything about it. Why, he'd read MacLaine's book and she was nothing special until she'd had her first out-of-body experience, floating over her hot tub.

Encouraged by his mother's interest, he began instructing Barbara, teaching her how to dress and telling her what books to read. She was slow at the reading, but he had expected she would be, was prepared to lovingly spoon knowledge into her as if she were a child still eating soft foods. He thought her slowness was an advantage. She wouldn't learn things on her own; she would be taught exactly as he wanted her taught.

They met at least twice a week at the office. He pulled down the cot, which had recently replaced the sleeping bag, from the rafters; and willingly, even the first time, she had allowed him to take her. She wasn't a virgin, but she might as well have been for all she knew about sex.

Because he liked to get off quickly the first time, he taught her to take his prick in her mouth and suck it until he came. "You want me to put it in my mouth?" she said, and he'd laughed at her. "Honey, you are so new at this, aren't you? Hold it tight at the base baby, with your hand, and play with the balls, honey, yes, with your fingers, lick it, honey, lick all of it, from the balls up the shaft, and take the head in your mouth and suck like you were suckling at your mama's breast." He explained everything he was doing as he was doing it, and the words thrilled her. "I'm going to lick your clitoris, honey. Can you say that word? Do you know where it is, your clit? Give me your hand, honey, and I'll put your finger on it, gently, yeees, honey, you didn't even know you had that, did you?"

She repeated the words he wanted to her to use. "I want you to lift up your hips, honey, to reach me, lift them up, so I can cup your ass with my hand while I drive into you, yes, that's it, and tell me what we're doing, honey, tell me, say, fuck, say it, honey, fuck, fuck, fuck, fuck." And she did, until she was too excited to talk and her sweet breath began to come in little honeyed gasps. He loved the smell of her mouth. She was the only woman he'd ever known who was as beautiful as Melody. He liked to pull out of her before she could come and told her to turn over, on her knees, with her ass up in the air, so he could enter her from behind. Trembling and moaning, she did what she was told, she always did what she was told. To reward her, he fucked her good and hard until she bit her lower lip and made it bleed.

When he held her afterward, he told her things. "I've killed a man," he said, and she looked at him solemnly, understanding that what he'd told her constituted a bond between them, a homicidal intimacy, which would deepen, an intimacy which could never be penetrated by anyone else. "I've killed a man," he said. And she asked him, "What did it feel like?" She didn't ask him why.

"Well, Doctor, does this bring back memories?"

He looked out the window. They were driving along Highway 157 where it curved into Edwardsville. Did they think he'd been stupid enough to come in through town, advertising himself? Hadn't it occurred to those pissants there was a back way in?

"No," he said. "I don't believe I've ever been to Edwardsville. I hear it's a very nice little town. Is it?"

*   *   *

Without a clear-cut plan, he had fixed her up with James Boyle, a dentist he knew from the clinic at Union Electric. She was anxious to go out with a better class of man than she'd met on her own in bars, and he had wanted her to have the chance. At first Jimmy hadn't wanted to go on any blind dates, but finally he'd consented. Of course when he saw Barbara, a vision in a white piqué sheath dress with crisscross straps on the back, he'd fallen for her. She and Jimmy had been dating pretty steadily when she'd come into the office one day and told him she *thought* she might be pregnant. By this time he had his hands full with Sandy, and Ruth Jolley had come into his life. She didn't look as good as Barbara, but she had no match in the sack. His life, he thought, was complicated enough, so he sat Barbara down and told her how to get her dentist to propose. She was still nineteen when she walked down the aisle of Main Street Methodist Church in Alton, Illinois, wearing a chantilly-lace sheath dress and a diaphanous veil attached to an orange blossom crown floating around her head. He was one of approximately one hundred invited guests. In marrying her off, he felt that he'd put her in a safe haven for the time being, not that he was giving her away. Briefly he considered murdering her husband, then changed his mind. He was a professional man and too many questions would be asked. That's when he really began forming in his mind the criteria for murder.

She brought the baby girl to the office to show him. Carmen was there one day, and they told Carmen the baby was theirs together. He thought Barbara was very caught up in being a dentist's wife, especially after the twin boys were born a few years later. She dressed her boys in matching clothes that coordinated with their sister's dresses. He saw her picture in the *Globe* one day. She was modeling at a fashion show put on by the Women's Auxiliary of the St. Louis Dental Society. He clipped out the picture and the two lines about her in the article. Mrs. Boyle collects baby teeth for experiments at Washington University Medical School and likes to bowl with her girlfriends. He smiled. The Mrs. Boyle he knew liked to do something other than bowl.

Shortly after that picture was published, she called and told him she was getting a divorce. Her Jimmy, she said, had been playing around with someone else or at least she was afraid he was because he wasn't interested in her anymore . . . while she bowled with her girlfriends, went shopping, had her hair done, dressed the children, did the things she was supposed to do. He remembered how shellshocked she had looked the first time he'd seen her after she moved into that little apartment in Wood River. "I don't deserve this," she had told him. "I deserve better than this"; and he had agreed. "You deserve it, honey," he'd told her, "and I can help you get it; I can give it to you." No other man could do for her what he could do, no other man would kill for her. He knew she was ready to take their intimacy to a new level.

He blinked in the sunshine. It was 4:15 P.M. and uncomfortably warm and bright for someone accustomed to prison. One of the deputies held onto his elbow and guided him up the steps. Another photographer was taking his picture, this one a portly, middle-aged fellow.

"I can walk, you know," he said to the guard. To the photographer, he called, "Reporters and photographers are nothing but pimps . . . pimps of the press. Why don't you find an honest job?"

Inside the jailhouse he looked around for her. She would be wearing an orange jumpsuit too. But he didn't see her. Perhaps they were deliberately keeping him apart from her. That would be the kind of plan they would pride themselves on developing. Divide and conquer and so forth. He did see Melody. She smiled across the room at him, and his heart picked up, the way it always did when he saw Melody. She was the only woman he ever should have trusted, the only one who hadn't betrayed him. Only Melody would drive all this way just for a glimpse of him being led in chains.

He was held at the jail until Thursday, when he appeared before the grand jury. His testimony took five minutes. He reserved his constitutional right to plead the Fifth Amendment. Later, he was indicted on the same charges as Barbara, three counts of capital murder and three counts of conspiracy to commit murder, but his subpoena gave him immunity for arraignment while in Edwardsville. He was transported back to Jefferson City.

"Once the extradition hearings take place, you'll be back over here, Doc," the deputy said with satisfaction. "I hear your buddy Handy got a pretty good deal. It must look even better to him now that Weber's asking for the death penalty. What do you think, Doc?"

He thought Ruth was to blame for all of it.

St. Louis, Wednesday, November 7, 1984

McGarvey looked around Freddy O's, the bar on Eleventh and Olive that was the unofficial watering hole of the federal agents. It was a nondescript bar with orange industrial carpet, red vinyl bar stools, and maple mate's chairs around Formica tables. The drinks were cheap and the popcorn was free. He recognized a few faces, but the place was largely deserted.

"Jeez," he said to Sheila, the waitress, "where is everybody?"

"You're a little early today, aren't you?" she asked, setting another Scotch in front of him. "It isn't even five yet. Bad day?"

"Nah, routine."

He'd been coming to Freddy O's since the days of go-go girls dancing in cages, and Sheila had been there since the first time he'd walked into the place. Yet her brown hair hadn't gotten gray and her smooth skin hadn't wrinkled. He caught sight of himself in the mirror behind the bar and took note of the gray hairs he'd grown since he first heard the name Glennon Engleman. He lit another cigarette and picked up the Scotch. He and his boss, James Elder, had driven to Edwardsville that afternoon to turn over the tapes and transcripts of the conversations between Doc and Ruth to a circuit state's attorney. Madison County had issued an order requiring him to produce them; and so, with Edler's authorization, he'd complied. Barb's lawyer, F. Lee Bailey, had requested them as part of the discovery process.

He was reluctant to part with the tapes. As long as they'd remained over here, he felt that he had some control of them. He and Elder had cautioned the attorney the material was sensitive and suggested he make arrangements with the court to have Barb's attorneys listen to them under the supervision of the court.

"You can be assured we'll handle them with the utmost of care," the guy had said.

McGarvey had almost laughed. Nothing else had been handled with the utmost care in Madison County. Before Don Weber had been defeated in the November elections, he had threatened to expose the attorney with whom Barb had allegedly been having an affair and attempted to determine the paternity of her daughter. Cooler heads had prevailed, but his efforts at scandal-mongering were still generally known within the community, famous for its love of dirty politics and sexual scandals.

Without waiting for him to ask, Sheila put another drink down in front of him.

"Hey, when are they going to trial in Illinois?" someone called from across the room.

"They're anticipating January," he said, shrugging his shoulders. "But I doubt they'll make it. They don't even have a prosecutor assigned yet. And Bailey is trying to get the charges against Barb dismissed on the basis of prosecutorial misconduct."

He heard a few scattered laughs and turned back to his Scotch to avoid further questions. It was barely possible that Bailey— who, it was rumored, had been paid a quarter of a million dollars in cash—would get Barb out of it on the basis of Weber's handling of the case. A gag order had been imposed shortly after her arrest because of his statements to the press. Jesus, he'd even heard that Weber used a slide presentation referring to the Gusewelle murders as a form of educating the grand jurors in their duties. It was barely possible, but possible, that Bailey would get her out. Meanwhile, she was still in jail, unable to meet the bond he'd yet to get reduced. Ron's brother was also suing her for his estate. Smart of Bailey to get his in cash—and, it was also rumored, to deposit the cash in a bank account outside the United States.

McGarvey swallowed his Scotch. He really had disliked turning over those tapes. In spite of everything, he wasn't proud of the tapes—or at least a portion of those tapes. That he had listened to a man have sexual relations with his ex-wife was bad enough— but that he had made it possible for other people to listen was worse. The tapes had accomplished their purpose, nailing a killer and getting him off the streets . . . but he still wasn't proud of it. Even leaving the sex aside, he had felt like a voyeur while listening to the ordinary domestic chatter of a family that would soon be split, thanks in part to his efforts. It was the right thing to do. It was justified but it wasn't pleasant.

He signaled Sheila for another Scotch. "Same old shit, Bill?"
"Yeah, Sheila, same old shit."

What bothered him about the Illinois side of the investigation
was the way everything had become so public. Sure, you had a
responsibility to inform the public about the crime, but not about
some of the sordid personal details. That, in his opinion, was
voyeurism. Hell, Buckles hadn't even listened to the sex portions
of the Engleman tapes because he didn't want to be a voyeur. It
wasn't necessary, he had said.

Everyone involved in the arrests and prosecutions on the Missouri side could tell stories, and did among themselves. Dempsey
and the prosecutors, ATF agents, and county and city cops had
drunk together and, yes, laughed at some of the intimate information they'd gathered on Doc and the group surrounding him.
Sometimes you had to laugh. At the party Dempsey had thrown
for the participants after Doc's last trial, they had exchanged
drinking stories into the morning. Dempsey's little son by his
second marriage had grown bug-eyed when McCrady showed him
his gun. But none of them had been anything less than professional in their handling of the investigations or trials. It was one
thing to speculate on whether Doc had actually fathered the illegitimate kids he claimed he had—and another to threaten to
take that speculation to the press.

"Bad day, huh?" Sheila asked, leaning her elbows on the counter in front of him; and he grinned.

Edwardsville, Tuesday, December 18, 1984

Bailey had finally gotten Barbara's bond reduced from three million dollars to one million dollars. After posting the required ten
percent, a cashier's check for $100,000, she was going to be free
until the trial. Her hands shook as she pulled on the new panty
hose Jamie had brought her. She was putting on her own clothes;
and she was, finally, going home.

Her friends had told her what was being said about her, but her
lawyers said, Ignore that, don't think about it, don't worry about it.
As soon as she was arrested, people began remembering little
incidents that they said proved she'd done it, like how she'd put

her Pepsi can down on Ron's casket at the wake. Well, so what if she had? People were hugging and kissing her. She had to put the can somewhere. Her lawyers said to ignore the gossip, they were going after Weber. They were going to prove he'd jeopardized her right to a fair trial by negative publicity. And maybe they would prove it. They'd gotten the federal charges dropped, hadn't they? They'd said the federal charges were merely a ploy to get her extradited quickly, and they'd been right about that, hadn't they?

Her friends said people were talking about how she had ruined the Gusewelle family. Well, let them. Her lawyers said talk couldn't kill her. She could see fat little Donna telling the neighbors how she had hounded Ron to make a will after his parents died, how she had threatened to divorce him if he worked with Rich to run the farm. Yes, she had insisted the farm become a liquid asset. Glen had given her the phrase, "liquid asset" . . . Yes, she had, and so what? Her lawyers said that didn't prove anything at all.

She pulled a tan leather belt tight around her waist, pleased she'd lost weight. They said she was a party person who loved to go drinking at bars and could dance all night. She patted her stomach. Yes, she had lost weight. She would look good in the pictures they would take of her walking out of jail.

Her knees were weak as the matron, smelling of old toilet water and older sweat, led her down the corridor. "Why did you do it," the old bitch said. Barbara stiffened and didn't say a word. Glen had always told her, Look pretty and keep your mouth shut. She didn't say a word. The old bitch had no right to ask, no right at all.

"So why are you doing it? Why are you getting married?" a woman she knew only slightly, another blond divorcée, had asked her over two Lite beers at Phil's Lounge in Wood River. It was 1976, mid May, just before she and Ronnie got married on the twenty-eighth. She didn't stop there often anymore, but this afternoon she had popped in on a whim. Maybe she still did think there was the chance she'd find Prince Charming. Some of her friends accused her of that. "Why? Why are you marrying Ron Gusewelle? When you describe him, he doesn't sound like what you were looking for."

"I'm going to wear a big lacy hat this time instead of a veil," she said. "I think you only get to wear the veil once." She pulled at the corner of the beer label. It was so wet, the upper half of the label pulled back as soon as she'd tugged it. "Isn't that what you think?"

"I think I don't get it," the woman said. "I remember meeting you a couple years ago, and you said you didn't like the men you were meeting, you wanted to marry a professional man. It sounds like you're giving up."

"What would that be to you if I were?"

"I don't know. Nothing I guess." The woman hesitated. Suddenly her belligerent attitude was gone. "It's just that I guess it will happen to me too. I'll give up and the truth is I'll be lucky to find anyone at all."

"When I got divorced," Barb said, "I thought he would have to take care of me better than he did. I didn't understand how the law works, you know?" The woman nodded her head vigorously. "I was scared. When I found out how it was going to be, I'd already taken the kids and left him, and he was telling people I was moody and had a split personality, happy some days and sad the next. Well, who isn't? What woman isn't? I want to know." She ripped the rest of the label off the bottle and signaled the bartender for two more. "I knew he wasn't going to take me back, not that I wanted to go. But I was scared. I had three little kids, the twins were only three and a half, and I didn't know how I was going to live or make ends meet."

"I know," the woman said, tears as much of sympathy as her own self-pity welling in her eyes. "My youngest was eighteen months. Why couldn't the bastard have discovered he didn't really like living with me before I had that one? Why are they always willing to ram it into you as often as you'll let them, whether they like you or not? That's the one thing I don't understand about men . . . Well, that and why they're so proud of their penises."

"I *know*," Barbara said, giggling slightly. The beers were put on the counter, and she pulled out two dollars, waving the other woman's dollar away. "I know. I didn't know how to do anything, had no job skills. How do you get job skills when you marry at nineteen and have a baby the next year? My mother didn't have anything to help me with; and I think she was disappointed in me anyway. She told me one day I let a dentist get away. That's how I began to feel—like Barbara, you fool, you let a dentist get away. I lost touch with all my friends in St. Louis, except one person. Only one person still cared about me for me myself and wanted to help me."

"I know," the woman said. "You were lucky to keep one friend. I lost all mine with the divorce. It's like they're afraid you'll rub off on them. They don't want to look at you or they wouldn't be able to look at their own husbands without wondering, Hey, what's going on here? Is he a jerk too? Am I next?"

"I know," Barbara said, eagerly picking up the narration. "And I wanted to be a real mother to my kids, be home with them, not like some of these high-toned bitches going out to work when they don't even have to and leave their kids to fend for themselves. I wanted to be with my kids. I've always done that. You know, I've been a room mother for all the kids and I've helped with the Scouts. What you do for one, you have to do for all of them; and I did it. I did what you were supposed to do, and look where it got me. I remember how I felt when the divorce was final and I looked at that paper and it gave me almost nothing. When my father died two years ago, it was the same thing. He'd given me almost nothing since he left us when I was a kid, and it was no different when he died. He didn't even have insurance for me. Can you believe that? Wouldn't you think he'd know I was alone with three kids and needed something? I took my kids to church. I had a real nice life. They could take it away from me just like that."

"Men. I know. Men have all the power. When they're through with you, that's it," the woman said, downing her beer and ordering two more. "It was the same for me. I was lucky to get a job as a secretary, and I got that through some woman I met right here in this bar. Can you believe that? All the men I met and dated and went to bed with—and some woman found me a job in her company. Weren't you able to find a job?"

"No," Barbara said, hesitating a moment, then deciding what she had to say was safe to say. "I had a friend, a man in St. Louis. He gave me money and helped me out so I could stay home with my kids."

"You were lucky," the woman said. "But you couldn't marry him?"

"No," Barbara said, abruptly closing her purse, picking up her car keys. "No, it wasn't like that."

"Oh," the woman said. Barbara read on her face the answer she thought she had: You've been kept by a married man and now the ride's over, so you're marrying the first guy who asked. "Listen," she said, as Barbara was walking out the door. "Good luck. I mean it. It will probably work out fine."

She thought about that conversation walking down the jailhouse corridor in Edwardsville. Even then, she hadn't been tempted to set the woman straight. Let her think what she'd wanted to think. She had never told anyone anything, and she wasn't about to start now. The only person she talked to was Glen. She remembered the sheer relief, the release of tension as the words spilled out when she was with him, like orgasm . . . just like he said, like orgasm. Homicidal intimacy, he called it. He talked a lot about intimacy. Well, he talked a lot, period. Glen was smarter than anyone else. He would not talk to the cops. They could not make him say anything he didn't want to say. Like he'd told her if three people knew this intimate secret and none of the three ever talked, no one else could possibly know it.

The matron unlocked a door. She saw her daughter Jamie waiting, teary-eyed. "Good-bye," she said sweetly to the old bitch, as if she were leaving a place where she had voluntarily stayed. The judge who had reduced her bail had cited her "highly exemplary" behavior in the various jails where she had stayed, and she was offended that this woman would dare treat her badly after she had behaved so nicely. Well, she wouldn't give it back in kind; she would behave in the ladylike manner her mother had taught her. When she and Jamie were walking down the steps together, she wondered if the woman at the bar had ever told anyone about their conversation. People would turn on her now. She could expect that from everyone and anyone, anyone except Glen. Jamie put an arm around her waist and squeezed. It was 10:50 A.M.

"I know it's a little early," she said to her daughter, "but let's go out to lunch."

St. Louis, Tuesday, March 5, 1985

> A Madison County judge denied motions Monday to dismiss murder charges against Barbara Gusewelle Boyle and to move her trial out of the county because of publicity.
> But Circuit Judge P. J. O'Neill criticized the handling of the case by former Madison County State's Attorney Don W. Weber, calling some of his conduct a "clear ethical violation." —St. Louis *Post-Dispatch*, March 5, 1985

McGarvey folded the paper in half and continued reading the story while he drank his coffee. The accompanying photo of Barb, taken during her recent travails, made her look even more attractive than her wedding pictures had. She'd lost weight since the fat days of her marriage when Ron Gusewelle reputedly offered her a candy-red Corvette if she'd lose fifty pounds. Black Widow Barb had caught the public's attention more than the other widows in the Engleman murders. That was a sure thing. He still found himself looking at her picture and trying to figure out why they wanted her worse than they wanted the Doc across the river.

He was waiting for Bob Trone, the Illinois prosecutor assigned to the case now that Weber, defeated in a messy election, was out of the picture. A lean and weathered man, almost Lincolnesque, Trone lived outside Springfield, Illinois, near the Sangamon River and appropriately, down the road from Salem, where a young Abraham Lincoln practiced law. As convinced of Barbara's guilt as Weber had been, he still didn't feel personally involved in the case as Weber had.

According to the *Post* story, Weber had been slapped on the hand for offenses that included improperly commenting to the press and lunching with the grand jurors. Bailey also decried the collusion with the feds and joint "trickery" that allowed Barb to be extradited quickly. McGarvey thought back to the trial in Hermann, which had been declared a mistrial for less. If the general feeling in Illinois wasn't going so heavily against Barb, Weber's shenanigans, added to the bias against feds, which Bailey could easily have whipped up to a froth, might have been enough to get the charges dismissed.

When Trone came into the office, he stood and shook hands.

McGarvey liked this man, who was redeeming their reputation in Illinois, and he was always glad to get someone else's fix on Doc and the principals.

"I saw Doc at the motion hearing the other day. He was sitting in court reading a book, trying to appear oblivious to the world," Trone said, laughing. "His lawyer, one of the young public defenders, files more motions than Bailey does. Now that the charges against Barb have been upheld, I think Doc's real worried."

"He filed for dismissal too, didn't he?" McGarvey asked, lighting a cigarette.

"Oh, yes. He knows the case against him won't be dismissed if they're trying Barb. The pretrial publicity was focused on Barb not him." Trone leaned back in the chair while McGarvey filled Styrofoam cups of coffee and pulled some more files. Weber hadn't been producing the material Trone needed as quickly as he could have, putting the man at a disadvantage going in to trial. "I wonder if he might plead, especially if he could arrange to stay in Missouri. What do you think?"

"It would be against the grain for him," McGarvey said. Everyone expected Doc to go to trial. He had maintained his innocence since the first time he was questioned in 1959, hadn't he? "Confession doesn't seem to fit his profile, but you never know."

"He didn't take the stand in the Berrera bombing. When it comes right down to dying, he's as scared as the next guy. He could get death in Illinois and probably will if it goes to trial. And I don't think he wants to go to jail over there. He'd end up in Menard. He wouldn't stand a chance of calling the shots in that prison population," Trone said. "But I expect everyone's right about him. I'd be real surprised if he did plead."

"Did he give you any hint he might plead?"

"No. He's still talking like he expects the charges to be dismissed, but he's just going through the motions. The man is scared. I was surprised when I got my first glimpse of him. He looks old and tired, finished. I was expecting him to look younger and healthier, more intimidating." Trone paused to take a sip of the black coffee. "He shambles along now. I think you'll be surprised when you see him in court next time. He asked me my astrological sign," he said, putting his head back and laughing heartily. "When I told him my birth date, he said, 'Oh, you're a Scorpio. I always have a bad time going against Scorpios.''

"Sounds like he can still bullshit," McGarvey said, laughing too, as he began opening files and pushing them across the table. Trone was a good solid lawyer, not even particularly worried about going against F. Lee Bailey. He seemed to have the right take on Barb and the Illinois situation. "What's happening with the lie-detector test Barb took?"

"Bailey keeps working behind the scenes to get it admitted as evidence, but he's had no luck. And I think he won't. The test wasn't properly administered. The man giving it didn't ask the right follow-up questions. She won't take it again, of course." Bailey, a recognized authority on the use of the lie detector and proponent of its admissibility as evidence, claimed he'd taken the case because Barb had passed the test. "We're just lucky the whole issue hasn't been publicized. You know what Weber says about that, don't you? If Bailey was influenced by Barb's test results, then he took the case for two hundred fifty-*one* thousand little reasons."

They laughed, and Trone added he would be lucky if Weber didn't make *that* little comment to the press too.

"There'll be a hue and cry over here if the Doc pleads," Trone said.

McGarvey agreed. The Missouri prosecutors who wanted to put him on death row would scream. But he could see why Madison County would be glad to take the plea, if such an un-likely thing happened. Murder trials were expensive, and the county didn't have money to waste on prosecuting someone who was already in prison for life. Even if they succeeded in putting Doc on death row, appeals would probably keep him alive until the diabetes got him anyway. Why spend money to move a man from one prison to another? They would be happy if they could put Barb away long enough to make sure nobody would want to marry her when she got out.

Alton, Illinois, Closing Arguments, Saturday, April 13, 1985

"Ruth Engleman was the key. She offered a lot of corroboration to the statement of Handy's as to the

APPOINTMENT FOR MURDER / *273*

*relationship between Engleman and Mrs. Boyle. She offered
corroboration as to the planning of the murder." —Robert
E. Trone in an interview with the *Alton Telegraph*,
Monday, April 15, 1985

The trial had lasted two weeks, and the participants, with the exception of Trone, appeared weary. Each day they'd had to push their way through crowds of camera-toting spectators to get inside the packed courtroom. A special sign, DO NOT STAND AND LOOK THROUGH THE DOOR!, written in Magic Marker, had been posted on the double doors separating the throng who couldn't get seats and munched candy bars while they waited for news from the people who were related or knew someone and always got in. Though she had maintained a blank expression throughout most of the proceedings, Barbara was showing the strain. The fine lines around her eyes and mouth had begun to eat more deeply into her flesh. Bailey—who was at the point in life where his age showed cruelly unless he was taking scrupulous care of himself— looked more puffy around the edges. The parade of witnesses had come and gone, with Ruth turning in her expected good performance and Handy claiming remorse for his part in the murders. Bailey had produced Andre Jones, who recanted his recantation and said he knew who killed Ron Gusewelle but couldn't say who for fear of reprisals to his family while insisting Mrs. Boyle did not do it.

Bailey had also obtained a letter Handy sent to Engleman the week before, apologizing for what he had to do in the trial.

"For what I am going to say, your ghost will be following me forever," he'd written. "I have got to say some bad things about you, and you have been like a brother to me."

To the court Handy had said, "I think there is hope for Engleman. He has many good qualities, and I feel sorry for the man. I despair for what he did and I despair for my part, but I can't give away a chance to clear my conscience."

In his closing arguments, Trone recounted Handy's testimony. Standing before the jurors, he took them through the stages of conspiracy with Robert Handy as their guide. The hardworking, country-lawyer manner he affected had served him well as a foil to

Bailey's courtroom style during the trial, and he maintained it to the end. While the short, dapper Bailey, in his immaculate three-piece suits, had paced smartly before the witnesses and jurors, delivering each question and comment in a staccato voice as devoid of regional accent as a newscaster's, Trone lolled back in his chair, hands behind his head, long legs outstretched, emphasizing by his posture his considerable height and down-home character. In closing, he hammered hard on the evidence, speaking in the thunderous, heavily accented voice of a revival minister, reminding them that Handy's description of the murder weapon matched the .38-caliber pearl-handled revolver that Ruth Engleman had stated disappeared from her home at the same time as Ron was killed.

During the trial, he had asked most of his questions from the table, but he walked leisurely back and forth in closing arguments, working the jury like a congregation, stopping at each end of the jury box to enumerate evidence, one piece at a time, putting it down like a judgment-day bricklayer building the last wall.

At one point, he turned abruptly, faced the jury head-on, and said, "You heard Bob Handy say that Ronald Gusewelle looked toward the back door of his home after he was shot. You know who was behind that door with towels to mop up the blood."

For a full minute he allowed his shoulders to slump inside his wrinkled suit and looked at the jurors, making eye contact with each of the six men and six women in turn. *You know who was there* . . . And his expression seemed to say, You and I both know Robert Handy is guilty too and lucky to get off as easily as he did, but we know who is *really* guilty here, don't we? We know that this man's *wife, his partner in holy matrimony*, stood behind the door waiting for him to die so she could clean up his blood . . . And we don't need to know anything else.

"If you don't believe she was part of the murder conspiracy, you must think she had a strong premonition about his death." Trone turned again and picked up some notes from the table. "She forged his name to the applications for one hundred ninety-three thousand dollars' worth of insurance before he died. You might say she came out of this family tragedy smelling like a rose. She came out with five hundred ninety-eight thousand dollars."

He looked deeply into their eyes again.

Pointing to Barbara, who did not flinch, he said, "There is a woman who set up her own in-laws, her own husband, and boy, has she done well."

Bailey met the same eyes and must have known he was looking at people who were proud to say they didn't give a hoot for big Eastern cities or big Eastern lawyers. Never mind the East Coast crap, the fancy cross-examination technique that only proved Bob Handy wasn't as smart as F. Lee Bailey. They just wanted to get to the truth, that was all. And $598,000 was a lot of truth. If Barbara had made off with as little cash as Ruth Bullock, or Sandy Frey, or Carmen Miranda, or if she'd suffered like Carmen, they might have forgiven her. Instead she sat stoically in front of them every day, wearing good clothes bought with blood money. They couldn't forgive the pretty suits, the matching shoes and bags, the earrings glinting in her ears.

Bailey showed the jury a list he had made, a list of twenty-nine elements of Handy's testimony he claimed were contradicted by facts. Then he began to pound away at those discrepancies as he had when Bob Handy was on the stand. The jury listened politely. Finally he returned to Andre Jones, declaring the recantation unbelievable, another Weber ploy.

"In order to bring charges against Mrs. Boyle, the police and Don Weber had to go out and unsolve the case and then come back and re-solve the case," Bailey said, "Andre Jones knows too much and Robert Handy doesn't know enough. And if you can't eliminate Andre Jones, you needn't go any further." His voice raised an octave higher, he began emoting as if there were television cameras pointed in his direction. "I wouldn't believe Andre Jones if he told me this was East Alton unless you had a lot of proof. I wouldn't believe Robert Handy if he said this was the state of Illinois without some corroboration! I don't suggest you take one word either of these two liars—admitted liars—said to you!"

A surviving Gusewelle relative said under his breath to a friend, "I'm not sure he *does* know he's in the state of Illinois."

The jury began deliberation at 2:15. Barbara, dressed in an off-white suit, left the courthouse with her mother and three children. On her last night of freedom, they went to a restaurant and ordered friend chicken, family-style, all-you-can-eat, but they didn't eat very much at all.

Sunday, April 14, 1985

The knew the jurors had reached a verdict and would announce it shortly. Breaking away from the grasping hands of relatives and friends, Barbara went alone into the chilled courtroom. Dressed in a different tailored off-white suit, this one a deeper shade of cream, she sat at the defense table for several minutes before Bailey joined her. He put his hand on her back and whispered to her. She had paid for his elegant consolation, and she was receiving it in full measure. As the jurors filed in, he kept his hand in place. Across the courtroom, Richard and Donna Gusewelle held hands.

After fourteen and a half hours of deliberation the jury acquitted Barbara Gusewelle Boyle in the killing of her husband's parents—and found her guilty of her husband's murder. About one hundred fifty spectators gasped audibly as Judge P. J. O'Neill read the verdict. Jamie Boyle, seated behind her mother, burst into tears. Barbara turned, put her arm around her daughter, and whispered, "Hush, baby, it's all right . . . it's going to be all right . . . it's all right."

O'Neill ordered the building cleared and court adjourned before Barbara was to be led out. Crying silently, she removed her earrings and handed them to Bailey, who had begun patting her back again and whispering in her ear. "Give my daughter my earrings," she said. Jamie's sobs were still audible, coming from the hallway.

A deputy handcuffed and leg-ironed Barbara Gusewelle Boyle and led her outside through the small crowd requesting autographs from F. Lee Bailey, who had assured the press, "We will appeal," and past a larger group of onlookers who cheered as she was helped into the waiting van. After she was gone Trone and Bailey shook hands. The two lawyers, who'd developed a genuine liking and respect for each other during the trial, arranged to meet for a drink. Following an emotional meeting with the Gusewelle family, McGarvey joined them.

PART TEN:

Doc

"Notoriety isn't all it's cracked up to be. It forces a man to live inside himself."—Glennon Engleman

The Plea, Edwardsville, Wednesday, June 19, 1985

*The book is closed on Glennon E. Engleman.
The final chapter was written June 19 when the former
dentist from south St. Louis pleaded guilty to committing three
callous, calculated murders in Madison County.
As far as prosecutors and law enforcement authorities are
concerned, no more murders will be blamed on Engleman,
who treated the working class and socialized with those less
educated than he. Engleman, 58, will spend the rest of his life
locked up in the Missouri Penitentiary; he will not stand trial
again."*—St. Louis Post-Dispatch, Thursday, June 20.

The phone rang at ten A.M. in Trone's modern, gray frame house on the bank of the Sangamon River. You'd better get down here fast, he was told, the Doc wants to plead. He called McGarvey, the Illinois cops involved in the investigation, and the Gusewelle family and arranged to meet them in Edwardsville. Unless they strongly disapproved, he would take the plea.

While the plea shocked everyone, including Dick Dempsey,

who had defended Doc in the Missouri murder trials, none of the people Trone questioned that afternoon in Edwardsville believed the state should pursue a trial. In exchange for a plea of guilty to each count of murder, Doc agreed to take three consecutive life-without-parole sentences. He would be allowed to continue serving his time in Missouri.

When he entered the courtroom to make his formal plea, the onlookers included the group Trone had assembled, the press, and the few curious Edwardsville citizens who had heard the word on the street. Doc's plea didn't excite the interest in downtown Edwardsville that Barbara's trial had, so the crowd was smaller. His wrists shackled to his belt, Doc shambled up the center aisle with a deputy on each side. He wore an orange jumpsuit and the pasty, ashen look of a man who has lived in prison for a few years on darkness and starch. When the judge asked, "How do you plead?" he replied, "Guilty" three times. The process took less than ten minutes.

"Doc, would you sit down and talk to me about this?" Trone asked.

"I'll talk to you," he said. "I'll talk to you if it's just you alone in a room. No cops. I'm not talking to any more cops."

As Doc was being led away again, McGarvey joined Trone.

"He looked worn down," McGarvey said. "I've never seen him like that, resigned and complacent." He shook Trone's hand. "Well, it's over."

Driving back to St. Louis, McGarvey envied Trone the chance to talk to Doc, one on one. Aside from Ruth, he knew he was the person Doc most hated—and the one he'd least likely talk to. "That federal pimp," he called him. He'd never forgive him for bugging his bedroom, his "sanctum sanctorum," never forgive him for really turning Ruth against him. Everything else he considered fair, but not the bugging of his bedroom. It was ironic that Doc, a man who described his sexual adventures in graphic terms, was so offended about this. Well, at least the plea would be good news for Ruth, McGarvey thought. She was tired of reliving the past, and now she would not have to testify again.

Robert E. Trone and Glennon E. Engleman sat across from each other on wooden chairs at a small table in an interrogation room at the Madison County jail. Trone often told people he had a knack for getting along with "these guys," the defendants in the murder trials he prosecuted. He could chat about firearms with a man who had shot to death his entire family. Like Engleman, he performed manual labor on his own property, a house with a rugged façade set at the end of a dirt road otherwise inhabited by shanty dwellers. Inside the house was spectacular: a cathedral-ceiling living room, an abundance of space and lush carpets, expensive furniture in an eclectic blend of antique and modern, and huge green ferns. Bob Trone was like that house, and Engleman trusted the simple, rugged façade.

"Was Handy telling us pretty much the straight story on the murders?" he asked.

"Handy is a good man, a good friend. He's really good people. I bear him no ill will for what he's done. I want you to know that," the Doc began. Trone had expected him to ramble, to control the conversation, and he did from the start. "Handy has the courage of a lion. He isn't a leader, he's a follower, and so he has to have someone to lead him. This has been a hard thing for Handy, but he has more courage, more courage than any man I've ever known. He's fearless."

"I like Bob Handy," Trone said, and it was somewhat true. Like Engleman, he didn't regard Handy as a particularly bright guy, but then he thought the Doc exaggerated his own intelligence. According to the I.Q. tests administered at the penitentiary, the dentist was only at the top of average. His exalted vision of himself was just that, a vision. That he hadn't been caught until he let rage get the best of him when he murdered Sophie wasn't entirely because of his own planning. He had been right about one thing, the real core of his murder philosophy: kill an ordinary man who isn't worth much money in a manner that can easily be written off as accidental, and few questions are likely to be asked. "What I'm curious about, Doc, was he in the house when the parents were murdered? Or did he wait outside like he said he did?"

"Handy was in the house," Doc said, grinning. "He came in right after I got inside, and he was ransacking the bedrooms while I killed them." His face grew animated as he talked about the murders. "He told the truth about the rest of it. I put on my suit and told them I was from the Farm Bureau. They opened the door and let me in, laid right down on the kitchen floor when I told them to, just as pretty as you please, and I shot them. Handy was inside, ransacking the house. It was over in a matter of minutes. It went real smooth."

"You shot both of them? Handy had no part in it except ransacking the house?"

"That's right. I killed them. I killed them both," he said smugly. "I like to kill. Not everyone has the strength, the guts, to kill. It sets a man apart from his fellow man if he can kill."

"You took a big chance, didn't you, Doc? What if someone had come along while you were in the house? The way that property's situated, you couldn't get out of the driveway without being seen."

"You have to take chances, don't you? I planned everything well. I always planned carefully. I liked to say I planned my crimes from the witness stand back, and if it weren't for Ruth betraying me, we wouldn't be here now. You don't think I'd go out to those farmhouses without a backup, do you? Ruth was waiting in another car at the end of the lane. She was at the end of the driveway both times when I committed those murders." His face took on a reddish hue, and his voice grew louder. "Ruth, Ruth was my partner! That woman has the finest criminal mind of anyone I've ever known. She's the one who's getting away with a crime by taking my own son away from me . . ."

Trone let him ramble for a while about Ruth, waited while he vented his spleen on the woman he considered responsible for his fate. He thought McGarvey was right, that you had to discard whatever the Doc said about Ruth because he hated her so much he'd say anything, and maybe believe it himself too. After several minutes, he began to wind down a little, and Trone interjected another comment.

"What about Ron's murder, Doc? Did it go down the way Handy described it?"

"Well, I don't know where Handy got the idea Barb picked us up at a shopping center in Fairmont City. He was never good at remembering locations. She met us at the Troy Truck Stop on

162. There's more traffic in and out of a truck stop. It was a natural place. Handy was wrong about that. Why would we meet at the Venture store out in the open?"

"Is that all? Did he have the rest of the story straight? You killed Ron while he stood by and watched."

"I shot him, but Handy picked up the hammer and hit him in the head," he said, grinning triumphantly again. "Think about it. Which one of us was the carpenter? He just did it without thinking about it, picked up the hammer and hit him on the way down to be sure he was dead. Ron was a big man, and he wanted to be sure and so forth."

"What about Barb's role in the parents' deaths? How much did she know?"

"Did you ever see anything so pretty as Barb?" he asked. "She's a beautiful thing, a golden girl. She's very brave too. Barb will never crack, never talk. She did what she was supposed to do; and she was tight, a rock. She's a good girl, had a rough time . . ."

Trone tried rephrasing the question, but he couldn't get a solid answer on how much Barb had known about the parents' deaths. Perhaps Doc thought her silence indicated she was standing by him, and he meant to stand by her. For an hour and a half, Doc talked. Most of it was the kind of talk everyone associated with the case had heard before, but he had told Robert Trone what he hadn't told anyone outside his intimate circle: *I killed them. I like to kill. It sets a man apart from his fellow man if he can kill.*

"Why did you plead, Doc?" Trone asked. "You surprised us all. We thought you'd take it to trial. What made you plead?"

"You're a Scorpio, Mr. Trone. I knew I didn't stand a chance against you. No, Mr. Trone, I knew I was whipped this time."

When the *Post-Dispatch* wrote the "final story" on the Doc, they did not quote Robert E. Trone, the only man to whom he had ever confessed. Perhaps the *Globe*, which had ceased to exist, would have called him. The saga of the Doc had really been the *Globe*'s story. But the *Post* quoted Gordon Ankney as saying he was upset about the Madison County prosecutor's agreement with Engleman not to seek the death penalty in exchange for the guilty pleas. "The only reason to indict him was to hang him," Ankney said.

Their story implied the end was tidy, that all the questions had been answered, when really they had not. Two women, Barbara Gusewelle and Ruth Bullock, the last and the first widows, had maintained their silence about the details of their participation in the murders of their husbands. Their vow of homicidal intimacy had not been broken—and quite likely never will be. Perhaps Ruth Bullock's silence, encouraged by the attitudes of St. Louisans in the '50s, led directly to the murders of those very ordinary young men, Eric Frey and Peter Halm.

The *Post* reporters also asked several of the principals why they thought the doctor *did* commit seven murders. It was the typical last-roundup question and elicited no surprise answers. Perhaps the best response came from Dempsey: "No, his motives were not money. He would treat people for nothing, and there were acts of kindness and charity in his background. I think probably his desire to control individuals was his driving force—to make all the little dummies walk in line and sing at the same time."

Surely even the acts of kindness and charity were motivated by the same desire to control. They did not quote the Doc because he wouldn't talk to them. He sent a message to the reporter who'd driven three hours from St. Louis to Jefferson City to see him: "I'm sorry that you were so presumptuous to drive up here without an appointment. One of the few personal dignities which we are allowed here is privacy."

EPILOGUE

A detective, slight of build, age thirty-three, of the St. Louis Police Department, Homicide Division, got interested in the Bullock murder in the spring of 1987. Over the years other detectives and reporters have been drawn to the case, which, like all officially unsolved cases, has seductive allure. He was putting in a routine, and boring, shift on night duty, and he began flipping through the files of unsolved cases to pass the time.

"I was actually looking for pictures of old cars," he says, twirling the end of his mustache as he talks. "I wasn't drawn to the Bullock case because I'd read about a book being done on Engleman, not at all. I was curious about how the old Buicks were built."

A restless man looking for something on which to hook his personal sense of injustice, the detective was still irked by a promotion he hadn't received the year before and a divorce he had been granted at his wife's instigation. He discovered in his early perusal of the Bullock files that a young lawyer who worked for a firm that had been involved in a peripheral way in the Bullock case was the same man, a much older lawyer now, who had represented his wife in the divorce.

"A lot of things began coming together for me when I read that file," the detective says. "I thought the evidence was there, and I wondered why they'd never closed that case. So I decided to reopen the investigation on my own."

His investigation convinced him that John Daly, one of the reputed hit men, had actually pulled the trigger. He based his theory primarily on the testimony of Ivan Deckard, who allegedly had heard Daly confess to the crime when the two happened to be staying at the same prison facility some thirty years ago. Deckard, convicted of various crimes over the years, was being held in the spring of 1987 at an undisclosed prison location in New York as a protected government witness. In other words, Ivan Deckard, like Robert Handy, was a snitch, but a snitch on a larger scale. He had been involved in drug-smuggling operations.

The young detective and Deckard, who was negotiating a book and movie deal for his life story, hit it off well. The Bullock murder stuff, he said, would go down nicely with the drug smuggling, wouldn't it? He remembered everything John Daly had told him in detail, the story he had told, then recanted—and also remembered he had been promised payment to change his story at the time. Who would pay him to protect Daly, convicted of armed robbery, and why?

The detective began calling people, including his wife's lawyer "and leaned on him, to shake him up a little."

He says, "I got great satisfaction in calling him. I told him I knew the truth had been suppressed to protect people in high places, and I suspected the firm he worked for had a hand in suppressing it. He said he didn't remember Bullock's name, and I said, 'How about my name, do you remember that name?'" The lawyer didn't remember his name either.

The detective was having a good time anyway. His search took him next to a midwestern suburb in search of Mrs. Bullock. In a car parked some distance from Ruthie's house, he kept her under surveillance for a few days. He took pictures of her, now a chunky middle-aged matron, the mother of grown children. Then he called her on the phone and told her the Doc was going to break his silence about the Bullock murders. He took the pictures with him when he visited Glennon Engleman at Jeff City.

"That's my Ruthie," Doc said. "She's put on a little weight, of course, but that's her."

The detective told him, "I know you didn't pull the trigger. You and Ruthie hired Daly to commit the murder, and I expect to have indictments on the three of you within a few weeks. I have a witness."

"You're not going to take this one away from me, now are you? Why, it took Sputnik to get me off the front pages in the late '50s," Doc exclaimed, and other than giving the young cop advice on psychic matters, that was all he said.

Doc was led back to his cell. He began laughing as soon as the door to the interrogation room closed behind him. His laughter grew harder and harder until he was cackling, flapping his elbows up and down like a demented bird.

The detective returned to St. Louis and met on two separate occasions with two different reporters, whom he gave copies of the seventy-page report he had prepared. He expected, he said, to have indictments within weeks. If he didn't get them, he wanted the story "leaked."

"This case was never solved," he confided, "because Ruthie had sexual affairs with two prominent people, men she'd picked up in bars on the DeBaliviere Strip." He named the prominent people. "The move was made to squash the investigation because of those men," he said.

He described searching for James Bullock's grave in the dark one night and being unable to find it because the marker was gone. His attempts to question Bullock's aunt, Geraldine Duerbeck, who was nearing ninety and infirm, had proven as fruitless as his graveyard search. Her granddaughter told him she'd suffered enough and shut the door in his face. But, he swore, he would go tell her the news as soon as the case was officially solved. He thought he owed it to her, that she would sleep better if she knew the truth.

The circuit attorney's office reviewed the new file he had assembled, found it contained nothing new, and refused to indict. When he went public with his story, the circuit attorney hastily called a news conference. The case was now considered solved, *closed*, he said, though there would be no indictments due to the passage of time. The *Post* ran a story on the young detective.

Geraldine Duerbeck's granddaughter said it really didn't make a lot of difference to them anymore. What's done is done, and who's dead is dead. You couldn't change it by taking a lot of old people to trial. Her grandmother's mind drifted in and out, she said, and the rest of them hardly remembered Jimmy at all. There wasn't anything special about him, she said, anything you could fasten onto and hold for thirty years. He was just a nice boy, a good boy. What's done is done. God will take care of it, she said.